THE THEORY MESS

03/01/01

HERMAN RAPAPORT

THE
THEORY
MESS

deconstruction in eclipse

COLUMBIA UNIVERSITY PRESS
NEW YORK

Columbia University Press
Publishers Since 1893
New York   Chichester, West Sussex

Copyright © 2001 Columbia University Press

Library of Congress Cataloging-in-Publication Data

Rapaport, Herman, 1947–
    The theory mess : deconstruction in eclipse / Herman Rapaport.
        p.   cm.
    Includes bibliographical references and index.
    ISBN 0–231–12134–2 (cloth)—ISBN 0–231–12135–0 (paper)
        1. Deconstruction. 2. Derrida, Jacques—Criticism and interpretation. I. Title.

    PN98.D43 R37 2001
    801'.95—dc21

                                                                                    00–059336

Casebound editions of Columbia University Press books are printed on
permanent and durable acid-free paper.
Designed by Chang Jae Lee
Printed in the United States of America
c 10 9 8 7 6 5 4 3 2 1
p 10 9 8 7 6 5 4 3 2 1

for angelika and hanno

Nonetheless, all these people we are talking about here, all these criticisms, have in common that they present deconstruction as an enclosure "in the prison-house of language," which is — I don't know how to qualify it — blindness, bad faith, a stubborn refusal to read, which is an enormous symptom.

— *Jacques Derrida, "Deconstruction in America" (1985)*

[René Wellek's "Destroying Literary Studies"] belongs to a series or to what we might call a campaign: certain professors invested with a great deal of prestige, and what seems to them to threaten the very foundation of this power — its discourse, its axiomatics, its procedures, its theoretical and territorial limits, etc. In the course of this campaign, they grasp at straws; they forget the elementary rules of reading and of philological integrity in whose name they claim to do battle. They think they can identify deconstruction as the common enemy.

— *Jacques Derrida,* Memoires for Paul de Man *(1986)*

Here once again, if one relies on this ignorant and aberrant reading of "Deconstruction" or of my "practice," I have no way out. Whenever such a reader cannot deny my attention to context, to history, to biography, and so on, then s/he reproaches me for not being faithful to what s/he believes to be my "practice" or my "theory . . ." When s/he believes that I am faithful to what s/he believes or wants others to believe deconstruction means to say or to do, then I am reproached for decontextualizing, making meaning indeterminate and neglecting history. [. . .] Faced with those who do not want or do not know how to read, I confess I am powerless.

— *Jacques Derrida, "Biodegradables" (1989)*

For the first time in history, to my knowledge, there has been the spectacle of academics at universities other than Cambridge, not even in England, claiming to protect the institution [i.e., from Derrida himself], that of Cambridge, and of the university in general. They do this not by way of discussion and argument supported by reading and references, as one does in scholarly publications, but through the most powerful organs of the media, in a style reminiscent of the slogan or manifesto, the denunciatory placard or election propaganda . . . phrases fabricated from I cannot imagine what rumors. I challenge anyone to find in my writings the expression "logical phallusies" by which the signatories of this document [protesting an honorary doctorate for Derrida to be given by Cambridge], in what is a serious and dogmatic abuse of their authority in the press, try to discredit me. [. . .] And how can they say that what I write "defies comprehension" when they are denouncing its excessive influence and end up by saying that they themselves have very well understood that there is nothing to understand in my work except the false or the trivial?

— *Jacques Derrida, "Honoris Causa" (1992)*

The offensive launched by Wolin — *The New York Review of Books* — Sheehan was in fact unleashed against me only in order to get at my work and everything that can be associated with it, in an ideological campaign that began a long time ago. The archives of the magazine give eloquent testimony to this effect.

— *Jacques Derrida, "The Work of Intellectuals and the Press." (1995)*

CONTENTS

PREFACE

The Theory Mess is an account of the general reception of Jacques Derrida's work in Anglo-American academies, since the story of this reception provides insight into what has been happening in the field of critical theory within these academies over roughly the past thirty years. Whereas in the late 1970s there was some euphoria concerning the promise of a new theoretical episteme that might replace Enlightenment humanism, the late 1990s has reflected a time of intellectual deflation in which there is cynicism about an overproliferation of theoretical models that have rapidly come and gone. By the late 1980s it was clear that no new episteme from continental Europe was going to supplant Anglo-American pragmatisms or empiricisms and that at best we might see the success of compromise formations like New Historicism and postcolonial studies. The irresolution of epistemic differences — due in part to extremely different cultural traditions — has left us in a messy philosophical state with respect to criticism and theory. This theoretical messiness has pervaded the languages and literatures by a widespread subscription to a left-of-center politics that reflects a convergence of Marxist currents in recent European critical theories with the liberation politics of Anglo-American countercultural thinking. Under this political umbrella, figures like Jacques Derrida, Theodor Adorno, Michel Foucault, Louis Althusser, Drucilla Cornell, Fredric Jameson, Gayatri Chakravorty Spivak, Barbara Johnson, Trinh T. Minh ha, Edward Said, Henry Louis Gates Jr., and Judith Butler could be said to speak the same language. In fact, they do not.

In considering the vicissitudes of deconstruction, it is crucial to take into account Derrida's repeated remarks in a number of interviews and articles that warn us against imagining that theory could be anything other than a disseminative broadcasting of ideas that inevitably undergo multiple displacements, hybridizations, misroutings, misconstructions, and mutations. As Derrida has often said of deconstruction, it is not something that he could ever possess or control, since deconstruction is not a system, not a method, not a technology but rather a "differentiated movement" whose sites and resources change as it crosses various borderlines, whether institutional, disciplinary, political, or national. To imagine deconstruction as anything other than a bit messy from that disseminative perspective would be naïve.

Certainly, one has to be open to the kind of rhizomatic possibilities that are likely to result from what Gilles Deleuze and Felix Guattari would have called a "micropolitics of critical theory." Their notion of collective assemblages of enunciation or the idea that "there is no language in itself; nor are there any linguistic universals, only a throng of dialects, patois, slangs, and specialized languages" is quite apropos of the theoretical jargons one is likely to encounter. Derrida is in agreement with Deleuze and Guattari that "there is no ideal speaker-listener, any more than there is a homogeneous linguistic community."[1] One of the central conflicts we encounter within the humanities is the expectation that there should be a homogeneous linguistic community, whether of traditionalists along the lines posited by critics like Hilton Kramer or of social activist theorists, as posited by Terry Eagleton, who are politically in agreement and theoretically speak roughly the same language. No doubt, other interpretive communities could be imagined — pragmatists, New Historicists, semioticians, or theorists of postmodernism. Hence there has been a strong inclination to think in terms of a number of discrete homogeneous critical localities, or schools, as opposed to the kind of rhizomatic structure imagined by Deleuze and Guattari, in which the consistency of a language is made up of its variability in terms of territorializing and deterritorializing constellations of meaning, and in which variability necessarily implies the encountering of singularities around which meanings temporarily pool. No doubt, given the distribution of intellectuals within universities spread out across vast distances and the sometimes hit-or-miss influence of even very important studies, it is likely that variability in the form of misunderstandings and incomprehensions will emerge within critical works.

That said, Derrida has also been quite protective of deconstruction and has taken many opportunities to define and redefine it so that no one gets the wrong idea. In numerous texts Derrida has given definitions of deconstruction in order to set the critical record straight. Hence his idea that deconstruction is a "differentiated movement" would be typical of a definition that sets deconstruction apart by limiting, or at least orienting, how we are to conceive of it as an intellectual movement.

In terms of the moral debates surrounding the revelations of Paul de Man's career as a columnist for a Belgian newspaper that served the interests of the Nazi occupation during the Second World War, Derrida expressed anger over the purposive misconstructions and misapplications of his responses. In "Biodegradables" (1989), critics of Derrida were taken to task for their unwillingness to read carefully and accurately (to organize thoughts properly, to reconstruct logically — in short, to order) and hence their willingness to degrade academic discussion and life. In a very recent rejoinder to some Marxist critics of his work on spectrality in Marx's writings, Derrida again attacks his intellectual assailants for having purposely misread and falsified him. His comments on Gayatri Chakravorty Spivak are typical: "Some of her errors stem from an outright inability to read, exacerbated here by the wounded resentment of her 'proprietoriality about Marx.' Others are due to her unbridled manipulation of a rhetoric."[2] Apparently, for Derrida not *everything* is allowable, including bad hermeneutical prep work and the "manipulation of rhetoric." But if that's the case, hasn't Derrida brought about a call to hermeneutical reasonability? And isn't that a call to order that in principle violates deconstruction's very critiques of hermeneutical reasoning, as in, say, Derrida's critique of Hans-Georg Gadamer's hermeneutical conceptions of interpretive agreement?[3] Here it would appear that the classical protocols of hermeneutical analysis — attention to history, context, philology, structure, logic, and agreement — return as primary lines of defense at the moment deconstruction is maligned and Derrida's words are turned against him.

However, if one faults Derrida for retreating into the arms of hermeneutical fair play (given his critiques of classical hermeneutics), do we agree that everything is hermeneutically permissible? What permission does the other think he or she has to speak to us in such and such a way? What is permissible institutionally? What is permissible intellectually — but also hermeneutically and communally? In an interview with Gerald Graff that concluded the reprinting of "Limited Inc," Derrida addresses the question of what is not only critically permissible but theoretically required when he reassures Graff that, "I have never 'put such concepts as truth, reference, and the stability of interpretive contexts radically into question' if 'putting radically into question' means contesting that there *are* and that there *should be* truth, reference, and stable contexts of interpretation." Derrida insists that it is not the stability of such interpretive contexts that he questions with all its norms, rules, and contractual possibilities. Indeed, it would be impermissible to deny such stability or to refuse to acknowledge it. Rather, in accounting for such stability, Derrida would be on the lookout for how it might also be destabi-

lized, since it cannot be natural, absolute, permanent, or eternal — "A stability is not an immutability."[4]

At this juncture, Derrida defines an interpretation as an "object of agreements" whose ties are demonstrable in their ability to link ideas to things, to
determine truth from falsehood. Indeed, what will concern me in the historical description of critical theory is an institutional constriction of the "object
of agreements" to the point where such objects are not generally demonstrable
because they make no consistent attempt to determine truth from falsehood,
much less an effort to work within a stability of interpretive contexts for the
sake of understanding the relationships, potentials, or limitations of concepts.
This will become clear in my sections on "subject-positions" in which the term
can be shown to be so conceptually unstable as to be methodologically useless.
For example, Stanley Fish's well-known understanding of interpretation as an
object of agreements is so solipsistic in its sectarianism that it collapses into the
authoritarianism of a "might makes right" mentality. This reduction of the object of agreements to individual will or communitarian self-interest has contributed to a fracturing of theory into numerous objects of agreement with
ever-shrinking constituencies and ever-expanding contradictions, causing conflicts with other constituencies and theories. Hence one might be justified in
referring to "objects of disagreement" wherein the inability or refusal of the
professoriate to come into general agreement about truth, reference, and the
stability of interpretive contexts serves in and of itself as a constant that, like
any stability, is not natural, absolute, or eternal. But how is this constant to be
impacted or destabilized? How does one destabilize what is already destabilized? It is here that the question of permissibility becomes relevant. A certain
reinstitutionalization and rededication to theory needs to take place wherein
theoretical work can be stabilized, which is to say, *refereed* by "objects of agreement" that are not competitively articulated to be out of adjustment with one
another but competently articulated and stabilized for the sake of philosophical principles that transcend a self-centered authorial (or performative) interest
aiming to stand apart as different and irreconcilable. Moreover, such stabilization would rest on a certain *Bildung* that is philosophically serious enough
(that is to say, logically compelling enough because sufficiently thought
through) to not only respect the protocols of stabilization but also embark on
the kind of critical work that Derrida imagines could be carried out.

If critical theory has been chiefly an object of destabilization and disagreement among academics, this is in no small measure because humanists

have increasingly been drawn to a competitive celebrity, or star, system that rewards people for not seeing eye to eye. Moreover, there is the troubling phenomenon of a star system that encourages academics to look the part of being an intellectual without necessarily doing all the work of an intellectual. Since the 1970s academics have increasingly started responding to representations, or simulacra, of intellectual behavior that glamorize theory in such a way that it becomes an attribute of desirability that has more to do with the individual critic's sexiness and popularity than with more mundane things like checking one's footnotes, reading one's peers, or getting an argument or theory reasonably right. If one considers the idea that disagreement is the admission price to an agonistic celebrity system in which each critic has his or her own product to sell (i.e., himself or herself), then it's no wonder that critical theory is less about a hermeneutical attempt to philosophically stabilize a conceptual field in order to patiently question aspects of that field than about matters of celebrity in which all that matters is who gets the best of whom. That the academic star system has contributed to both a theory mess and institutional strife is amply supported by Edward Said's plea for "restoring intellectual coherence" in a newsletter of the Modern Language Association of which he has been elected president: "All manner of fragmented, jargonized subjects of discussion now flourish in an ahistorical limbo." Moreover, "when reputable, distinguished departments of literature can no longer function without terrible, paralyzing disagreement on the smallest as well as the largest issues, something is quite wrong."[5]

Although one can blame the theory mess on an egotism of celebrity that has become more and more commonplace — everyone, it seems, is an author who has articles and books in print — Said's remarks reveal a growing concern with a much more vexing underlying set of issues that addresses the present state of intellectual communities characterized by what Christopher Fynsk has called "an absence of distress about the absence of community" within universities.[6] That is, given the acrimonious fissuring of community, many faculty just want to be left alone. Indeed, to them a phenomenon like the theory mess is the condition upon which they justify opting out of academic debate to retreat into the restricted research interests of their choice. But one may well wonder why they acquiesce so willingly to this option, given that the absence of community is an enormous sacrifice to make for enjoying a mutually deferential isolation. More curious, according to Fynsk, is the extent to which there has been substantial tolerance for the failure of linkage between faculties of the humanities and public debate concerning our general cultural and historical situation at the end of the twentieth century. Hence there was a bloodless acquiescence on the part of faculties within universities not only to the loss of their own general community but to their alienation from the society at large.

In *The University in Ruins* (1996) Bill Readings took some of this a step further in pointing out that academic community has been replaced by administration. "Professionalization deals with the loss of the subject-reference of the educational experience by integrating teaching and research as aspects of the general administration of a closed system: teaching is the administration of students by professors; research is the administration of professors by their peers; administration is the name given to the stratum of bureaucrats who administer the whole."[7] Appeals to excellence, according to Readings, are bureaucratic jargon that work toward "deferentializing" value, since "excellence" is a vacuous term that means something different to everyone; at the same time, it is used as an overarching criterion to commission and decommission faculty, curricula, programs, departments, and degrees by administrative fiat. Readings argues that the replacement of community by bureaucracy destroys the intellectual fabric of a community of scholars by turning the university into a parody of itself, imposing a corporate model whose bottom line is cutting cost and maximizing output, something that requires "dereferentializing." Indeed, what I call "the theory mess" is a direct expression of such an administrated space within which questions of critical-theoretical truth are rescinded for the sake of breaking down barriers to the circulation of products (different intellectual commodities) and hence creating uncontrolled intellectual market expansion, something that Readings associates with the university in ruins.

Back in the 1980s Derrida had already been worrying about the fragility of university communities, citing their hypersensitivity and inability to tolerate difference — for example, even ordinary political differences (such as, in America, Democrat versus Republican). Here again, the question of community and interpretive agreement is striking, because there is a problematic contradiction between what Readings sees as administrative "dereferentializing" in the service of an uncontrolled (i.e., "free market") intellectual expansionism and the isolation of fractured academic groups that have become so hypersensitive to differences of opinion that their tolerance for even variations of difference can be quite low. This, of course, is where the encouragement of intellectual latitude conflicts with an absence of permissibility and may be why despite a plethora of different critical theories there has been little attempt at synthesis or a coming to terms.

Of course, it is always much easier to identify problems than solve them. For example, I don't believe that Said's recent call for a return to the academic politics of thirty years ago is viable. Nor do I agree with Fynsk that a return to Heideggerian conceptions of language and being is going to save us from the communitarian crisis we are facing. I also don't agree with Readings that the paradigm of the university is totally in ruins and that we have to embrace a "community at loose ends" in which there is no common identity upon which to found what he calls "a shared possibility of communication." Readings's idea of "*transience*, the solidarity of those who have nothing in common but who are aggregated together by the state of things" is untenable. What this enables for Readings is "the heteronomous horizon of dissensus," which is to say, the suspension of a politics of consensus that, in Readings's view, is necessarily authoritarian.[8] Unfortunately, dissensus is itself authoritarian to the extent that it prohibits a certain kind of hermeneutical work that some might call constructive.

That said, Readings's concept of "dissensus" raises one of the major problems crucial to my project. Invocation of a theory mess implies a dichotomy between disorder and order that immediately presses the issue of having to choose between two alternatives. The term "theory mess" appears to require either an apology for the messy, decentered conditions within which theory finds itself today or an advocacy of a return to critical order with all the logocentric, totalitarian, and transcendental baggage that it entails. But, of course, both are problematic options for deconstruction. On the one hand, the theory mess has been particularly disadvantageous for deconstruction, because, strictly speaking, it isn't answerable to what Derrida calls "objects of agreement," something that is politically vexing when deconstruction gets critiqued or eclipsed because of wild analyses that cannot be reasoned with, let alone entirely comprehended. On the other hand, deconstruction, with its emphasis upon decentering and dissemination, does not really have the option of invoking a rational, metaphysical recovery of truth in the hermeneutical tradition of someone like Wilhelm Dilthey. Given this dilemma, if it turns out that deconstruction is articulated in such a way that there is no possibility for critically taking a phenomenon like the theory mess to task, then deconstruction certainly reveals some major limitations within a rather basic predicament.

Although Derrida himself has appealed for a call to order when on the defensive ("Biodegradables") and a call to dissemination and *différance* when on the attack ("Some Statements and Truisms [1990]), I wonder if he hasn't overlooked the fact that deconstruction has not fared well in the rather decentered and pluralist universe of Anglo-American critical theoretical thinking, despite the fact that a common dominant point is the rejection of a totalizing notion of Grand Theory, if not a general disgust for logocentricism (i.e., "metaphysics" in its most reductive sense). After all, feminists, pragmatists, postcolonialists, queer theorists, post-Marxists, and many other designated subspecialties in the criticism-theory nexus share Derrida's antipathy to closure and appear open to "otherness." But, as we will see, deconstruction has taken a beating in precisely this arena of supposedly like-minded critical orientations whose state, or overall condition as an archipelago of differentiated critical ensembles, often mirrors Derrida's own prescriptions for liberating us from order.

In coming to terms with the dilemma of deconstruction as posed by the theory mess, I conclude that one ought to think through the theory mess from a phenomenological perspective in which the mess is not an antinomy to something better but a horizon of understanding in and of itself that has order, though not the totalizing, logocentric, or panoptical kind of order loathsome to deconstruction. This is not to fall into the temptation of simply arguing for the idea of order as disorder and disorder as order. Nor do I want to make a case for an undecidability of order and disorder. Rather, I think it is wiser to argue that the theory mess is another way of naming the difference between order and disorder as a conflict that is sustained as a horizon of critical apprehension if not comprehension that follows and brings into relation disparate historical currents, rather than attempting to reduce itself to the task of making a decision between two alternatives.[9] Only when this difference explodes as a flashpoint that forces the issue of *either* this *or* that does it pose itself as a crisis that demands adjudication. But at that point the difference no longer poses itself *as* a horizon of apprehension but rather as the specific event of a determination or decision *on* the horizon of apprehension. That this event is itself comprehended by the horizon line of difference within a much larger expanse of relations is what brings it back within the fold of differential relations generally. As horizon, the theory mess characterizes and hence delimits ensembles of relations that have specific trajectories, like the history of deconstruction's negative receptions in the U.S. and U.K. At least, such is the view that I develop in the penultimate section of this book on reconceptualizing the theory mess.

Given the split screens of reading that a history of contemporary theory more or less requires, I have written a modular text in which I look at symptomatic critical engagements or disengagements. Although there is no attempt to totalize, there is nevertheless enough of a linear (or horizonal) historical sketch for those who are interested in reading about the unfolding of theory over the past three decades. While I look at individual approaches or views, it should be kept in mind that I am all the while addressing the conflicts of mind within an intellectual community of academicians in the U.S. and U.K. that has not been eager to force the issue of theoretical incoherence, let alone the distorted and often hysterical attacks on deconstruction. Certainly, one could cynically hypothesize that the question of incoherence and incompetency is never forced, because many academics are hopeful that critical theory will self-destruct if it subjects itself to enough conflicts and contradictions. More charitably, one could hypothesize that we seem to be living at a time when it is more professionally advantageous to tolerate wildly differing views within a supermarket of ideas than to insist on some kind of intellectual reckoning. Again, this raises questions about conceptual permissibility and the limits of theory.

Because I want to underscore my view that we are generally in a bad state of theory, if not a bad state of intellectual community, the overarching thread of my accounts will be the permissibility of the bewilderingly negative reception that deconstruction has received — or what amounts to concerted attempts to eclipse (misrepresent, overlook, patronize, abuse, forget) deconstruction — despite the theoretical breakthroughs and "paradigm busting" that deconstruction has self-evidently brought to pass. In speaking to Christopher Fynsk about my plans to write such a history of attempts to eclipse deconstruction, he wondered whether anything positive could come of such an account and why anyone would want to pursue such a study. His point was well taken. However, I think that the history of deconstruction's drubbing in academia and the media is remarkable enough to merit some sustained attention, if only because it suggests not only that deconstruction has hit a philosophical nerve in many quarters but also that the theory mess is itself the overdetermination of a crisis of judgment that has yet to be adequately acknowledged or addressed in university communities. After all, the sustained attack on deconstruction is largely the expression of a crisis concerning values at whose heart is the inability to know good from bad, right from wrong, and true from false. The attempts to eclipse deconstruction are also reminiscent of the kind of intolerance that Western societies have expressed during their darker historical moments. This parallel suggests that the fight over ideas is never simply academic and that other motives — often passionate motives concerning religious, moral, and political beliefs — put theorists and theories at odds or into agreement.

Last, I'm fully aware that Derrida doesn't need anyone to defend deconstruction for him. Yet few people have openly defended deconstruction against its adversaries. What I have attempted is a sympathetic though not uncritical counterreading of deconstruction that relates many of the major developments in critical theory over the past thirty years. Such an assessment is merited because we have entered a period of general disaffection with critical theory that has expressed itself in a reactionary attempt to turn back the clock. Quite symptomatic is the revival of cold war humanism, of pre–cold war aestheticism, and of Shakespeare worship by latter-day traditionalists — Harold Bloom in the form of a Johnsonian revaluation of Shakespeare's plays, and archtraditionalist Helen Vendler in the form of a book on Shakespeare's sonnets.[10] Then, too, there has been a budding poetry appreciation movement that argues that the reason students in school don't appreciate poetry is because great literature has been ruined for them by the instituting of literary critical analysis. Instead of critically "picking poems apart," teachers of poetry appreciation say we should focus on the positive experience of relishing the feelings that poetry stimulates within us.

Such tendencies are symptomatic of what some might call a "theory bust," which is to say, the assumption that now it can be admitted criticism and theory are as bankrupt as communism was after the end of the cold war. Such thinking assumes that historically everything that has happened in criticism and theory since the 1960s has been, as was once said of William Blake, the wild effusions of a distempered brain, and that now it is time to return to more reasonable (that is, literal) forms of analysis and understanding. However, in place of entertaining the fantasy that one could turn criticism and theory into a historical chapter that can be closed, I believe it is much more realistic to analyze what has happened by way of a descriptive analysis, if for no other reason than that so much has happened so quickly in the field of critical theory over the past three decades that analysis is merited in order to come to terms with the twists and turns of the recent past and what these might mean for an understanding of how contemporary academics have practiced critical thinking.

I wish to acknowledge the Society of Humanities at Cornell University for awarding me a year-long fellowship that enabled me to write most of this project. I especially wish to thank participants in the Society for their good fellowship and encouragement, with special gratitude to Dominick LaCapra and Mary Jacobus for their many kindnesses. I am grateful to the secretarial staff of the Society without whom my year there would have been far less enjoyable and productive. I am also grateful to the National Endowment for the Humanities and to Wayne State University for funding that enabled me to work on this project. Also, I wish to thank staff and faculty here at the University of Southampton who have made my transition to the United Kingdom easier. Of course, I want to thank everyone who responded to my drafts; most constructive were the anonymous evaluators and the board of Columbia University Press who gave me substantial critiques that led to considerable revision. Last, I am very grateful to Jennifer Crewe for her support of my project.

THE THEORY MESS

THE THEORY MESS

INTRODUCTION

As a catchword, "deconstruction" has been a rising star among neologisms in our culture. At least, it seems that everyone now wants to deconstruct something, whether an administrative structure, an economic plan, an educational procedure, or, as in the case of Woody Allen's *Deconstructing Harry*, a neurotic movie character. As a philosophy, however, deconstruction has fared less well in the popular imagination, since it not only sounds hectoring and violent but has been associated in the press with the demise of tradition in the liberal arts. Given the contradiction between the widespread acceptance of "deconstruction" the catchword and the equally widespread rejection of deconstruction the philosophy, our immediate interest will be to dwell on the conflicted reception of deconstruction within institutions of higher learning and, insofar as it is relevant, the general culture.

This will be significant for several reasons. First, we can see what happens when a new body of ideas is introduced into a culture such as ours that praises itself for tolerance, objectivity, and civility. Second, we can examine the extent to which deconstruction's reception has been tied to a general legitimacy crisis in the humanities regarding ideological, methodological, and conceptual conflicts. Third, we will notice a certain incoherence in the field of critical theory that makes various encounters with theoretical bodies of thought problematic. Fourth, we will see how deconstruction has and has not been eclipsed within a layered and often contradictory array of theoretical approaches and views that are themselves quite unaware of the intellectual historical contours in which they occur. I am interested in this condition of critical incoherence, because it is and isn't what one might call a "theory mess," since the mess has a kind of logic relating to questions of receptivity, engagement, and interlocution that we often do not consider when we talk about the history of theory.

In beginning to talk about the theory mess, I can think of no better place to start than with a passage by Ann duCille, an African-American critic, who clearly sees into the kind of problem I want to investigate:

> So I have arrived at what for me is at the heart of what's the matter. Much of the newfound interest in African-American women that seems to honor the field of black feminist studies actually demeans it by treating it not like a discipline with a history and a body of rigorous scholarship and distinguished scholars underpinning it, *but like an anybody-can-play pick-up game performed on a wide-open, untrammeled field.* Often the object of the game seems to be to reinvent the intellectual wheel: to boldly go where in fact others have gone before, to flood the field with supposedly new "new scholarship" that evinces little or no sense of the discipline's genealogy.[1]

What bothers duCille and what should bother us is a certain failed encounter with African-American studies, if not black feminism, when critics ignore disciplinarity, history, and intellectual genealogy and write whatever comes to mind, as if the study of African-American women was little else than an "anybody-can-play pick-up game" that is subject to no restrictions whatsoever. It is the emphasis on the failed encounter that I will be coming back to throughout my account. Indeed, what duCille notices about the study of African-American literature is, in fact, a general condition of literary scholarship that affects all its areas of study, particularly critical theory. Because we are in a profession that expects prodigious publication, there is real incentive *not* to respect the intellectual history or genealogy of an area of study and to act as if anybody can play at anything, whether it be interpreting Toni Morrison's *Beloved*, Jacques Lacan's "Mirror Stage," or the situation of subalterns in Southeast Asia. DuCille is right when she argues that when people write without putting in the required homework, they end up writing pieces that, for all their purported sophistication, are selectively ignorant explorations of a topic that ensure a general failure of engagement, or, what Derrida has called a "*faux bond*," or "no show."

My working thesis is the idea that over the past thirty years critical theory has obeyed the principle of the *faux bond*: the false bond, no show, failed encounter, or missed interlocution that creates some kind of linkage, despite itself, say, the angry linkage expressed by duCille who sees a certain bad faith in the *faux bond* that bonds itself with other kinds of bad faith that one could imagine to be of relevance in terms of race; for example, disavowal, avoidance, disrespect, or taking for granted. Indeed, whereas the *faux bond* is most troublesome in this context, it is the case that *faux bonds* are quite common in academia. Consider the *faux bond* of a bad translation. Walter Benjamin's *Trauerspiel* is currently in an unusable English translation, which means there will be a failed encounter with that book for those who cannot read German.

Consider a conference that might be arranged on a campus from which someone on that campus was eclipsed as a speaker—an expert, as it turns out, who has more expertise in the field than anyone who was invited to speak. It's a *faux bond* that sometimes occurs, and one that can have political consequences, given that the eclipsed party might be annoyed that there are those who think that scholarship is an "anybody-can-play pick-up game." The *faux bond* can also take place when a text misses the point or somehow fails to engage the crux of a complex of issues. For example, Frank Lentricchia's *After the New Criticism* failed to acknowledge even one feminist critic at the end of a decade when feminism was arguably among the most important (if not *the* most important) critical developments of the 1970s. Getting much of the history of recent theory right, Lentricchia's book, in retrospect, is a dud: a misfire or *faux bond*. In truth, many important books are duds in this respect, and that they can be influential is itself problematic, since they function to misdirect or disorient us in terms of what at any given time is, in fact, of most conceptual significance.

The *faux bond* can be more subtle, as in the case of the Yale School, which for over a decade played false friend to Derrida. The de Man scandal is an instance where the problem of the false friend surfaced rather dramatically. De Man, it turned out, was and wasn't a cognate or friend to deconstruction; was and wasn't of the intellectual genealogy that could or should identify him with deconstruction. Of course, whenever a critic is influenced by another critic or belongs to the school of a certain kind of criticism, a close look at that person's writings will always betray him or her as a false friend and the writing as a *faux bond*, for there is a sense in which something does not exactly match up or exactly bond. In *Glas,* Derrida situated the *faux bond* within his own text as the false relation of his two columns, the one on Hegel and the other on Genet. They talked past each other. They were no shows for each other. They were false friends to each other. And yet they collide, intersect, match up in places, overlap. The *faux bond,* then, resembles two ships passing in the night. They may miss. But even so, they come into proximity.

It's the two ships together we are talking about, the missing of an encounter whose meeting place was at least staged and whose conditions were at least partially realized.

In "Limited Inc." (1977), Derrida develops the idea of failed critical encounters as a means to exploit the vast number of ways in which intellectual confrontation takes place even as it does not happen. This essay is a vitriolic response to John Searle, who had written "Reiterating the Differences: A Reply to Derrida" (1977) in which Derrida's critiques of speech act theory are dismissed as nugatory and irrelevant to speech act theory per se.[2] In challenging the premise that speech acts are always predicated upon an encounter between an addresser and an addressee, Derrida writes, "What I like about this 'confrontation' [between Derrida/Searle] is that I don't know if it is quite taking place, if it ever will be able, or will have been able, quite, to take place; or if it does, between whom or what." Who speaks for speech act theory when Searle speaks on its behalf? Is it Searle only? Or is it a group of "auto-authorized heirs of Austin" for whom Searle is the front man? Are we talking about a one-to-one encounter or the politics of a debate between deconstruction and speech act theory or, to put it in even more political terms, a debate between French and Anglo-American philosophy? Derrida asks,

> Is it because the confrontation never quite takes place that I take such lasting pleasure in it? Because I, too, think as much, almost that is, almost but not quite? Or is it, on the contrary, because I am very excited, I confess, by this scene? But the speech acts of the *Reply*, by their structure composed of denial, seduction, coquettishly fascinating underneath the virile candor, initiating a "confrontation" by saying that it has not taken place and, moreover, that at (*and in the*) *present*, between the late Austin and myself, *it does not take place*, or at least not entirely, *not quite*, both because I have missed the point, missed him, and because he was already dead . . . when I missed him, so that in fact I did not have much of a chance. The speech acts of the *Reply* do their utmost, apparently, to insure that this confrontation will not have taken place and, moreover, that it shall not (ever) take place, or at least not quite; and yet they produce it, this confrontation that they sought to avoid, that they declare to be non-existent without being able to stop themselves from participating in it, from confirming and developing the event through the very gesture of withdrawing from it.[3]

Indeed, Searle's instantiation of the *faux bond* characterizes an attempt to eclipse deconstruction that has been repeated in many different ways during the three decades in which Derrida's intellectual influence has been felt outside of France. However, as the quotation from "Limited Inc." demonstrates, Derrida is quite capable of turning this strategy to his own advantage by calling attention to the umbra of a *faux bond*, which is to say, to the problematic casting of the analytical philosophical shadow over deconstruction, since that shadow is the umbra of a false encounter staged by a certain philosophical hubris whose blindness is made manifest in the very attempt to overshadow and hence negate what analytical philosophy does not understand. In other words, the umbra of the *faux bond* marks the place of a willful failure to understand, an eclipse that the critics of deconstruction hope to use to advantage.

Ann duCille's complaint that African-American studies have been taken up at will by those who have no in-depth training in the field speaks to this general problem. For such an appropriation, too, is less about incompetence than about the hubris of those who wish to speak for and hence eclipse black feminist studies, a *faux bond* that marks, say, the opportunistic ascension of the "anybody-can-play" politically correct critic in the place of a willful failure to understand. That this is a usurpation and not just an eclipsing of black feminist studies ought to be considered, because the goal of the appropriator is to arrogate for oneself what one has successfully blocked from view by way of a failed encounter. However, as Derrida's "Limited Inc." demonstrates, this strategy can be turned around in such a way that what has been negated or eclipsed returns within the discursive field of purposive misunderstanding and supersession as the unassimilable unthought that ruptures the lie. Hence, as quoted above, "The speech acts of the *Reply* do their utmost, apparently, to insure that this confrontation will not have taken place and, moreover, that it shall not (ever) take place, or at least not quite; and yet they produce it, this confrontation that they sought to avoid."

BEGINNINGS

In addressing Jean-Paul Sartre, Derrida once wrote, "What must a society such as ours be if a man, who, in his own way, rejected or misunderstood so many theoretical and literary events of his time—let's say, to go quickly, psychoanalysis, Marxism, structuralism, Joyce, Artaud, Bataille, Blanchot—who accumulated and disseminated incredible misreadings of Heidegger, sometimes of Husserl, could come to dominate the cultural scene to the point of becoming a great popular figure?"[4] We might transpose this statement by asking what it says of us as an academy that we have misunderstood and rejected so many theoretical and literary events of our time—let's say, deconstruction, postmodernism, Lacanianism, Marxism, but also structuralism and formalism—and have accumulated and disseminated such an incredible number of misinformed readings of Irigaray, Deleuze, Derrida, Lacan, Foucault, Adorno, Lukács, Benjamin, that this very same society of scholars has come to dominate the cultural scene to the point of becoming celebrated? What is it about the *faux bond* as the purposive failure to comprehend that enables an individual or a group to come into prominence as a cultural celebrity?

As Elizabeth Roudinesco has chronicled, the Johns Hopkins encounter with deconstruction in "The Languages of Criticism and the Sciences of Man" symposium (October 1966) almost didn't happen.[5] Invited at the last minute, Derrida came to America to read a paper that in the years to follow would have the impact of a manifesto. Derrida called it "Structure, Sign, and Play." In an encounter that immediately raised a couple of eyebrows, the question that may have occurred to people was whether Derrida annihilates the social subject as a precondition for embarking on a deconstruction of a text. Hence Serge Doubrovsky complained:

> It is not One who speaks, but "I." And even if you reduce the I, you are obliged to come across once again the concept of intentionality, which I believe is at the base of a whole thought, which, moreover, you do not deny. Therefore I ask how you reconcile it with your present attempts?

Derrida replied:

> The subject is absolutely indispensable. I don't destroy the subject; I situate it. That is to say, I believe that at a certain level both of experience and of philosophical and scientific discourse one cannot get along without the notion of subject. It is a question of knowing where it comes from and how it functions.[6]

This rejoinder to Doubrovsky has had the same fate as many of Derrida's qualifications over the past thirty years: none of his detractors has either heard or wished to hear Derrida speak in these terms. Therefore, according to the logic of the *faux bond*, Derrida has been eclipsed; that is, he has been treated as if he had claimed different positions on the question of subject-hood, positions that foreclose precisely what he is not foreclosing in the comments above.

In the series of interviews entitled *Positions* (1972), Derrida is told by his interviewers, Jean Louis Houdebine and Guy Scarpetta, that he was the focus of attention at a conference in Cluny and that critiques were leveled against him. His critics charged that Derrida's attachment to Heidegger's legacy came at the expense of considering other figures (like Marx) and that his critiques of metaphysics textualized history to such a point that the real world was effaced from consideration. Derrida responded by pointing out that he was considering the metaphysical character of history as a "system of implications (teleology, eschatology, elevating and interiorizing accumulation of meaning, a certain type of traditionality, a certain concept of continuity, truth, etc.)." Metaphysics, he said, cannot exist by itself. It has to be situated or instantiated in the historical. As if to predict the advent of New Historicism, Derrida argued that "there is not one single history, a general history, but rather histories *different* in their type, rhythm, mode of inscription—intervallic, differentiated histories."[7] "History," as it was used in the Cluny colloquium, referred to a homogeneous master narrative, a "Hegelian" conception of history that Derrida was opposing. Here was the emergence of some very disruptive conceptions that would only become relevant in the 1980s: the end of master narratives, the pluralization of histories, and the critique of closure. All of these points would become foundational for cultural studies and allied specializations in the 1980s, feminism and postcolonial studies among them. Yet, Derrida would be eclipsed—accused over and over again of being ahistorical, antihistorical, unhistorical.

Some will recall that Derrida was not noticed very much in the United States until 1972, when a paperback edition of the 1966 conference became widely available under the title *The Structuralist Controversy* and rumors about Derrida's brilliance and pathbreaking thought had begun to circulate in both language and philosophy departments where theory was an issue. Derrida's stunning work on Husserl, *Speech and Phenomena* (1967), was already translated and published by 1973 in an edition that also included the crucial essay

"Différance." Indeed, it was hard at the time to transpose the critique of Husserl into a literary critical framework, if it was possible at all. And it was even more difficult to grasp the significance of "Différance," which David B. Allison, its translator, and Newton Garver, its commentator, failed to contextualize in terms of its most obvious though somewhat recondite intertexts— namely, Plato's dialogue on difference and identity that comes toward the end of *The Sophist*, Hegel's *Logic*, Martin Heidegger's *Identity and Difference*, and Ferdinand de Saussure's *Course in General Linguistics*.

Here, no doubt, the failure to allow deconstruction to have an interlocution with its immediate contexts served to obscure Derrida's thinking. Still, Garver wrote a very insightful and careful introduction that situated Derrida and, by extension Husserl, in the context of Wittgenstein and ordinary language philosophy. "Our attention must focus on Wittgenstein," Garver said, "since his own philosophical development, with respect to the foundations of language, is in many ways parallel to the movement in Continental philosophy from Husserl to Heidegger to Derrida."[8] This view was quite ahead of its time—so much ahead, in fact, that it could not usefully situate Derrida's work for an audience outside the sphere of ordinary language philosophy who would have benefited from some of the more fundamental intertextual relationships that were more directly in line with Derrida's conceptual trajectories.

That aside, it is a shame that Garver's sagacious definition of deconstruction would be routinely overlooked by the literati who would appropriate Derrida for their own purposes. "In its negative component," Garver wrote,

> the core of Derrida's analysis, or "deconstruction," is a sustained argument against the possibility of anything pure and simple which can serve as the foundation for the meaning of signs. It is an argument which strikes at the very idea of a transcendental phenomenology. The move is parallel with Wittgenstein's rejection of the idea of simples (which is also the core of the negative component in his later work); but whereas the simples Wittgenstein came to reject were logical atoms . . . the simples that Derrida rejects are the simples of transcendental phenomenology . . . viz., experience that is pure in the sense that it can be fully understood as it is found in our private mental life, without reference to transient circumstances or actual empirical objects.[9]

Allison's introduction was similarly wise in its pronouncements (although, once more, it is a pity that literary critics were not influenced by his reading either):

> What is striking in Derrida's claim is the objection that linguistic meaning can never be completely present. There can never be an absolutely signified content, an absolutely identical or univocal meaning in language. All these values are denied to meaning once we admit its dependence upon nonpresent elements. *Meaning can never be isolated or held in abstraction from its context, e.g., its linguistic, semiotic, or historical context.*[10]

This last sentence, which I have italicized, flies in the face of a daisy chain of remarks by the uninformed that for some twenty-five years have accused Derrida of promoting a referenceless free play of meaning detached from any context or reality whatsoever. Exactly how such a counterfactual reading of Derrida could gain currency is something that we shall investigate, though for now we may venture the safe guess that British empirical resistance to Continental philosophy aside, there is considerable resistance to the emergence of "theory" as a practice of writing that draws upon competencies and talents that are alien to the old-fashioned scholarship practiced by academics earlier in the century.

An allergy to deconstruction aside, of significance in the positive early reception of Derrida was Paul de Man's essay, "The Rhetoric of Blindness: Jacques Derrida's Reading of Rousseau," wherein he reviewed Derrida's *Of Grammatology.* Anyone wanting a reliable introduction to Derrida's work could have turned to de Man's reading, which was careful to underline the following points:

1. Derrida's compatibility with standard scholarly evaluations of Jean-Jacques Rousseau and its confirmation of Derrida's arguments concerning Rousseau's metaphysics;
2. Derrida's meticulous close readings in which the process of reading (its protocols, its systematicity, its blindspots) was itself examined as part and parcel of its capacity to posit readerly constructions upon which valorizations are then based; and
3. Derrida's careful attention to the historical (diachronic) and structu-

ral (synchronic) relations that placed his analysis of Rousseau in correspondence with an analysis of Claude Lévi-Strauss, where certain general deductions about the valorization of writing and reading as preconditions for understanding could be posited as problematic for hermeneutics and, by implication, for Western philosophy.

De Man immediately saw Derrida as a key figure for the future of literary criticism. Telling, of course, is that de Man's chief interest was Derrida's rigor: his formalizing capacity to transcend mere formalism and talk about it (as reading and as writing) while in the process. What de Man did not admire, however, was Derrida's avant-gardist side as a writer of strange new texts that broke with traditional philosophical protocols.[11]

As it turned out, de Man's scrupulous and very accessible description of Derrida's work fell on deaf ears. Instead, American readers were fascinated with Marxist Fredric Jameson's overview of intellectual currents in France entitled *The Prison-House of Language*. Published in 1972, just a year before the appearance of the English translation of *Speech and Phenomena*, Jameson's book attempted to survey Russian formalism, structuralism, and what some people were already calling poststructuralism. Instead of developing a rigorous analytic, typical say of de Man, Allison, and Garver, Jameson wrote a slapdash account of all the new theories he had encountered in Paris. Starting with the idea that "the Anglo-American approach has of course its philosophical and ideological roots in the long tradition of British empiricism," Jameson says that the French approach begins with the idea that perception is limited to what a perceptual model permits us to see: "The methodological starting point does more than simply reveal, it actually creates, the object of study."[12] A view that would become influential in America some years later by way of Michel Foucault, Jameson cited it in order to argue that structuralism was inherently a semiotic prison-house.

In his discussion of Derrida, Jameson pointed out that Derrida had gone beyond the formalist limitations of Saussurean linguistics by questioning the function of presence in relation to the self-identity of language. That is, Derrida was a postformalist. However, instead of pointing out that Saussurean difference had ensured the self-identity of linguistic elements by putting them in strict opposition to other elements that fixed them in place—whereas Derridean *différance* introduced a destabilization of the distinction between identity and difference that threatened the self-referentiality of language (and hence its solipsistic or prison-house quality)—Jameson, who did not fully grasp Derrida's project, decided to talk about how, in Derrida's own words, "Meaning is in its very structure always a *trace*, an already happened."[13] In other words, Jameson decided to explain *différance* as a palimpsestic forestructure that always defers the origin of meaning in a way that makes the signified inaccessible. Jameson thus decided to explain *différance* in such a way that language would expose itself as *mise en abyme* (a bottomless pit of self-reflexivity) and thereby reveal itself as the very prison-house of language that Derrida had taken pains *not* to construct. This is but one of a large number of distortions in Jameson's account that, unfortunately, eclipsed Derrida's argument and was taken very much on faith by readers who were eager to inform themselves of developments in France. As such, Jameson's account instantiates a failed encounter with deconstruction that would be repeated for some three decades, often in the public press.

It is odd, given the academy's purported interest in careful if not painstaking reading that Jameson's off-base reading wasn't put in check by either Allison and Garver's remarks, de Man's review of *Of Grammatology*, or Jonathan Culler's authoritative analyses in *Structuralist Poetics* (1975), where he emphasized that the Derridean free play of the signifier is always subjected to the protocols of conventions and contexts. "The meaning of a sentence," Culler wrote,

> is not a form or an essence, present at the moment of its production and lying behind it as a truth to be recovered, but the series of developments to which it gives rise, as determined by past and future relations between words and the conventions of semiotic systems. Some texts are more "orphaned" than others because the conventions of reading are not so firm as to provide a stepfather. To read a political speech, for example, is to submit to a teleology, to take the text as governed by a communicative end. . . . But literature, foregrounding the text itself, gives freer play to the "essential drift" and autonomous productivity of the language.[14]

Culler's distinction between literary and political texts is significant in that it recognizes degrees of referentiality and does not lump all discourse into a single category (i.e., language) within which we're supposedly locked up.

CO-OPTING DECONSTRUCTION

Back in the early 1970s, deconstruction was still very much an unknown, a philosophy as yet to be defined. However, there already had been attempts by outside forces to appropriate or eclipse deconstruction by as early as 1967. The Tel Quel group, for example, had assumed that the economy of writing, as Derrida described it, could be viewed as a materialist account of signification that had parallels in psychoanalysis and Marxism, where language could be seen as a base rather than a superstructure—or, the primary mode of production upon which all other modes of production were modeled. The voice/writing distinction, which Derrida had elegantly critiqued, was thought to open the way for a materialist understanding of writing as a grammatology that took distance from idealist or metaphysical understandings of communication that were inherently incompatible with Marxist praxis. By 1970, Derrida would alienate Tel Quel by explicitly rejecting the base/superstructure division as philosophically naïve. He had distanced himself from critics such as Philippe Sollers, Julia Kristeva, and Jean-Joseph Goux for whom the working assumption had been that language, understood semiotically, was at the base of not only cultural but material production. Then, too, in the Points edition of his *Ecrits* (1970), Jacques Lacan had made an indirect reference to Derrida as someone who had plagiarized Lacanian psychoanalysis. Lacan suggested that deconstruction was an impostor and that it should be eclipsed by Lacanian psychoanalysis. His jealousy aside, it is telling that Lacan had read enough of Derrida to make a claim on his contributions.

Meanwhile, to the French philosophical community Derrida was to be appropriated in terms of a Husserlian phenomenological tradition that, given the French history of contemporary philosophical thought, embraced Hegel and Heidegger as well. Clearly delineated in this intellectual context is (1) Derrida's juxtaposition of various "constructions" in analysis that resist the very synthesis they presuppose (hence the indebtedness to Husserl); (2) Derrida's dismantling of dialectics and of existential presuppositions of self/other relations (hence an indebtedness to Hegel's *Logic*); and (3) Derrida's critiques of metaphysical foundations (hence the indebtedness to Heidegger and, by extention, Nietzsche). Of interest in all these conjectures is the elusiveness of deconstruction as a philosophy that escapes apprehension and determination by a system of thought that is already in place. That is, no philosophy already in place can countersign for deconstruction or take itself for deconstruction's entelechy. This is also true in terms of the Yale School's eclipse of deconstruction by treating it as a literary philosophy compatible with late New Criticism, which by 1970 had entered an antiformalist phase.

Of course, by the early 1970s some American critics started realizing that "theory" could stand for a higher form of criticism that self-reflexively asked questions about its own formal procedures. "Theory" was somewhat akin to a "systems analysis" approach that when applied to critics such as T. S. Eliot, Rosemond Tuve, and D. C. Allen made them look rather ridiculous, since it was obvious that as critics they had never thought about criticism as a formal structure that imposes strictures upon an interpretation. Derrida's "Structure, Sign, and Play," de Man's "The Rhetoric of Blindness," and E. D. Hirsch's *Validity in Interpretation* (1967) were important texts of the 1960s that introduced American critics to hermeneutical questions of what it means to think of criticism as an analytical system.[15]

Indeed, there are places where Derrida has referred to deconstruction as a systems theory. For example, in "There is No *One* Narcissism" (1986), Derrida tells us:

> Deconstruction concerns, first of all, systems. This does not mean that it brings down the system, but that it opens onto possibilities of arrangement and assembling, of being together if you like, that are not necessarily systematic, in the strict sense that philosophy gives to this word. It is thus a reflection on the system, on the closure and opening of the system.[16]

"Structure, Sign, and Play" (1966) is perhaps Derrida's most determinate use of deconstruction as a systems theory whose thesis is that analytical totalities are metaphysical fictions. It is well known that this essay implicitly demolished a considerable amount of literary criticism by calling the terms of its structural validation into question. Derrida's postulation of a *logocentric fallacy* dealt a death blow to the credibility and legitimacy of what many people in America called "scholarship" (e.g., synoptic historicism supported by formalist analysis). His arguments concerning decentering, supplementarity, marginalization, circularity, and differentiation were structural critiques or systems analyses that, once explained, could no longer be ignored by those who were serious about questions of validity and truth. Despite the fact that many American critics wrote in blissful ignorance of Derrida's analytical demonstrations—anyway, could they change course after building reputations on a discredited method of scholarship?—his writing did contribute to a crisis of judgment. This was reinforced by a large number of Continental theorists who become known in the United States during the 1970s, Michel Foucault among them.

In the early 1970s, then, deconstruction was, from an American perspective, the farthest outpost of the French structuralist adventure—structuralist linguistics, structuralist anthropology, structuralist literary criticism, structuralist Marxism—whose critique of traditional rationalist forms of critical analysis was decisive. If this sounds a bit odd today, we should remember that structuralism did not precede Derrida in America. Rather, French structuralism of the 1950s was being introduced into the United States some twenty years after the fact, while work by a younger generation—Baudrillard, Derrida, Eco, Foucault, and Kristeva—was *also* being disseminated. This was confusing, to say the least. In addition, particular attention was being paid to hermeneutics, since of major importance to some American critics of the 1970s was the question of what one might call "critical sophistication"—the search for methods that were not based on simplistic formal assumptions of agreement (structural coherence, historical identity, or universal value).

By the early 1970s, Derrida stood out for having made a most decisive structural critique that invalidated institutional practices in full swing. However, this did not mean that many on the losing side of the critique were aware of Derrida or, if they were, that they were going to surrender themselves up to the prescriptions of some little-known Parisian thinker. Hence even though Gayatri Chakravorty Spivak, in her translator's preface to *Of Grammatology* (1976), outlined an elaborate account of how Derrida transvalued the methodologies of Hegel, Nietzsche, Husserl, Freud, Heidegger, and de Saussure, her explication did not register.[17]

Therefore, it was possible for Derrida to be absolutely on the mark with a substantial critique of major scope and yet be effectively eclipsed by those who had the most to lose by it. Suffice it to say that whenever there is a great disparity between a correct critique and false social practice, it is always the false social practice that wins out, given that politics always triumphs over truth—at least in the short run. And therein lies the basis of the various failed or eclipsed encounters with deconstruction: it has not generally been in the interests of Anglo-American critical establishments to embrace a critique that invalidates ongoing critical practices upon which major careers have been and could be based.

Given that by the late 1970s it was becoming less and less possible to dodge the challenge of deconstruction as a systems critique, it is not surprising that Jameson's prison-house of language was resurrected by conservative critics as if it were the glaring blind spot of deconstruction that spelled its demise.

THEORY AS POSTPHILOSOPHY:
ROSI BRAIDOTTI, GEOFFREY HARTMAN, AND ANNETTE KOLODNY

Before we turn to Meyer Abrams's attempts to eclipse deconstruction in "The Deconstructive Angel" (1977), we need to address a much more significant issue, namely, the decline of philosophy as the ground for the human and natural sciences. Derrida himself wrote political tracts during the late 1970s in the hopes that the French government would not cut philosophy from the Lycée curriculum. In America philosophy is usually not part of the high-school experience; and as a result of its tenuous, if not endangered, standing in the university, some humanists have agonized over the demystification and dismissal of conceptual doctrines that form the foundation of Western arts and letters. Having debunked reason, God, and the human as the fundamental grounds for philosophical inquiry we are, in Rosi Braidotti's words, "epistemological orphans." Braidotti has written that

> The ontological insecurity we suffer is our unavoidable historical condition. Afflicted by the melancholy which henceforth marks the end of this millennium, haunted by a feeling of loss, philosophy is no longer the queen of knowledge, nor is it the master-discipline anymore. At the most it can claim the status of a merry widow, sadly trying to find her place in the new cynicism of postmodern society.

For traditionalists such as Allan Bloom, E. D. Hirsch, George Steiner, Roger Shattuck, and John Hollander this represents a major intellectual catastrophe that can only be salvaged by a new renaissance—rediscovering the intellectual wealth of the past. However, for Braidotti, "the state of intellectual 'crisis' we are in is not necessarily the sign of the imminent death of theoretical practice."[18] That is, for Braidotti the word "theory" stands in for philosophy's wake and as such is itself the afterlife of philosophy.

Hence, despite a general crisis of philosophy, there is nevertheless a will to go on theorizing. Undoubtedly, there is an advantage to keeping the term "theorizing" rather undertheorized, because then one can think in terms of a philosophy as yet to come, a philosophy that goes by the name of theory, which, unlike traditional philosophy, in and of itself isn't as yet critically determined (i.e., conceptually, logically, historically). Moreover, a name for this theory which is on the way to becoming a philosophy—the philosophy to come—might very well be "deconstruction," insofar as we are talking about theoretical practices that emerge after the demise of grounding concepts such as man, spirit, truth, and reason. To that extent, "theory" takes place between a philosophy that has been and a philosophy that is as yet to be. This is why "theory" takes place outside the law of system building, logical coherence, subject centeredness, self-reflexivity, and metalanguage. In fact, such a theory occurs outside the law of self-identity. A definition of "theory," then, is extremely vexed, because its determinations are not answerable to laws of self-identification—for example, the intellectual biography of the theorist who theorizes, concepts of method, stable philosophical vocabularies, logical structures, or the overall coherence of a philosophical oeuvre.

This understanding of theory is much more advanced, of course, than the systems analysis approach espoused by those studying semiotics, structuralism, hermeneutics, and deconstruction in the 1970s for the sake of building a better theoretical mouse trap. Indeed, what Braidotti calls "theory" can be related to that indeterminacy of deconstruction that has kept it separate from, say, Yale School literary criticism, Tel Quel, or Jamesonian cultural analysis. In texts such as *Glas* (1974) and *The Post Card* (1980), Derrida embarked on what he himself has recognized as an *écriture* that cannot be justified or understood in terms of any academic genre of writing. Similarly, Maurice Blanchot's texts on neutrality, disaster, and absence of the book reflect a mode of theorization that makes the most sense when one thinks of it as a writing that comes in the wake of philosophy's death. Hölderlin's critical fragments, Nietzsche's *Nachlass*, Wittgenstein's *Zettel*, and Artaud's notes written in madness remind one of cuttings or conceptual outtakes that are philosophical scraps of what comes after the fall of philosophy and the demise of the humanities. As such they exemplify a will to go on theorizing. One can detect this same willingness in the writings of Marguerite Duras, Hélène

Cixous, and Charlotte Delbo. One could also consider the performance writing of Meredith Monk, Karen Finley, or Ping Chong—a writing that gathers after the death of theatrical writing. Analogously, consider how the hyphenated identitarianism of postcolonial writing, the decentered condition of postmodern writing, and the polylingual condition of borderland or nomadic writing are occurring in the wake of literary criticism's demise, if not the fall of literature itself.

Still, if the advent of theory in the wake of an empire of signs sounds radical to Braidotti and others, it also reveals the fact that this very same indeterminacy of "theory" has a conservative dimension that we could call the eternal return of "criticism." It may turn out, after all, that the New Criticism was aberrant in its presupposition that its mode of criticism could be more systematic and rigorous than the critical trends of the nineteenth century. After all, unlike philosophy, criticism is in essence a discourse that is supposed to elude systems and bypass logic in order to make brilliantly inspired and singular insights that, in retrospect, cannot be made any other way and hence not be proven to anyone's satisfaction. Criticism has always been a blend of authoritarianism (unwarranted self-assertion) and the haphazard (the unaccountable, the surprising). It has always snatched insight (made brilliant connections no one else would ordinarily see) at the expense of misrepresentations and oversights (misreading). Typical are Samuel Johnsons's essays on Shakespeare, Novalis's aphorisms, or Oscar Wilde's remarks on life imitating art. Paul de Man himself summed this up when he said that in order to see something has to be overlooked, as if insight were always beclouded by blindness.

Such criticism is most in its own element when it is belletristic—conceited (talented, unaccountable), blithe (unsystematic, vagrant), prescriptive (moral, aesthetic, political), and dubious (skeptical, ambivalent, self-critical). Therefore, criticism has always been postmetaphysical, insofar as it has never been beholden to ratiocination, systematization, and identitarianism. Criticism is analytical, even utilitarian, but loosely so. It can be illogical, biased, impressionistic, impassioned, reductive, and evocative. In Geoffrey Hartman's *Saving the Text* (1981), which is an analysis of Derrida's *Glas*, we experience such criticism taken to the limit. Indeed, what Hartman says of Derrida at the outset could be said of Hartman himself: "His *discours de la folie* blurs genres or engages in so interminable a mode of analysis that the sanity of writing— its indebtedness to evolved conventions, as well as its apparent realism—is threatened."[19] What Hartman writes about is the larger issue of what I am (after Braidotti) calling "theory," the place where philosophy and criticism intersect. It is a place that can elude realism and sanity, if not sobriety. More to the point, theory is a discourse that in threatening the sanity of writing threatens us with unreadability if not unrepresentability.

Elsewhere in *Saving the Text* Hartman advances a rumination whose significance is quite striking. He speaks of a "literary evolution of the vulgar or vernacular tongues" that is "essential for an understanding of the concept of dissemination." These vulgar or vernacular tongues "clearly belong in a differentiated series with imitation, translation, contamination, secularization, and (sacred) parody." Whereas the appropriation of vernaculars is usually imitative, in the case of Derrida "[dissemination] is now directed *analytically*—prosaically, if you wish—*against* the mimetic principle."[20] Such writing cannot be very utilitarian, because it refuses to disclose itself as research in the scientific sense wherein vernaculars are purged and a bureaucratized lingua franca substituted in their place. Again, Hartman seems to be glossing himself, given that he has been playing fast and loose with vernacular expressions throughout his commentary. There is, he says, something antimimetic or unrepresentable in a disseminative vernacular play that withdraws itself from our understanding and hence our capacity to know, much less our ability to adequately appropriate, imitate, or formalize the vulgar tongues. Hartman's heteroglot criticism and Derrida's heteroglot philosophy are therefore both instantiations of theory in the sense of a discourse that is and isn't methodologically rigorous and that, as such, cannot be appropriated as a formally reproducible analytic.

If I have invoked Braidotti it is because she is not only a theorist but also a feminist who seems to be aware that feminism is itself more a part of what she calls "theory" than the disciplines that precede it. That, of course, is not how such theory played itself out in American universities, where feminists took a position more in tune with the conservative filiation to criticism that we have already considered. Relevant in this context is Annette Kolodny's "Dancing Through the Minefield" (1980), which is a landmark assessment of feminist criticism that inaugurates the advent of a newer critical dispensation in America known as "pluralism." Kolodny wrote that the task of American feminists is "to initiate nothing less than a playful pluralism responsive to the possibilities of multiple critical schools and methods, but captive to none, recognizing that the many tools needed for our analysis will necessarily be largely inherited and only partly of our own making."[21] This follows Kolodny's correct assessment that the diversity of feminist inquiry

> easily outstripped all efforts to define feminist literary criticism as either a coherent system or a unified set of methodologies. Under its wide umbrella, *everything* has been thrown into question: our established canons, our aesthetic criteria, our interpretive strategies, our reading habits, and, most of all, ourselves as critics and teachers.[22]

New Criticism, Marxism, semiotics, biographism, constructivism, confessionalism, moralism, and Yale School deconstructionism were among the "many tools needed for [feminist] analysis." Hartman might well have called them "vernaculars." For Kolodny and many like-minded critics, the perception that no unified set of methodologies was appropriate for a social study as diverse as feminism meant that one had to embrace pluralism and diversity. Theoretical texts, therefore, would be polyglot; they would cultivate what Hartman called "vernaculars" in the sense that they would incorporate diverse critical approaches that were both high and low. Theory, therefore, implicitly transgressed class lines, something which became more obvious in the 1980s when feminists and African-Americanists began to purposely harry the class line.

In order to justify her position, Kolodny did, however, require a three part article of faith. We must accept first that "literary history (and, with that, the historicity of literature) is a fiction"; second, "insofar as we are taught how to read, what we engage are not texts but paradigms"; and third, "since the grounds upon which we assign aesthetic value to texts are never infallible, unchangeable, or universal, we must reexamine not only our aesthetics but, as well, the inherent biases and assumptions informing the critical methods which (in part) shape our aesthetic responses."[23] In other words, history, textuality, and experience are *relative* to social consensus and are constantly being renegotiated and reconstructed by means of ongoing intellectual analyses. Putting this all together, it appears that relativism and pluralism go hand and hand with the writing of a criticism that can claim "neither definitiveness nor structural completeness." What criticism can claim, however, is "usefulness in recognizing the particular achievements of woman-as-author and their applicability in conscientiously decoding woman-as-sign." Again, "different readings will be differently useful, even illuminating, within different contexts of inquiry."[24]

Kolodny's essay marks a significant moment in literary criticism, since it both objectified and justified a pluralist and relativist ideology that was indebted to philosopher-historians such as Hans-Georg Gadamer, Michel Foucault, Thomas Kuhn, Paul Feyerabend, and Hayden White. That her thinking makes possible a certain kind of theoretical writing that conforms to Braidotti's idea of a theory in the wake of philosophy is also highly significant, though not more so than her relativist philosophical ground that many mistook for deconstruction, the basis from which feminists and multiculturalists supposedly derived the kinds of principles Kolodny outlined in her tip toe through the minefield of critical differences. At least what no one can deny is that her views of history, textuality, and experience followed rather closely the sore points of various critiques that had been leveled at deconstruction from early on in its career. That said, what still needs to be underscored is the paralleling of deconstruction by a feminist theoretical orientation that does and does not have affinities with the Derridean project. Moreover, we need to be sensitive to the fact that feminism, like deconstruction, conforms, albeit not rigidly, to what Braidotti calls "theory," and that, as such, they both swim the same waters.

Of course, of major importance is the way in which "theory" has been doubly inscribed as disciplinary—methodological, positioned, eclectic, pluralizable—and postdisciplinary—as a writing that comes after certain disciplinary forms of writing have passed into obsolescence. By 1981 Hartman is himself on the cusp of these two understandings of theory and tries to relate them in *Saving the Text*. Derrida, however, publishes "Of an Apocalyptic Tone Recently Adopted in Philosophy" (1981), which pushes the kind of theoretical understanding that Braidotti has in mind to extremes. An "interlacing of voices," Derrida will "bundle" this apocalyptic text together with a book on Joyce, an essay on Babel, the *envois* of *The Post Card*, and a text on Celan that as an ensemble defies categorization and traditional modes of comparative analysis.[25] Cixous, in a much later text (*Rootprints* [1994]) will speak of "a double listening" that tries to "perceive, to receive, excitations, vibrations, signs coming from sexed, marked, different places, and then, in a certain place—barely a point, a full stop or a semicolon—the difference gives way to (but it is rather that the two currents mix, flow into each other, so as only to be) what awaits us all: the human."[26] In her "life writing," Cixous hasn't yet determined entirely what the human means; hence, it is an unrealized concept whose meaning is as yet to come or on the way. The human is not a thing, quality, or entity. It is, as the structuralists used to say, a "floating signifier": a signifier at sea in language. This, of course, is not what Kolodny had in mind when she talked of "different readings," though I imagine she would have hardly shut Cixous out of her understanding of criticism. The only problem is that in Kolodny's world, Cixous would be inherently fixed or positioned as a perspective or approach, not a free-roaming discourse. This points to a perspectivalist reduction endemic to a pluralism whose ideological ground is the market place of commodities wherein truth is in the eye of the beholder.

THE MISCONSTRUCTION OF DECONSTRUCTION: GERALD GRAFF AND FRANK LENTRICCHIA

While by 1980 we can already begin thinking in terms of what Rosi Braidotti has called "theory"—whether of the pluralist or postdisciplinary kind—a dominant American white-male understanding of critical theory, completely oblivious to feminism, was doing its best to discredit deconstruction and its ilk as destructively self-absorbed and unpragmatic. Although William Pritchard had already talked of a "hermeneutical mafia" at Yale in a *Hudson Review* article of 1975, and Murray Krieger had rejected Derrida in *Theory of Criticism* (1976), it was Meyer Abrams who in "The Deconstructive Angel" (1977) wrote the first widely read assault on deconstruction.[27]

The politics of this attack was rather obvious. By the late 1970s the Yale School's ascension to prominence in the field of critical theory was so apparent that traditionalists like Abrams had no choice but to try and take Yale down a notch or two and break what was beginning to look like a critical monopoly on sophisticated and "legitimate" literary analysis. In fact, Abrams was trying to settle a score with J. Hillis Miller. In taking Miller out back behind the woodshed, Abrams decided that, while he was at it, he might just as well pull up deconstruction root and branch.

Taking up where Jameson left off, Abrams characterized *différance* as an "endless play of generated significances in which the reference is interminably postponed." Abrams, moreover, borrowed Jameson's prison-house metaphor, though with a bit of dissembling to cover his tracks. "Derrida's chamber of texts is a sealed echo-chamber in which meanings are reduced to a ceaseless echolalia . . . ghostly non-presences emanating from no voice, intended by no one, referring to nothing, bombinating in a void."[28] Evidently, Abrams's main concern was Derrida's challenge to British empiricism and the consequences this would have for "norms, controls, or indicators which in the ordinary use and experience of language set a limit to what we can mean and what we can be understood to mean."[29] In short, Abrams was concerned with hermeneutical validity insofar as he wanted to preserve those norms, controls, or indicators that are key to the kind of intellectual legitimacy and power that conservative critics in the saddle were reluctant to give up. Nothing was more threatening to Abrams than the idea that "What Derrida's conclusion comes to is that no sign or chain of signs can have a determinate meaning." At risk was the institution of criticism as a hierarchy wherein the validation and legitimation of a traditional scholarly episteme is accepted without question. Hence Abrams fights fire with fire. He suspends the rules of a competent reading of Derrida for the sake of countering a critical mentality that he suspects has done the same thing. "What is one to say in response to this abysmal vision of the textual world of literature, philosophy, and all other achievements of mankind?"[30]

With the ground prepared by Abrams, Gerald Graff in 1979 published *Literature Against Itself.* The work was an attack on the self-defeating uses of literature as a politics of individualistic estrangement from capitalist society; it was also a conservative recuperation of tried and true empirical researches into the meaning and value of literature as a mimetic window onto capitalist society and all its evils. Like Abrams before him, Graff suspended the rules of scholarship: sufficient research, adequate knowledge of the cultural and intellectual context in which works are written, adequate comprehension of an argument. He therefore studiously avoided an informed encounter with de Man's *Blindness and Insight* in which Derrida is lucidly and patiently explained, ignored the double introduction by Allison and Garver to their 1973 translation of Derrida's *Speech and Phenomena,* and purposely spoofed Gayatri Chakravorty Spivak's introductory essay to her translation of *Of Grammatology* (1976) by quipping about the number of times the locution "always already" turns up in the translation. In brief, Graff simply refused to learn from either Derrida or his expositors. This suggests that the politics of deconstruction was such that its detractors were self-consciously avoiding any readings other than the misinformed conclusions arrived at by Jameson. Apparently what they wanted to create was an eclipse of deconstruction that would spell its quick and easy demise.

Because he presented overly simplified and distorted accounts of deconstruction that could be consumed and dismissed at one go (among them, the strict identification of deconstruction with metatextuality), Graff's book gained considerable currency and popularity. With Jameson and Abrams ringing in his ears, Graff wrote that for deconstructors literature was

> a vehicle for a nihilistic metaphysics, an anti-didactic form of preaching. In a world in which nobody can look outside the walls of the prison-house of language, literature, with its built-in confession of its self-imprisonment, becomes once again the great oracle of truth, but now the truth that there is no truth.[31]

In supposedly addressing Derrida's remarks in *Of Grammatology* that it is impossible to simply step outside of metaphysics, Graff wrote that "nothing is conceivable without them [metaphysical notions] . . . if language is incorrigibly a naïve realist, how can we profess to challenge this realism without talking nonsense?"[32]

Garver, it has to be said, raised precisely the same question but put it as follows:

> Readers are bound to ask whether Derrida has succeeded in eliminating all metaphysical presuppositions from his deconstruction. The question arises most forcefully when Derrida is discussing what is real and what is unreal, a question which it hardly seems possible to deal with without having a conception of reality in one's mind. . . . No doubt the answer to this question will depend in part on epistemological views as well. Derrida *seems* at times to embrace a nominalism combined with a sort of radical empiricism.[33]

Garver isn't sure what to make of this and leaves the issue open for further clarification by Derrida at a later time, if not for further analysis via philosophical intertexts, Husserl's and Wittgenstein's among them. However, Graff, whose epistemology is what a philosopher would call "precritical," concludes that Derrida's position is "nonsense" and shuts down all possible inquiry as quickly as possible.

Unlike Abrams, Graff attacked deconstruction because he thought that Derrida and the Yale School were taken in by a modernist high culture that could not deal with the harsh realities of recent history and, in particular, World War Two. This is the view maintained by Georg Lukács who in *The Destruction of Reason* (1954) insisted that modernism escaped historical reality by repudiating reason, representation, and meaning. Echoing Lukács, Graff wrote that "criticism has had to repudiate objective methods of analysis and firm standards of taste. It is by these routes that humanistic culture has so often deprived itself of the critical perspective it might well contribute to the larger society."[34] As with existentialism before it, deconstruction was viewed by Graff as a philosophy of personal alienation that is politically harmless and shapes attitudes of consumption:

> Though he may operate on the loftiest level and may even call himself a revolutionary, the vanguard professor-intellectual fits in: he hands on the "alternative" ideas and "life-styles"—that is to say, the consumer tastes, which mark the approved modes of social estrangement. He enacts an exemplary drama of powerlessness which gives him considerable power in the cultural sphere—power to shape the styles of powerlessness.[35]

Graff's moral, then, is that "our radicalism is diverted from legitimate targets—injustice, poverty, triviality, vulgarity, and social loneliness—to a spurious quest after psychic liberation."[36] To put this another way, deconstruction, with its emphasis on free play, is psychically liberating but socially irresponsible and hence spurious. By the mid-1980s, this view would become widespread in the humanities.

Just a year after Graff's highly influential complaint appeared, Frank Lentricchia published *After the New Criticism* (1980). Lentricchia's tract was philosophically more sophisticated but roughly equivalent to Graff in its assessment of Derrida and the Yale School. Moreover, like Graff, Lentricchia had very little understanding of that aspect of French intellectual history within which deconstruction becomes comprehensible. Lentricchia's descriptions of Sartrean philosophy, for example, are quite rudimentary homespun accounts that do not reflect a mind trained in the field. In other words, *After the New Criticism* was amateur intellectual history at best. Typically problematic in this book is Lentricchia's version of the "official" history of what came *after* New Criticism, which, like Graff's account, omits the importance of feminist criticism during the 1970s. There is no mention of Kate Millett,

Elaine Showalter, Judith Fetterley, Jane Gallop, Gayle Rubin, Sandra Gilbert, Susan Gubar, or, for that matter, the very influential Adrienne Rich. Instead, critical theory is presided over by four male critics: Paul de Man, Harold Bloom, Murray Krieger, and E. D. Hirsch. In looking back at the 1950s, Lentricchia dwells on the work of Northrop Frye but has nothing to say about Susan Sontag, Alfred Kazin, Leslie Fiedler, Lionel Trilling, Irving Howe, or George Orwell, who were all oriented with the political interface of literature and society in a way that Frye, with his timeless archetypes, was not. Hence Lentricchia was unable to account for the preconditions for a sociological turn in literary study that came after New Criticism in the 1970s, and, therefore, he was unable to see the sociological relevance of structuralism, semiotics, and deconstruction. Instead, Lentricchia set his sights on Murray Krieger, last of the New Critics, who was indebted both to the formalist orientations of 1950s structural critical practices and to the philosophy of existentialism. In the chapter on Paul de Man, Lentricchia wanted to show how someone with the same kind of indebtedness to American formalism and European existentialism as Krieger could develop differently while still holding to the same essential romantic view of "an aesthetic medium free from representational responsibility."[37]

Even if Lentricchia advanced a ridiculous thesis (in fact, de Man and Krieger did not share the same intellectual formation), he did offer a close reading of Krieger's work in order to successfully elucidate a romantic isolationism in which the "fictional play" of the literary text set itself off from reference to the real world. Lentricchia rightly saw that Wallace Stevens was an enormous influence on late New Criticism and that not only Krieger, but J. Hillis Miller and Harold Bloom subscribed to the poet's view. "The final belief," Lentricchia quotes Stevens, "is to believe in a fiction, which you know to be a fiction, there being nothing else."[38] According to Lentricchia, this nominalist isolationism was itself the prison-house of language that not only Derrida but Krieger, Miller, Bloom, Hartman, and de Man inhabited—a prison-house of language that had its predecessor in an existential flight from the horror of reality that was not only supposedly core to Murray Krieger's writings but typical, according to Graff, of modernism as a whole.

Although Lentricchia took the more circuitous, if not tortuous, route, he ended in the same place as Graff: New Criticism and deconstruction were to be considered nominalist, relativist, isolationist, and escapist textual theories summarizable in terms of Lentricchia's view of de Man:

Literary discourse achieves the effect of a "self-reflecting mirror": by pointing to its own fictional nature it separates itself from "empirical reality." This art of self-reflection, this unique self-deconstructive ability of literature to speak of its own fictionality or mediating character de Man believes "characterizes the work of literature in its essence."[39]

Like Graff and other detractors of Yale School criticism, Lentricchia ends up dismissing close reading in a supposed "text for text's sake" context.

Whereas Lentricchia was quite aware of the differences between Derrida and New Criticism—"Derrida more typically emphasizes that deconstruction is not free-playing, joyful destruction"[40]—the odd overall lesson of *After the New Criticism* was that text criticism (Derrida's included) had cut itself off from reality: "On the matter of history, the deconstructionist position—despite the awesome historical learning of its Yale proponents—appears equivalent to the position of the literary know-nothing, newly reinforced with a theory of discourse that reassures him that history-writing is bunk."[41] This deliberate attempt to eclipse the viability of deconstruction by means of a flagrant distortion enters as a critical cliché into the culture, given that it will become recycled by David Lehman and others some years later in the more heated attacks on deconstruction.

Apparently, Graff's *Literature Against Itself* and Lentricchia's *After the New Criticism* both failed to grasp the significance of a new way of thinking about theory that is evident in deconstruction and feminism. Instead of imagining theory as something that could not be entirely formalized, Graff proposed a very utilitarian vision in which literary study would become, in essence, a form of applied social science. The unstated message of Graff's book is that literature is boring for undergraduates and that teachers have to make it more interesting by introducing more current affairs into the classroom. The idea of literary study as a political embarrassment made the path to legitimation much easier for certain feminists in the late 1970s and early 1980s. Indeed, even though particular critics were insensitive to feminist issues in the late 1970s, they did make a strong case for a political turn within the languages and literatures that helped to justify a rejection of literary hermeneutics in favor of a sociological approach akin to one that Graff himself undertook in *Professing Literature* (1987), an examination of English department politics spanning the twentieth century.

DEMONIZING DECONSTRUCTION:
WALTER JACKSON BATE, RENÉ WELLEK, AND DAVID LEHMAN

Although no one realized it at the time, the 1980s would become the most turbulent and significant decade for critical theory in America during the century. This is the decade that feminist literary criticism came of age, the decade that saw a genuine turn toward the inclusion of African-American literature in the American literary curriculum, the decade that saw a major political turn within the languages and literatures, and the decade in which literary criticism went into decline and canon wars flourished. It is the decade of identitarianism and the rebirth of the concept of the subject. Ethnocriticism, which for decades was held beneath contempt, was instantly in vogue. Suddenly, it was okay to be Jewish American, Asian American, or Mexican American and to talk about it in one's research. Queer theory was following upon the heels of feminism. Postmodernism, just a quirky concept owned by Ihab Hassan in the 1970s, became respectable as a *Weltanschauung* in the 1980s. Powerful movements in architecture, painting, performance, and creative writing were behind the postmodern revolution. Then, too, by 1985 many academics had turned in their typewriters for word processors, and the sheer volume of publications soared. More books were published than anyone could read, even within niche specializations. Many were published in a new field that would become increasingly more visible in the 1990s: cultural studies.

While all this was beginning to congeal, traditionalists started to get alarmed about the "state of the humanities." In 1982 and 1983 Walter Jackson Bate and René Wellek both hit the panic button by publishing heated polemics against deconstruction and the state of the languages and literatures, which, according to them, was in crisis. Bate's "The Crisis in English Studies" was originally published in *Harvard Magazine*: "The humanities are not merely entering, they are plunging into their worst state of crisis since the modern university was formed a century ago in the 1880s." Like all true conservatives, Bate's view was Olympian and acknowledged in true Spenglerian form that the downhill slide in intellectual spirit encompassed centuries; in fact, it went all the way back to the Renaissance, which, according to Bate, was a time when the human letters (or "letterae humanitas") were in full flower. The short version of Bate's long-winded argument is that as time progressed, the *letterae humanitas* broke down into smaller and smaller specializations, which, in the present day, have led to intellectual vapidity:

> The truth is that, with the fading of the Renaissance ideal through progressive stages of specialization, leading to intellectual emptiness, we are left with a potentially suicidal movement among leaders of the profession, while, at the same time, the profession sprawls, without its old center [the humanist integration of life and letters], in helpless disarray.[42]

Symptomatic of the suiciding of the profession is predictably nothing less than deconstruction, given that to Bate deconstruction sounds a lot like culture assassination. Simplemindedness aside, what matters is Bate's definition of deconstruction, since it is a definition that will be often repeated in the popular press and broadsides in literary supplements, such as *The New York Review of Books*, and education chronicles, such as *The Chronicle of Higher Education*:

> Deconstructionism—whose presiding spirit has been the puckish Parisian, Jacques Derrida—unites structuralist concerns for very special kinds of pattern with what comes down to a nihilistic view of literature, human communication, and of life itself. The building blocks of an author, say Shakespeare—are reduced to a sequence of signs (words) the "meaning" of which has no real relationship to the author's own intention or imaginative vision or to the world in general. Interpretation is open to anyone (anyone at all?—exponents never seem to draw the line firmly) who "deconstructs" the text, sweeps the ground clear and then creates, through criticism, another (presumably more valid) work of art: this procedure gloriously free of any necessary relationship to history, to philosophy, or to human lives (apart from that of the deconstruction).[43]

As if that is not enough of a dismissal, Bate adds, "Derrida significantly never turns to the really major philosophers except to snatch at stale pessimisms (e.g., Nietzsche), which appear to deny the possibility of finding truth."[44]

Quite remarkable, of course, are the sheer amount and degree of inaccuracies in Bate's account, as if he himself were the example of scholarship gone to the dogs. Notice, for example, the following obvious rejoinders. If

"Derrida significantly never turns to the really major philosophers," what does it mean that *Speech and Phenomena* (1967) is a meticulous engagement with Husserl's *Logical Investigations*, or that "The Pharmacy of Plato" in *Dissemination* (1972) is a lengthy excursus on "The Phaedrus," or that "The Parergon" in *The Truth in Painting* (1978) takes up Immanuel Kant? Are these not major philosophers? Would Derrida's "Spurs" (1976), an essay on Nietzsche, be a snatching of pessimisms when, in fact, it is a detailed analysis of Nietzsche and questions of gender? Is deconstruction the nihilism Bate says it is, or is it a critique and analysis of nihilism? What about Derrida's writings on the "yes" at the end of James Joyce's *Ulysses*? Isn't it anything *but* nihilistic? How can Bate claim deconstruction is decontextualized and estranged from the historical? Note, for example, Garver's assertion, "Meaning can never be isolated or held in abstraction from its context, e.g., its linguistic, semiotic, or historical context." Or, better yet, consider Derrida's *Of Grammatology* (1967), where the life of Rousseau and the history of eighteenth-century Europe play such an important part. And what about *The Post Card* (1980), in which the autobiography of Derrida himself is of central importance to the philosophy of the envois? Hence, when Bate argues that "the aim and tradition of literature is to give the whole experience of life," how can he fault Derrida whose *Post Card* does precisely that in no uncertain autobiographical terms? In retrospect, whose account is it that has no real relationship to the author's own intention or to reality in general? Isn't it Bate's account that lacks all connection with facts and realities?

Derrida had reason to question not only Bate's credibility but also his honesty as a scholar, teacher, and colleague. Similarly, Derrida had reason to question the honesty of René Wellek's characterizations, which mirror Bate's to a very large extent. Wellek's "Destroying Literary Studies" was the lead article in an issue of *The New Criterion* late in 1983 and invoked the by now tiresome Jamesonian cliché:

> The new theory states that man lives in a prison-house of language that has no relation to reality. It seems to be suggested or at least buttressed by a few passages in Nietzsche where, for example, he speaks of "truth as a mobile marching army of metaphors, metonymies, and anthropomorphisms, illusions of which one has forgotten they are illusions," and by an interpretation of the *Cours de linguistique générale* of Ferdinand de Saussure who considered the referential function of language irrelevant

for a science of linguistics but who did not doubt language's relation to experience and reality.

In a violently reductive accusation, Wellek lashed out: "In its extreme formulation, which looks for the abolition of man, denies the self, sees language as a free floating system of signs, the theory leads to total skepticism and ultimately to nihilism."[45]

A notable borrowing in Wellek's essay is the quotation of precisely the same passage Abrams cites from Derrida's "Structure, Sign, and Play" in "The Deconstructive Angel." That Wellek is tacitly quoting Abrams (but perhaps also Graff who mechanically cites exactly the same passage)[46] is quite evident, given that Abrams cuts into Derrida's sentence in a way that is idiosyncratic and that Wellek exactly repeats. It begins, "a Nietzschean *affirmation*—the joyous affirmation of the freeplay of the world and without truth, without origin, offered to an active interpretation. . . ." Derrida, who had obviously noticed that neither Wellek nor Bate had read him, argued in a footnote in *Memoires for Paul de Man* (1986) that a political smear campaign had begun in 1982 with the mission of destroying the influence of deconstruction at any cost. It was a smear campaign that, as it turned out, would have a nasty legacy, given that Bate's and Wellek's inaccuracies have been repeated in the academic and popular press to such a degree that for many they have by default become deconstruction's definition.

As if all this unpleasantness from the conservatives wasn't enough, in 1987 Derrida would be shocked to learn that a young scholar in Belgium had been researching back issues of the Belgian newspaper *Le Soir* wherein he came across nearly two hundred articles by the young Paul de Man. Apparently, de Man had been writing cultural essays for the newspaper when it was under the control of the National Socialists during the Second World War. Even though de Man resigned from the paper quite a bit before the war ended and was exonerated of wrong doing after the war by officials, the fact is that in one of the articles, written during the period of the Holocaust, there are very anti-Semitic remarks whose drift is quite in tune with the Final Solution. That de Man had never apologized for this past while an American academic caused considerable hand wringing and outrage once the news became public. Derrida himself was the first to announce the revelations, and a year later a lengthy anthology of commentary on the de Man Affair appeared in a volume entitled *Responses* (1989). The commentary in the public press that preceded this publication was heated, if not extremely inflammatory. Suddenly, deconstruction was treated as if it were public enemy number one and a chorus of "I told you so" rang out from all conservative quarters.

In February 1988 David Lehman, a poet with an ax to grind, published a savage article in *Newsweek* entitled "Deconstructing de Man's Life: An Academic Idol Falls Into Disgrace." The article began:

> During his 13 years at Yale, Paul de Man perfected the role of the influential literary critic. Until his death in 1983, he was the high priest of the arcane philosophy known as "deconstruction," a controversial analytic method which turns literature into a play of words, robbing it of any broader significance.[47]

This trivializing characterization was followed by the observation that "critics have long seen deconstruction as hostile to the very principles of Western thought that make moral philosophy possible" and "the deconstructivist view of the past was ably stated by automobile magnate Henry Ford: history is bunk." The "critics" who have "long seen deconstruction" are none other than Bate and Wellek, and the Henry Ford allusion had its source in Lentricchia. Following the hatchet job on deconstruction was Lehman's announcement that de Man had collaborated with the Nazis during the Second World War and had kept the fact of his collaboration a secret. Lehman happily crows, "Opponents of deconstruction think the movement is finished."

It would have been more accurate to say that they *hoped* it would be finished, a hope that in many circles motivated the outrage and self-righteous moral posturing in the wake of the de Man revelations. That many academics wanted to take the moral high ground in order to advance their own intellectual projects at the expense of deconstruction was extremely apparent to everyone, especially to Derrida. Particularly evident is that cultural studies advocates were going to benefit from the fall of de Man; and, with him, the deconstructive legacy of Yale would be eclipsed. Indeed, Lehman says as much:

> Frederick Crews in looking to the future sees "the new militant culturalist materialism of the left." That school prescribes the study of books not because of the moral or esthetic value but because they permit the profession to advance a political, often Marxist agenda. Crews contends that there is more than a trace of deconstruction in the "New Histori-

cism"—which is one reason traditional humanists hope that it, too, will self-deconstruct in the wake of the de Man disgrace.

There is no doubt that the de Man affair was taken by many in the languages and literatures for permission to make a dramatic turn toward cultural studies, including, of course, multiculturalism, alterity politics, and identitarianism. Their cause was only helped by Derrida's tactic of publishing "Like the Sound of the Sea Deep Within a Shell: Paul de Man's War" (1988) whose critical sophistication was not appreciated because what most academics wanted to hear was an unambiguous repudiation of what de Man did as a young writer for a fascist newspaper, something Derrida did not quite do.[48] Of course, Derrida, who had just published a booklength project, *Memoires for Paul de Man* (1986), found himself in the awkward predicament of having been betrayed by de Man's past, given that Derrida's enemies were using that past as the proof that only a highly corrupt intellectual would ally himself with something as supposedly problematic as deconstruction. For Derrida to attack de Man and thereby align himself with his enemies would have been equivalent to self-betrayal: the admission that, yes, there is something not right about deconstruction, given that it was the philosophy of a collaborator, Paul de Man. But to support de Man in the face of criticism was also not a viable option, since Derrida's enemies would accuse him of irresponsibility and historical revisionism. Derrida's only option, therefore, was a middle-of-the-road position that he took by way of talking about de Man's internal war with himself and the singularity of this war, which only he could have known. Derrida certainly did not condone de Man's wartime writings. But he also did not condone the political advantage that academics tried to gain by protesting de Man's life-long cover up and the narrow minded moralism, which thought that life is easily divided into categories of right and wrong, when matters were always far more complicated for those civilians in occupied territories who had to survive during World War Two. Morally shocked, a clear majority of American academics did not see matters this way. They wanted Derrida to condemn de Man unequivocally, so that one could rest assured that there were instances in which deconstruction would not hang itself up on undecidabilities. As it turned out, Derrida would disappoint them.

While the de Man scandal and the Heidegger affair (a rehash of an "affair" that was amply discussed shortly after the end of World War Two in France) grabbed headlines, the cold war came to an end, and literary study began to fizzle out as a viable form of academic scholarship. By 1990 publishers would be cautioning literary critics that literary criticism does not sell and that an age of close literary reading was over. Apparently, literary criticism had been replaced by cultural criticism, which reflected what nineteenth-century comparative literary critics thought the study of literature should be like: anthropological in scope, multicultural in orientation, and politically savvy. Even during the preeminence of contemporary literary interpretation, cultural study had been active. It was sanctioned in the 1970s by structuralism and Marxism. Roland Barthes, Umberto Eco, Julia Kristeva, Fredric Jameson, Louis Marin, Michel de Certeau, and Edward Said were all engaged in forms of cultural study. Indeed, in the 1960s both the Birmingham School and Tel Quel were largely dedicated to breaking down the disciplinary borders between cultural history, economics, social theory, linguistic theory, and literary practice for the sake of an analytic that could bring economic, psychological, and linguistic theory into powerful relation. And back in the 1930s, art critics such as Meyer Schapiro, who belonged to the Communist Party, had already been thinking in broad culturalist and political terms, as had Kenneth Burke, whose critical essays had often interrogated cultural discourses that were not literary per se.

Given that even as late as the early 1980s, cultural studies had not quite come into dominance, it occurred to Terry Eagleton that if one was to clear the way for cultural as opposed to literary study, one would have to do more than practice close cultural readings. One would have to aggressively discredit and push aside literary hermeneutics altogether. This is the aim of Eagleton's *Literary Theory* (1983). Among the literary hermeneutical targets was, not surprisingly, deconstruction, which Eagleton associated as much with the Yale School as he did with Derrida, hence perpetuating the error of conflating the two. In addressing deconstruction, Eagleton elevated Jameson's critique to that of a dogma assumed by deconstruction itself: "One advantage of the dogma that we are the prisoners of our own discourse . . . allows you to drive a coach and horses through everybody else's beliefs while not saddling you with the inconvenience of having to adopt any yourself." Furthermore, deconstruction "smacks of a jaded resignation to the impossibility of truth which is by no means unrelated to post-1968 historical disillusion."[49] That Eagleton (from the Left) is at least as crude as Lehman (from the Right) is most evident: "Literature for the deconstructionists testifies to the impossibility of language's ever doing more than talk about its own failure, like some barroom bore. Literature is the ruin of all reference, the cemetery of communication."[50] Like Graff, Eagleton had a not-so-hidden agenda to promote the destruction of literary hermeneutics (a part of what he calls "liberal humanism") for the sake of advancing "political criticism." Literature as well as literary theory is, according to Eagleton, an "illusion":

> It is an illusion first in the sense that literary theory . . . is really no more than a branch of social ideologies, utterly without any unity or identity which would adequately distinguish it from philosophy, linguistics, psychology, cultural and sociological thought. . . . The one hope it has of distinguishing itself—clinging to an object named literature—is misplaced. We must conclude, then, that this [Eagleton's] book is less an introduction than an obituary, and that we have ended by burying the object [literature] we sought to unearth.[51]

Eagleton would end up arguing that "*any method or theory which will contribute to the strategic goal of human emancipation, the production of 'better people' through the socialist transformation of society is acceptable.*"[52] This view has greatly convinced many English-speaking language and literature professors to hold the position that anyone who is not teaching literature for the sake of promoting social justice is not doing anything worthwhile. Hence, because deconstruction is thought to lack any reference to the real world, it is useless. Not history but philosophy is bunk!

AMERICA IS DECONSTRUCTION?

It was in the midst of all these cross-currents, some peaking and some just emerging, that in 1985 Derrida began arguing that America is the "historical space which today, in all its dimensions and through all its power plays, reveals itself as being undeniably the most sensitive, receptive, or responsive space of all to the themes and effects of deconstruction."[53] America—land of deconstruction? As if to insist on the point, Derrida even put it this way in the English translation of his book on Paul de Man: "L'Amérique, mais c'est la déconstruction." One wonders: Could this be the unconscious reason why American critics get so nervous about the impact of deconstruction in America? That it's *too* American? That Americans might be *too* susceptible to deconstruction? It's a mistake, Derrida said, to think that deconstruction occurred first in Europe and then in America. "Contrary to what is often thought, deconstruction is not exported from Europe to the United States. Deconstruction has several original configurations in this country [the USA], which in turn—and there are many signs of this—produce singular effects in Europe and elsewhere in the world."[54] That America might be deconstruction's homeland was a proposition that involved the Yale School as well as the history of New Criticism. But Derrida was almost certainly thinking, too, of America as the home of postmodernism, if not as the home of a certain counterculturalism whose utopian horizons allow for the kind of intellectual and political free play that is more typical of the United States than, say, of France, Germany, or Spain. America is the home of not only a willingness to continually deconstruct the immediate past but to continually construct immediate futures.

In the interview, "Deconstruction in America" (1985), Derrida maintained:

> We can't understand the reception that deconstruction has had in the United States without background—historical, political, religious, and so forth. I would say religious above all. . . . So we can't understand what is going on regarding this issue without studying not only very long sequences of American history, but also a shorter sequence which is the history of the American university institution.[55]

These are striking remarks given that Derrida has been and will continue to be attacked for being ahistorical and unreferential. In fact, these remarks make one wonder if the charge of ahistoricism isn't a wish, the wish that deconstruction *not* examine the history of America, that it *not* question America's religious, political, and historical backgrounds, for fear of . . . well, what? It's here, of course, that the interface of deconstruction with so-called political correctness (that is, alternative readings of American culture and history) poses a certain danger for those who don't want these matters to become the basis for renegotiating how we represent the past and use that to chart our future. Less broadly, Derrida argues that the fate of deconstruction's reception is bound to "the profession of literary and philosophical study" and "the evolution of the [academic] market, to the economic and political sphere—the number of jobs, etc." He continues, "I'm persuaded that an analysis could show that all this comes into play in both the positive and negative reception given deconstruction, in the defense against it as well as in the acceptance which—it should be emphasized after all—has indeed been stronger in the United States than anywhere else."[56]

By 1985 Derrida had become very sensitized to the question of how the word "deconstruction" serves the interests of various groups, interests that are economic and political, interests that boil down to who does and doesn't get hired, promoted, published, and so on. Switching to the larger perspective, Derrida almost immediately then says:

> One finally realizes that there is no deconstruction in America quite simply because once one takes into account that the United States is today the place where deconstruction, or the reaction against deconstruction, has spread more markedly than anywhere else in the world, then at that point one can't give a meaning to the name "America" unless one takes into account that very symptom. And, consequently, I would say that the United States today is a place where something like this can take place. (And, moreover, it is remarkable that at least in a timid and scattered fashion, the word "deconstruction" has appeared in certain political contexts, as well as in certain newspapers like *The Wall Street Journal*.)[57]

As place, America is the site where *the dissemination of deconstruction becomes possible*. Europe, in contrast, has not been hospitable, the question of hospitality being one that Derrida will take up some ten years later in the context of the topic, monolinguism. By being the place that is hospitable to deconstruction, I think Derrida was already suggesting in 1985 that America is a place that is not monolingual, a place where there are enough "differences" (i.e., conceptual, political, religious) to enable the dissemination of deconstruction, in other words, a place where deconstruction could be argued about rather than just eclipsed. Then, too, Derrida, who in *Glas* appreciated the botanical metaphor of grafting, was open to the transplantation of deconstruction:

> Even my own work within the field of deconstruction is received very often on the basis of the American reception. So something has happened in the United States which is not a simple translation or impor-

tation of something European. I believe it has an absolutely new and original dimension in the United States, and therefore all the more difficult to put together. I don't think that there is something like *one* deconstruction. There are very diverse, heterogeneous phenomena which resemble one another, which in a way come together under that name, but only to a certain point. So we also have to take this great diversity into account.[58]

It's here that Peggy Kamuf interrupts Derrida in midstream. In fact, it's she who encourages him to restrict himself to the question of how the space of American intellectual life has been increasingly exiled and compressed into the space of the university, as if intellectual thinking were a specialty to be set apart from ordinary living, which, supposedly, is nonintellectual. In picking up on this, Derrida says, "This academic concentration explains why deconstruction reverberated much more strongly here than in France."[59] At this point, Derrida hints that in America intellectual thought is becoming an endangered species and that its gene pool (my metaphor for any body of thought that can replicate itself and that has an evolution and genealogy) is so small that any new genetic strain could potentially wipe it out. In other words, the situation is unique because intellectualism in America is actually very endangered and monolingual. Hence the university has turned into a hypersensitive space; it has become an intellectual sphere whose everyday condition is that of endangerment if not extinction, given that every intellectual nuance has the capacity to threaten the intellectual ecology.

In the interview, Derrida also reverses perspective, because he also sees French culture as *more* heterogeneous than American culture. In France, "an intellectual or cultural or literary milieu . . . was not defined by its links to the academy." In France, deconstruction "had an impact very quickly, but right away it dispersed and there were moves to interpret, to censure, to misread, to disassociate, but also to combine. Moves proportional to the diversity of intellectual milieu, of interests, schools, cliques—which weren't university cliques." In short, "deconstruction found itself dispersed right away, channeled into a highly diversified place." Hence, according to Derrida, deconstruction got watered down very quickly in France. In the United States, where there is intellectual concentration in the university system, deconstruction "reverberated much more strongly than in France."[60] This suggests that a less diversified intellectual field is actually superior for deconstruction.

Does this contradict Derrida's remarks on heterogeneity? That there can be no *one* deconstruction? Elsewhere in the interview, Derrida speaks of a "double gesture" that consists of counterposing one conceptual formation to another. Derrida's argument, in fact, is that in some respects America is more heterogeneous as an intellectual site than France, but in other respects it is also more homogeneous. There is no *simple* opposition. What is of interest to Derrida is the fact that the homogeneous and the heterogeneous are distributed and constituted differently in different places and that the dissemination of a philosophy—say, even of an "ism" (a body of ideas)—will not follow the same laws and patterns in one site as in another. At issue, then, is the diffusion, dissemination, or distribution whereby ideas are transmitted across unevenly constructed cultural sites.

The fact that deconstruction is a "rather heterogeneous movement" is in *its* interests, even if the *its* is problematic, given that "deconstruction . . . is neither a system nor a unified discourse. It's as you [Kamuf] say a multiplicity of gestures, of movements, of operations."[61] That deconstruction carries out several gestures that appear contradictory creates a certain irresolvable tension. In other words, the very gesture of maintaining more than one position—or, as in Husserl, more than one construction—concerns a fracturing or heterogenizing of a field of relationships that everyone may have presumed to be what in America is called "a level playing field," which is to say, a common site. Here, of course, it is the university that Derrida is challenging insofar as we consider it to be a homogeneous intellectual site made up of departments that have, relative to one another, the same status—the same rights, procedures, methods of organization, and so on. In fact, the university is, from an intellectual point of view alone, a highly heterogeneous site of many double gestures—multiple intellectual constructions—that defy logocentric recoveries, among them, a rationalist model.

Having taken such a viewpoint, Derrida then introduces his own double gesture—dropping the other shoe, as it were—about conserving tradition. "I feel very 'traditionalist' in a certain way because I am for memory, history, and in sum, everything of which the university is the guardian."[62] It's here, of course, that Bate, Wellek, and so many others have egregiously failed to engage Derrida at even the most basic level of understanding: that it's never a matter of either/or, but of a conflict of intellectual formations (conservative, radical) that are always actively at work side by side, operative as a "double gesture" that "doesn't designate the same thing each time." Whereas conservative academics assume that there is a fixed intellectual fault line where the altercation between deconstruction and traditionalism can be firmly situated, Derrida argues that the site of the encounter is never entirely identical to itself, that it is continually displaced and transformed, given that the intellectual domain of the university is a heterogeneous domain, politically, institutionally, disciplinarily, regionally, and culturally. As Derrida himself points out, different fields have different sensitivities, receptivities, and prejudices. Deconstruction could take root in literature departments in American universities because a certain prejudice against close reading had already been removed by the New Criticism. Yet, these same departments harbor prejudices against the infiltration of philosophy, what Derrida calls the "resistance to theory." In other words, even here on this heterogeneous ground there are double gestures.

NON-PLACET

The double gesture coming at deconstruction from the university is itself a typically Derridean double bind or aporia. In literature departments, deconstruction is rejected as too philosophical, while in philosophy departments under the sway of analytical philosophy, deconstruction is rejected as too literary and mush minded. It is on this point that Derrida responds to Bate and Wellek, who are by 1985 politically parallel in position to the conservative philosophers, Arthur Danto and John Searle. The common tactic taken by Bate and Wellek is to say that deconstruction is "going on somewhere else," that it is philosophy and hence bad philosophy, irrelevant to literary study; to the contrary, Danto and Searle say that deconstruction is going on in literature departments and that it is an outsider movement corrupting philosophy. In each case, deconstruction is positioned as outsider, as a viral attack that comes from another place like the Asian flu. Heterogeneous, if not stringently opposed in terms of their traditions, prejudices, and practices, traditionalists in philosophy and literature nevertheless resort to a homogeneous logic—that of thought-infection—in their attempt to blame each other for the advent of a new philosophical development that demystifies dearly held enlightenment assumptions.

Deconstruction's threat to the stability of disciplinary boundaries came to the fore in 1992 when the *Times* (London) ran the following open letter on Saturday, May 9 under the heading, "Derrida Degree a Question of Honor."

Signed by Barry Smith (editor of *The Monist*) and some eighteen other philos-ophers—among them Ruth Barcan Marcus (Yale), David Armstrong (Univer-sity of Sydney), and Willard Quine (Harvard)—the open letter stated unequiv-ocally that Derrida should not be given an honorary doctorate by Cambridge University, because although "M. Derrida describes himself as a philosopher," the influence of his writings "has been to a striking degree almost entirely in fields outside philosophy—in departments of film studies, for example, or of French and English literature." Accusing Derrida of introducing "tricks and gimmicks similar to those of the Dadaists or of the concrete poets" and of being an embarrassment to French philosophy ("his antics having contributed signif-icantly to the widespread impression that contemporary French philosophy is little more than an object of ridicule"), the signatories of the open letter to the *Times* call for Derrida's exclusion from any honors that might be bestowed by Cambridge: "M. Derrida's voluminous writings in our view stretch the normal forms of academic scholarship beyond recognition. Above all—as every reader can very easily establish for himself (and for this purpose any page will do)—his works employ a written style that defies comprehension."[63]

Of course, there is something rather amusing about analytical philoso-phers accusing Derrida of antics and trivialization, given that analytical philos-ophy itself is very open to such criticism. Gilles Deleuze and Felix Guattari sum up the matter rather well in *What Is Philosophy?* when they write, "Logic is al-ways defeated by itself, that is to say, by the insignificance of the cases on which it thrives. In its desire to supplant philosophy, logic detaches the proposition from all its psychological dimensions, but clings all the more to the set of pos-tulates that limited and subjected thought to the constraints of a recognition of truth in the proposition."[64] Indeed, what the signatories of the letter con-demning Derrida repudiate is precisely everything that logic has itself rejected—verbal plurisignation, psychological relays, illogical reading effects, and so on. Analytical philosophy is by definition so restricted in terms of specific logical problems that it can only respond dogmatically and uncomprehendingly to dis-courses that are not "propositionally detached." As such, analytical philosophy cannot award honorary distinctions to (because it cannot recognize) anything that lies outside its very rarefied confines. Hence Derrida can rightfully call his rejoinder, "Honoris Causa: 'This is *also* extremely funny,' " the funny thing being analytical philosophy's psychological projection onto another of its own triviality, its own logical antics, its own irrelevance, its own divorce from some-thing one might choose to call "philosophy."

The year 1992, of course, marks Derrida's third major publicity horror show in the Anglo-American arena, if one counts the Bate-Wellek smear campaign of the early '80s and the de Man affair of 1987 as its two major predecessors. Hence it is not surprising to hear Derrida insist that "what certain academics should be warned against is the *temptation of the media*." That deconstruction should be the occasion for one of the rare occasions when humanists can speak directly to the general public suggests, of course, that deconstruction is, *on the one hand*, not only affiliated with but being blamed for a crisis in the humanities, and, *on the other hand*, functioning as one of the only premises or grounds upon which lowly humanists are being encouraged to speak to the public at large. After all, there is no other intellectual (i.e., professional) basis upon which academics like Barry Smith could address the general public, given that it is highly doubtful that the general public has any interest whatsoever in the kind of thinking that matters to the pages of *The Monist*. Ironically, Smith only emerges from academic obscurity on account of deconstruction; he is only heard from by the public because of "M. Derrida's voluminous writings," not because of anything he himself has done as an academic. Without deconstruction, what would Barry Smith be? The same can be said of David Lehman, another minor figure whose fifteen minutes of intellectual fame was entirely parasitical.

In "Honoris Causa" Derrida speaks to the media's sudden interest in academic politics as follows:

> I call temptation of the media the compulsion to misuse the privilege of public declaration in a social space that extends far beyond the normal circuits of intellectual discussion. Such misuse constitutes a breach of confidence, an abuse of authority—in a word, an abuse of power. The temptation of the media actually encourages academics to use the media as an easy and immediate way of obtaining a certain power of seduction, sometimes indeed just power alone. It encourages them to appear in the media simply for the sake of appearing, or to use their professorial authority for purposes which have as little to do with the norms of intellectual research as they have with political responsibility.[65]

Deconstruction, in other words, becomes the occasion for academics to abusively wrest the power to profess in the name of their authority, which, in the context of deconstruction, is entirely bogus. Bate, Wellek, Lehman, and

Smith both maliciously and ignorantly proclaim falsehoods in ways that are entirely irresponsible and unethical. "This temptation of the media"—the temptation to make one an immediate intellectual super-star, the temptation to exert political power within the academy, the temptation to make one be an expert on things one hardly comprehends—"encourages these intellectuals to renounce the academic discipline normally required 'inside' the university, and to try instead to exert pressure through the press and through public opinion. . . ." Structurally, this affects the boundary "between what is inside and what is outside the university."[66] In "Deconstruction in America" Derrida, we recall, was wondering about the intellectual concentratedness of the American university, the physical separation of intellectuals from the culture generally, and the borderline that creates between inside and outside. In "Honoris Causa" he is forced to acknowledge the capacity of the media to break that border down in the interests of denunciation and scapegoating: "For the first time in history, to my knowledge, there has been the spectacle of academics at universities other than Cambridge, not even in England, claiming to protect the institution, that of Cambridge, and of the university in general."[67] That is, one has suddenly entered into a global-political struggle for the protection of a university's reputation, a struggle mounted by professors who are *not within* the institution at all. In a style that reminds Derrida of "the slogan or manifesto, the denunciatory placard or election propaganda," these philosopher-marauders "intervene" in a debate that is going on *within* Cambridge. Their "violence," Derrida points out, is "directed through the media at a colleague who in this particular case hadn't asked for anything and was not a candidate for anything."[68] In other words, the attack was not directed on anyone who had even tried to make any sort of claim or purchase on Cambridge, who had, in fact, not wanted anything to do with Cambridge. Rather, it was a group at Cambridge that had wanted to honor Derrida, that wanted to make an institutional connection with *him*.

This is a political situation in which the borderline between what is internal and external to the university is itself protodeconstructed. Moreover, and perhaps most importantly, the "Cambridge Affair" represents the power and willingness to dismantle the institutionalized relays of academic politics—relays that depend upon certain restrictions, limitations, and borders (consider the administration of the Ph.D. examination, which is not conducted in the public square for good reason)—in order to mobilize what Jean-François Lyotard has called the *differend*, which is to say, an interlocution whose very procedure prohibits redress. What makes the media so tempting for academics is that they can impugn, distort, and pervert the truth without being called into question. Roger Scruton's accusation—echoing Abrams, Bate, Wellek, and Lehman, among others—that deconstruction is "pure nihilism" can be proclaimed to millions of readers without Scruton (a philosopher of music) being called on the mat for his egregious refusal to read Derrida's work in a serious and responsible manner, a reading that would quickly disprove Scruton's claim. Derrida countered, "Let him discuss this using texts and quotations, let him take to argument and stop this throwing around of invective which it is impossible to respond to in the press."[69] Apparently, it is the lack of any accountability for the criticisms made by conservative academics like Scruton that not only characterizes the media as an inhospitable place for intellectual differences of opinion but marks the site where intellectual debate is by definition foreclosed, given the tempo of media sound bites and the general lack of responsible contextualization (checking facts, monitoring the plausibility of a view, providing balance, etc.). Moreover, the dissemination of even silly remarks takes on a life of its own in the media. "*The Observer* only has to call me a 'computer virus' for my photograph to appear a few days later . . . in *Der Spiegel* with the title 'wie ein Comptervirus.'"[70] What are the truth conditions of such a remark? The usefulness of such an analogy? The appropriateness of translating deconstruction into cybernetics? The stakes of ad hominem shock value? How does rampantly disseminative media-speak, outside of the protocols of academic debate and dissemination, reenter the academy as a legitimized aspect of what is often thought to be academic politics and debate? As Derrida suggests, "It is a question here not only of theoretical research but of praxis, of ethics, or of a deontology aimed at creating new kinds of contract."[71]

A WORLD APART: DERRIDA AND THE FRANKFURT SCHOOL

Not only has Derrida run afoul of Anglo-American analytical philosophers, he has also been harshly criticized by Jürgen Habermas of the Frankfurt School. In fact, Derrida's relation to the Frankfurt School is rather complicated in terms of the *faux bond*, because there too an encounter does and doesn't seem to take place. To get a general sense of this, it is useful to recall

Fredric Jameson's *Late Marxism: Adorno, or, the Persistence of the Dialectic* (1990) in which he points out that the 1970s,

> the age, in this country at least, of Theory and theoretical discourse . . . were essentially French; Adorno (along with Lukács and so many other Central European thinkers, with the signal exceptions of Benjamin and Brecht) seemed an encumbrance, not to say an embarrassment, during the struggles of that time, and prompting those still committed to him into elaborate translation schemes, to "reconcile" Adorno with Derridean orthodoxy.[72]

Jameson's point, of course, is that in the 1970s the French overshadowed the Frankfurt School. Yet, Herbert Marcuse was widely read during the early 1970s, and the journal *Telos* was actively promoting Frankfurt School thinking in America. Certainly, by 1975 there was considerable interest in Georg Lukács, Herbert Marcuse, and Jürgen Habermas; and, there was strong interest in Max Horkheimer, Theodor Adorno, Ernst Bloch, and Walter Benjamin, thinkers who were not yet widely translated.

Jameson's own *Marxism and Form* (1971) was a beacon of cultural Marxist enlightenment that transcended the orthodoxies of base and superstructure, if not class struggle. In retrospect, it is interesting that Jameson bundled chapters on Adorno, Benjamin, Marcuse, Bloch, and Lukács together with Sartre and not Althusser, Foucault, or Derrida. Yet, Jameson did mention Derrida, comparing his conception of the trace in *Of Grammatology* to Bloch's *Spuren* or proleptic figures of hope, as well as to Benjamin's "brittle world of script and allegorical fragment."[73] Also, in Jameson's introduction to *Marxism and Form* there is talk of the then heady French theoretical developments in Paris as a "form of extracurricular Marxist culture," meaning that officially Lévi-Strauss, Lacan, Derrida, and Foucault did not posit themselves as Marxists, but that, unofficially, they were very much influenced by Marx in ways that defy an orthodox Marxist understanding. The fact that the Tel Quel critics of the 1960s encouraged the hybridization of Marx + Freud + Husserl + Heidegger + Saussure meant that a Marxist-structuralist-psychoanalytic-phenomenology would have difficulty accepting figures like Lukács, Habermas, Marcuse, Horkheimer, and Bloch, whereas it could much more easily incorporate someone like Benjamin, whose language theory, archival sensibilities, and phenomenological understanding of Freud was coupled with an unorthodox Marxism akin to the extracurricular Marxist culture of Parisian intellectuals.

But if that is the case, why was the French reception of Adorno so unenthusiastic?[74] After all, Adorno was also very polymathic—he was a composer of atonal music, he was an astute cultural and literary critic like Barthes, he had credentials as a sociologist and as a Marxist— having had philosophical training in Hegelian dialectics and Husserlian phenomenology, as well as having been a close reader of Heidegger. Part of the answer, I think, lies in the fact that so much of Adorno's work is oriented toward music and not literature and that this implies an aesthetic in place of what some in the late '60s were calling a "semiology." This difference becomes very self-evident in Christoph Menke's *Die Souveränität der Kunst: Äesthetische Erfahrung nach Adorno und Derrida* (1988) [*The Sovereignty of Art: Aesthetic Experience After Adorno and Derrida*], which dwells on topics such as "the aesthetic experience of crisis," "the concept of beauty," and "the aesthetics of negativity and hermeneutics." Pronounced in Menke's interesting study is the subordination of French semiology, so relevant for Derrida, to the transcendental philosophizing so endemic to the German philosophical tradition. Indeed, Menke's entire project appears to be an attempt to bring both Derrida and Adorno back into the fold of German Idealism in its updated, contemporary hermeneutical forms. But this is made plausible only because of Adorno's aesthetic theory, which establishes the possibility for Menke's point that:

> The aesthetic object is the ground of an experience of aesthetic negativity only insofar as it shows itself to be that which is alien to attempts at understanding in these very attempts at understanding it. By releasing or unleashing [here Menke has Derrida's trigger effects from *La dissémination* in mind] . . . the processuality of such efforts and thus negating them, we generate the object of our attempts at understanding as the ground of both the formation and subversion of understanding. Thus what we term "beautiful" is an object that appears as both the ground and the abyss of understanding.[75]

In addition to Adorno's susceptibility of a certain transcendental philosophical recovery, there is the fact that his *Negative Dialectics* was not published until 1966, long after his thesis about Hegel could be deemed pathbreaking by French standards. To appreciate this point, one should consider

Derrida's "From Restricted to General Economy: A Hegelianism Without Reserve," which appeared in *Writing and Difference* (1967). This essay drew heavily from George Bataille's earlier writings on Hegel that concerned the uncontainedness of Hegelian negativity and its unrecoverability within the very system that operationalizes the negative, as if it were a restricted component whose function could be circumscribed. Hence, with Bataille in mind, Derrida writes:

> The blind spot of Hegelianism, *around* which can be organized the representation of meaning, is the *point* at which destruction, suppression, death and sacrifice constitute so irreversible an expenditure, so radical a negativity—here we would have to say an expenditure and a negativity *without reserve*—that they can no longer be determined as negativity in a process or a system.

Derrida notes that the point or limit of the nonreserve breaks apart the dialectic of positivity and negativity and hence "cannot be inscribed in discourse" without "exceed[ing] the logic of philosophy." This, as Derrida puts it, is the "no return of destruction," or "absolute expenditure." In other words, at the limit where Hegelian dialectics breaks open, one encounters a violence without reserve.[76]

Whereas Adorno also stressed the antisystematic systematization (as Jameson calls it) of the Hegelian dialectic that is unsuccessful in conserving and operationalizing all its parts, he does not glorify the destructiveness of negativity with the kind of dithrambic rapture that one detects in Derrida's style. Rather, Adorno stresses the unassimilated or estranged components of a nonidentitarian configuration or constellation of relationships whose inertia (rather than energia) is stressed. The vitalism of Bataille, which Derrida takes over in terms of a deconstructive and disseminative violence of a negativity without reserve, is utterly avoided by what Gillian Rose once termed Adorno's "melancholy science," which is to say, his saturnine brooding upon the inertia of things that can not be animated by transcendental philosophizing. As Adorno writes in *Negative Dialectics*:

> The task of dialectical cognition is not, as its adversaries like to charge, to construe contradictions from above and to progress by resolving them—although Hegel's logic, now and then, proceeds in this fashion.

Instead, it is up to dialectical cognition to pursue the inadequacy of thought and thing, to experience it in the thing.

Yet, Adorno also points out that "no single thing is at peace in the unpacified whole," which is to say, the "thing" is not at rest or, to use Derrida's terms, "nonreserved."[77] Here, too, a certain violence in the sense of disruption or rupturing manifests itself as essential to what the thing is in and of itself. Commenting on Adorno's style, Jameson once wrote that "density is itself a conduct of intransigence," that intransigence being the violence endemic to a disassimilation of identitarianisms.[78]

Although Michael Ryan's *Marxism and Deconstruction* (1982) revealed the striking affinities between Adorno and Derrida's postphenomenological, anti-identitarian projects for the sake of establishing a common Marxist horizon, Menke's study shows that Marxism need not be of relevance when considering Adorno in relation to Derrida.[79] This evacuation of Marx is also pronounced in two remarkable studies that bring Adorno into relation with Derrida: Jean-Francois Lyotard's essay, "Discussions, or Phrasings After Auschwitz," which he presented at the "Fins de l'homme" conference at Cerisy in 1980, and Drucilla Cornell's *Philosophy of the Limit* (1992). Lyotard's paper posits the logic of the *différend* developed in his book, *Le différend* (1983), in order to mark that place where negative dialectics and deconstruction exceed the confines of speculative thought. Cornell's book triangulates negative dialectics with Lévinas's understanding of the incommensurability of self and other and Derrida's reading of Lévinas in which the deconstruction of identity and difference figures so prominently. Whereas Lyotard attempts to exceed the logic of speculative philosophy to a point of no return, Cornell takes the more conservative approach of suggesting that speculative philosophy can be restored as an ethics of alterity at the limit of its deconstruction. As Ryan and others would undoubtedly point out, such studies have only managed to depoliticize negative dialectics. Lyotard, for example, instrumentalizes negative dialectics as a logical aporia of the relation/non-relation, whereas Cornell instrumentalizes it as a logic of incommensurability between knowledge and being. This leaves out the argument that Adorno's negative dialectics has a Marxist social, cultural, and political significance that exceeds an ethics of self and other fundamental to both Cornell, who is anxious to recover it in a speculative philosophy that is paradoxically anti-reflexive, and Lyotard, whose concept of the *différend* attempts to explain the dynamics of unethical social practices.[80]

Although the theoretical relation between Adorno and Derrida still has to be more or less invented in the place of its explicit absence, we do have some clear indication from Jürgen Habermas as to what he thought about deconstruction in the mid-1980s. In *The Philosophical Discourse of Modernity* (1985), Habermas made it clear that he suspected French theory (by which one is to understand the hegemony of theory as it arose in the 1960s in Paris) of being rather indebted to strains of fascist ideology. The fact that Derrida refers much more frequently to Nietzsche or Heidegger, rather than to the works of Marx, leads Habermas to understand that deconstruction's political undercurrents may be suspect. This argument relies on a strategy of guilt by association that has been commonly invoked by those who wish to delegitimize and eclipse Derrida's work in one blow. What I want to point out in my reading of Habermas's critique is that the tables could be easily turned on Habermas, particularly since his kind of argument works by way of retroactive political recontextualization whereby a contemporary discourse is imagined within another political and historical context of the past, namely, National Socialism. If the contemporary discourse "fits," it is to be considered problematic. Consider, however, what happens when we use *The Philosophical Discourse of Modernity* as our test case.

Habermas informs us that Heidegger's philosophy is politically National Socialist and that Derrida's interest in Nietzsche and Heidegger means that he belongs to a philosophical tradition that wants to undermine rationality, something that from a social point of view has already had calamitous political effects in the form of justifying fascism. To back up this theory, Habermas recontextualizes Derrida in a Germany of the 1930s by erroneously telling us that "Derrida's deconstructions faithfully follow the movement of Heidegger's thought" (including, one must presume, the infamous Rectoral Address of 1933). Furthermore, Habermas claims that, like Heidegger, "[Derrida], too, promotes only a mystification of palpable social *pathologies*; he, too disconnects essential (namely, deconstructive) thinking from scientific analysis; and he, too, lands at an empty, formulalike avowal of some indeterminate authority." In other words, deconstruction is fascist in inspiration (socially pathological, unscientific, formulaic, under the influence of an indeterminate and hence irresponsible authority, etc.). Hence, deconstruction is certainly *not* what Habermas calls *Sozialwissenschaften*. As is typical of the fascists (i.e., Heidegger), "[Derrida], too, degrades politics and contemporary history to the status of the ontic and the foreground, so as to romp all the more freely, and with a greater wealth of associations, in the sphere of the ontological and the archewriting." In other words, like the Nazis, Derrida supposedly privileges the originary signification of blood and soil. Finally, to round off the allegory, Derrida is thought to be even worse than Heidegger, because Derrida "stands closer to the anarchist wish to explode the continuum of history than to the authoritarian admonition to bend before destiny." (By destiny, here, he is referring us to Heidegger's "destiny of Being.")[81]

Right after the sentence I have just quoted, Habermas then tells us, "This contrasting stance [i.e., the anarchist wish to explode the continuum of history] may have something to do with the fact that Derrida, all denials notwithstanding, remains close to Jewish mysticism."[82] Exactly what remaining close to Jewish mysticism has to do with anarchism is completely unclear, because it is an illogical connection. However, it is clear that Jewish mysticism isn't a good thing in Habermas's mind if it has the deleterious effects he claims, though historically it would be hard to find a single example in which Jewish mysticism resulted in social anarchy, while it would be easy to prove that German tradition, in the form of those academics who upheld it for the sake of a National Socialist cause, was complicit in a politics that led to social catastrophe. Moreover, by saying that "Derrida . . . remains close to Jewish mysticism," Habermas is implying that there is some essential or foundational bond with Jewish mysticisim, presumably Derrida's identity as a Jew. This raises the unsettling paraphrase: "Because Derrida is a Jew, he necessarily will remain close to Jewish mysticism, which leads to social anarchy." Is that what Habermas is really saying? Certainly, it's a plausible reading. Consider the phrase, "all denials notwithstanding." It can be taken to mean more than "despite Derrida's remonstrations that he is not a Jewish mystic," because it resonates rather well with a past in which some assimilated or converted Jews, all their denials of their Jewishness nothwithstanding, were arrested, deported, and executed for being enemies of the state (i.e., anarchists). "Denials," in the context of anti-Semitism, means "they're Jews, and hence outlaws, despite all lies to the contrary." Is this what Habermas is saying to Derrida? That Derrida is a Jew and hence a mystic and not a genuine philosopher, denials to the contrary notwithstanding?

Given Habermas's recontextualization of contemporary thought within fascist contexts of the 1930s, consider the following retroactive historical construction. In Hugo Ott's well known political biography of Heidegger, there is evidence that a former colleague of Heidegger's, Erich Jaensch, wrote a memorandum to Alfred Rosenberg in order to alert the Nazi Party to the following concerns: "Heidegger's thought is characterized by the same obsession with hairsplitting distinctions as Talmudic thought. This is why it holds such an extraordinary fascination for Jews, persons of Jewish ancestry and others with a similar mental make-up." Not unlike Habermas, Jaensch appeals to the evils of Jewish religious thought, which Jaensch, too, will call "pathological." Heidegger's is a "special kind of sophistry, so extreme as to border on the pathological; one is constantly asking oneself how much of this is just eccentric and misguided in a normal sense, and how much already qualifies as the wanderings of a schizophrenic mind."[83] Jaensch concludes by saying that if Heidegger becomes too influential in higher education, an epidemic of mass psychosis will break out in the universities of Germany. The fear, as in Habermas, is anarchy.

As if echoing this kind of criticism, Habermas critiques Derrida by taking us on a rather long-winded excursion into Jewish thought in order to show its philosophical perversities. He notices a distinct relation between Derrida's "inverted foundationalism" (the bottomless pit of origins endlessly deferred) and Rabbi Eliezer's statement, "If all the seas were of ink, and all ponds planted with reeds, if the sky and the earth were parchments and if all human beings practiced the art of writing—they would not exhaust the Torah I have learned, just as the Torah itself would not be diminished any more than is the sea by the water removed by a paint brush dipped in it." Contrary to what Derrida has written, Habermas argues that the "a" in Derrida's term *différance* is the aleph mentioned by Rabbi Mendel and cited by Gersohm Scholem: "To hear the aleph is to hear next to nothing; it is the preparation for all audible language, but in itself contains no determinate, specific meaning."[84] As we have seen, for Derrida to refute this is futile, since, as in the Nazi period, Jews are to be accused in advance of making denials. Like Jaensch before him, Habermas objects to the hair splitting of a Jewish tradition that strikes him as pathological because, in Habermas's terms, it ends up "romping" in the "sphere of the ontological and the archewriting," which, according to Habermas, is intellectually insignificant, politically degrading, and, ultimately, an anarchist wish to explode the continuum of history.

At this point I want to clarify that I am *not* accusing Habermas of anti-Semitism or of writing a discourse that is politically suspect. After all, Habermas's credentials as an opponent of fascism are beyond dispute. Rather, I am challenging Habermas's tendency to retroactively recontextualize Derrida, since it is rather easy to distort even Habermas's own texts by such means. Clearly, if Habermas wants to take issue with what he perceives to be Jewish mysticism, then he ought to be able to call that into question without someone resorting to an ad hominem argument based on a reframing of the argument in terms of what the Nazis were writing in the past. Indeed, there is a problematic here that concerns the relation of texts within political contexts and how they are to be examined in relation to one another. Philip Watts's *Allegories of the Purge* (1998) is a recent study of French fascism that notes the elusiveness of such retroactive readings in terms of their allegorical and hence suggestive potentials. What becomes evident in that study, however, is that retroactive contextualization leads to shadowy paratexts and paraphrases, which is to say, to a discourse whose quasi truths are always open to speculation about whether something is really the case or not.[85] Hence, when Jeffrey Mehlman in "Perspectives: On de Man and *Le Soir*" accuses Derrida of genuflecting to the fascist trinity of Heidegger, Blanchot, and de Man, he advances the allegory of a church and its sacrament; and, when he accuses Derrida of subscribing to a paradoxical logic akin to the exculpating logic of collaborators during the "purge" after the Occupation of France, he is, yet again, practicing allegory by way of a retroactive recontextualization whose truth claims are merely analogical and, hence, figural rather than literal.[86] To return to Habermas, not only does he engage in an allegorization of deconstruction by means of a faulty analogy to Heidegger, but his illogical progression of arguments and crude reductive characterizations lead one to the obvious perception that Habermas either doesn't understand Derrida very well, has not made a serious attempt to read his work, or simply does not want to read Derrida. As Derrida himself wrote in a footnote to "Like the Sound of the Sea Deep Within a Shell: Paul de Man's War," Habermas's critique of deconstruction is simply "a fabric of counter truths."[87]

Of all the figures associated with Frankfurt, Derrida has only gravitated to the one who was of the famous figures perhaps most marginal to it, Walter Benjamin. This is not accidental, because like Bataille, Blanchot, and Derrida himself, Benjamin wrote philosophy across a number of nonphilosophical genres and in ways that are not systematizable. Furthermore, Benjamin's language theories include an understanding of writing—that of allegory—that is quite close in outlook to what Derrida once called "grammatology." Derrida's two main forays into Benjamin's work are to be found in "Des tours de Babel"

(1980), which is on Benjamin's essay "The Task of the Translator," and the short book *Force de loi* (1994), which pays homage to Benjamin's short essay "Zur Kritik Der Gewalt" (1921). In *Archive Fever* (1995), Derrida returns to Benjamin in order to develop Benjamin's ideas about Messianism within Jewish religious thought. Here, of course, Habermas's criticism of Jewish mysticism falls short yet again, since it fails to acknowledge the significance of this kind of thinking within Benjamin's corpus, something that again resists the kind of flat dismissal Habermas enacts. Without going into the particulars of the complex junctures between Benjamin and Derrida, one should nevertheless be directed to the introduction to the second part of *Force de loi*, which Derrida gave at the University of California at Los Angeles as part of a conference presentation whose theme was the Holocaust. Of some importance to Derrida was Benjamin's grafting of Marxist and messianic revolution, both of them announcing a new historical epoch purified of myth, but also of a Holocaust to come that escaped the horizon of representability that Benjamin nevertheless detected, just as Freud detected it in *Moses and Monotheism*. Here, too, mention of Adorno turns up. In a seminar entitled "Kant, the Jew, the German," Derrida says:

> I became very interested in what I then called the *Judeo-German psyche*, that is, the logic of certain phenomena of a disturbing sort of specularity . . . that was itself reflected in some of the great German Jewish thinkers of this century: Cohen, Buber, Rosenzweig, Scholem, Adorno, Arendt—and, precisely Benjamin. I believe that a serious reflection on Nazism—and the "final solution"—cannot avoid a courageous, interminable and polyhedral analysis of the history and structure of this Judeo-German "psyche." Among other things that I cannot go into here, we studied certain analogies, which were sometimes of the most equivocal and disquieting sort, between the discourse of certain "great German" thinkers and certain "great German Jewish" thinkers. . . . It is in this context that certain limited but determinable affinities between Benjamin's text and some texts by Carl Schmitt, even by Heidegger, began to intrigue me. Not only because of the hostility to parliamentary democracy, even to democracy as such, or to the *Aufklärung*, not only because of a certain interpretation of the *polemos*, of war, violence and language, but also because of a thematic of "destruction" that was very widespread at the time.[88]

Derrida then speaks to "force de loi" and the dismaying trajectory of Benjamin's self-destructive text "that lets no other legacy appear than the violence of its signature—but as divine signature. How to read this text with a 'deconstructive' gesture that is neither, today any more than it has ever been, Heideggerian nor Benjaminian?"[89] Here, then, is Derrida's Frankfurt connection as the link to a highly vexed rhetoric of destruction that cuts across German Jewish and German Non-Jewish writers in ways that disorient the sorts of distinctions someone like Habermas would take for granted, among them, a hard and fast political opposition between Jewish and Non-Jewish thinkers that obeys the laws of inclusion and exclusion pronounced by Nazism. In other words, Derrida's interest in Benjamin concerns the nonidentitarianism of political discourse that vexes the sorts of classifications that the purveyors of political correctness hold up as conceptual absolutes. And here, too, one can already detect the emergence of a certain "negative dialectic" within the political differences that make up political thought of Jewish thinkers between the two world wars.

1980–1987: A WORLD OF DIFFERENCE

While Derrida was still coming around to imagining the possibility of deconstruction as an American phenomenon, as opposed to, say, a Parisian or Frankfurt phenomenon, Jonathan Culler published *On Deconstruction* (1983), which evaluated the significance of Derrida's work within a number of American critical contexts. Given the negative press that Derrida's work was getting at around this time, Culler's book was more than an introduction to deconstruction—it was a defense and, perhaps even more than that, a rescue effort. Notable is Culler's nervousness about feminist critiques of deconstruction and, not surprisingly, the swerve toward essentialist critical stances that simply wrote off elaborate critical practices like deconstruction as abstract and irrelevant. While paying lip service to feminist moralizers such as Kate Millett and Judith Fetterley, Culler undermined their essentialist concept of "reading as a woman" by providing a deconstructive twist:

> For woman to read as a woman is not to repeat an identity or an experience that is given but to play a role she constructs with reference to

her identity as a woman, which is also a construct, so that the series can continue: a woman reading as a woman reading as a woman.[90]

According to Culler, deconstruction is a textual hermeneutic that is sensitive to writerly strategies that mask logical contradictions and, perhaps more importantly, moral injustices. This is why Culler focuses on Derrida's questioning of hierarchical oppositions and his strategy of reversing and hence dislocating them in order to liberate a subject that has been subordinated, if not repressed. For Culler, the result of a deconstructive reading is not just the production of an interesting interpretation, but the reestablishment of social justice. Hence Derrida's analysis of Freud allows us to see that "a deconstructive reading reveals that woman is not marginal but central and that the account of her 'incomplete sexuality' is an attempt to construct a male plenitude by setting aside a complexity that proves to be a condition of sexuality in general."[91] Culler's slant is politically motivated to the extent that he attempts to show that deconstruction is compatible with the various social movements (feminism, in particular) that started to become dominant in the early '80s.

Culler's stress on deconstruction as a questioning of hierarchical distinctions also enabled him to broach sensitive topics within the humanities, for example, the difference between literary language/ordinary language, the difference between reading/misreading, the difference between female readers/male readers, the difference between center/margin. Indeed, in questioning *différance*, Culler tried to make a common cause with politicized criticisms that were calling these and other power differentials into question for the sake of liberating marginalized concepts and subjects that have been structurally repressed by discursive and textual conventions whose normativity was no longer beyond question. In this sense, Culler was not so far removed from someone like Gayatri Chakravorty Spivak who also saw in deconstruction the hermeneutical possibility of calling multiple power differentials to account for their injustice. Of significance in terms of the history of recent theory is that by the early 1980s critics like Culler saw the need for deconstruction to get into the political arena or suffer the consequences for remaining Yale bound.

However, Culler was not about to cut ties to the 1970s. For example, he remained attracted to deconstruction because of its importance as a form of systems analysis. Here, of course, the early reception of deconstruction lives on to the extent that Culler applauds how "deconstruction arrives in the wake of structuralism to frustrate its systematic projects." And, "deconstruction, by these lights, reveals the impossibility of any science of literature or science of discourse and returns critical inquiry to the task of interpretation." Culler then summarizes: "One can certainly argue that American criticism has found in deconstruction reasons to deem interpretation the supreme task of critical inquiry, and thus to preserve some measure of continuity between the goals of New Criticism and those of the newer criticism."[92] It is here that the gesture in the direction of social justice is complemented by a commitment to close reading that academics leaning toward social studies wanted to abandon for the sake of an explicit social critique that would not be compromised by arty ambiguities and impasses. Culler's attempt to appease, if not seduce, politically radicalized academics with the power of an ultrasophisticated interpretive tool was widely appreciated at the time, but, given our hindsight today, politely rejected with a cool "No, thank-you."

Somewhat more successful at this strategy, however, was Barbara Johnson. Her book *The Critical Difference* (1980) was a collection of essays written in the late 1970s, some of them published while Johnson was still a graduate student at Yale. Of the generation of Yale students whose work was closely attached to the critical methodology of de Man, Johnson placed the most restrictions on herself. After all, an odd feature about Johnson's approach in both *The Critical Difference* and *A World of Difference* (1987) is a certain theoretical restraint that never ventures beyond the theoretical limits of Derrida's essay, "La différance." It is a remarkable case of self-confinement, given that as a brilliant translator of essays like "La double séance" and "La dissémination," Johnson had been exposed to some very adventuresome rhetorical applications of "différance," applications that she studiously avoided for the sake of a much more familiar plain style of critical writing that harked back to New Criticism. The gain is a brilliant clarity of expression as well as a thoroughness of purpose that was somewhat lacking in her mentors, de Man, Hartman, Bloom, and even Miller.

She was also far less protean and polymorphous than Derrida, who would never have formalized difference the way Johnson does. "Reading, here, proceeds by identifying and dismantling differences by means of other differences that cannot be fully identified or dismantled." This metadifferential approach to difference is, in effect, an attempt to multiply the frames of differential reference, to dwell, as it were, on the embedded differences *within* differences. "The 'deconstruction' of a binary opposition is thus not an annihilation of all values or differences; it is an attempt to follow the subtle, powerful effects of differences already at work *within* the illusion of a binary opposition."[93] In quoting Derrida's "La différance," Johnson fails to explain that the relevant philosophical context is Martin Heidegger's *Identity and Difference* and that the whole discussion of time and space speaks to much of Heidegger's work, *Being and Time* in particular. Then, too, Johnson ignores the very difficult discussion of difference taken up in Plato's *The Sophist* where the binary distinction, or logical of binaryism, promoted by the Sophist himself, comes under fire at a time *before* Aristotelian category distinctions were logically established. Here, of course, the formalization of difference (i.e., sophistry) is precisely what Plato calls into question.

Key to Johnson's work at this time was the much republished essay "The Frame of Reference: Poe, Lacan, Derrida," which emphasized a multiplication of referential frames that highlighted the question of difference as a structural instability. In her essay, "Mallarmé and Austin," she even goes so far as to box words in a poem by Mallarmé, whose constative frames of reference cannot contain the performance of the words within them. The linguistic differentials required for the production of meaning—one may recall Roman Jakobson's binary structural readings of Shakespeare—are brought into a parergonal interplay of multiple references that opens out upon what Johnson calls a monstrosity, which is to say, a reading so exploded into referential fragments that only an aggressive "writerly" reader (in Roland Barthes's sense, which Johnson has invoked earlier in her book) can salvage it. Still, however much Johnson has multiplied the frames of reference and the aporias of difference that they sometimes produce, one comes away with the impression that in the end Johnson has succeeded in doing what her predecessors at Yale had envisioned: the creation of a higher order of new critical analysis that displayed a virtuosic ability to distinguish between delicately nuanced fluctuations of meaning and to exploit them for the sake of showing how literature vexes classical understandings of identity and difference.

By 1987, Johnson had already left Yale for Harvard and had published her second book, *A World of Difference*, that starts out with essays that closely resemble *The Critical Difference*. Yet in this book Johnson makes a major turn away from her mentors at Yale. Initially, Johnson's book addresses both the bad press that deconstruction was getting from the likes of Denis Donoghue, Walter Jackson Bate, and others, as well as what I take to be a concern she must have had about her own work, namely, the use of deconstruction as an interpretive *techne* that the more refined it gets the more predictable it becomes. Her counterattack on Bate and other critical curmudgeons points out that their logic is based on simplistic binary distinctions of the all-or-nothing variety and that the poverty of their arguments is belied by the crudity of that logic. In turning to her own methodological concerns, Johnson included a very lucid and lengthy definition of deconstruction in which it becomes a kind of deregulated metatextuality: "Instead of according moments of textual self-interpretation and authoritative metalinguistic status, deconstruction considers anything the text says about itself to be another fiction, an allegory of the reading process." Just as late New Critics were more interested in what the text said about itself than in what the critic was interested in saying about the text, Johnson argues that deconstruction is more interested in looking for what the text says about itself as a fictionalized allegory of reading than in subordinating the text under whatever is calling itself "deconstruction." Hence "the text subverts the possibility of any authoritative reading by inscribing the reader's strategies into its own structures that often, for de Man, ends up being constitutive of literature as such. Deconstructors, therefore, tend to privilege texts that are self-reflexive in interestingly and rigorously unreliable ways."[94]

It is curious that Johnson talks of critics in terms of being "deconstructors," as if deconstruction could be a subject or agent of this kind, since nothing could be more alien to Derrida's own formulations of deconstruction. Never has he referred to himself or anyone else as a "deconstructor." Also, we should not overlook the fact that Johnson extends a political assumption that is dear to the New Critics, namely, that literature is subversive and that *explication du texte* is inherently antiauthoritarian. Recall that R. P. Blackmur once distinguished between dogmatic readings, which were imposed on the text by moralizing critics, and subversive readings, which were immanent within the texts themselves. De Man, in Johnson's context, similarly points to a subversive aspect of the text that resists a dictatorial, dogmatic imposition of intentions and meanings upon the text. Deconstruction, apparently, is a term that marks the furthest reaches of such a liberation of meaning from the dogmas of reading.

However, by the time we get to the end of chapter 11, "Les Fleurs du Mal Armé," one cannot help but notice that a sea change has occurred in Johnson's critical allegiances and outlooks: "In conclusion, I would like to look briefly at two poems that carry out, in very different ways, a female revision of the Western male poetic tradition of poems about the female body and, in particular, the breast."[95] First, she quotes from Clément Marot and Edmund Spenser whose conventional praises of the female body belong to a classical rhetoric of erotic praise that is highly familiar. In contrast, she also quotes Anne Sexton's "The Breast," which deflates such erotic stereotypes ("Something between/my shoulders was there. But never enough"), and Lucille Clifton's "If I stand in my window," which introduces the issue of race: "and if the man come to stop me . . . saying I have offended him / I have offended his / Gods / let him watch my black body / push against my own glass . . ."[96] Here, again, Johnson is multiplying frames of reference. But now they are multiplied not for the sake of a Derridean principle (*la différance*) but for the sake of a social studies orientation that is much closer to moralizing critics who tally up gender references, inventory images, and diagnose stereotypes for the sake of promoting social equality as opposed to close reading and abstruse philosophizing.

Whereas difference was once so subtle an issue it required a somewhat Byzantine multiplication of referential frames that ultimately served to destabilize our confidence in referentiality and reality, all of a sudden we notice the upsurge of a determinate difference—i.e., color difference—that suddenly requires a very oppositional and static understanding of social positioning. For example, "the man" who watches the naked black female speaker of Clifton's poem is presumably a white policeman. That it is the woman who speaks inverts the traditional power play of the male gaze. "The male gaze is returned and judged by the female speaker, the object turned subject." This reversal is, in fact, but a simple inversion of relations in which the male is to "learn the experience of exclusion, alienation, dispossession. He must discover himself as other." I say this even though Johnson argues that "Clifton's revision is not a simple symmetrical reversal."[97] For the fact is that in the poem, as in Johnson's reading, role reversal is the *dominant* logic, even if the woman is more compassionate toward the man than the man is toward the woman.

What has happened to difference? Apparently, Johnson concluded at some point in her researches that socially articulated differences are differences of identity that do not dissolve into "*la différance*," which is to say, *A World of Difference* describes a range of possibilities for the concept of difference that makes up a complex field of different conceptualizations and theories of difference that are all embedded within the word "difference." Hence, a *world* of difference. Now, of course, we can see the major implication behind Johnson's restricting herself to Derrida's theoretical excursus, "La différance." Derrida's theorizations may well require the kind of lengthy meditation and development that means one has to stay with only one essay for many years. It is in this sense that Johnson has made an enormous contribution to theory: she has demonstrated that only a sustained and restricted study will do justice to the working through of theory and that the fugitive hopping around from one theoretical frame to another is not in the interests of a serious investigation of a topic.

Politically, Johnson's book carried much weight with the languages and literatures in that it could be read as a deft recantation of Yale School criticism, if not to say, a switching of parties, as it were, from a text-based theory (*la différance*) to a social studies approach (identitarianism). Given her critique of how a feminist understanding of gender was missing from Yale School criticism and her introduction of essays that engaged African-American literature and current affairs issues like abortion, Johnson was telling her profession that despite the fact that deconstruction was politically enlightened, the passing bell had nevertheless rung for it. That the de Man affair coincided with the publication of Johnson's book made this wink to the profession all the more authoritative, even if Johnson could not have calculated the coincidence of her project with the flap over de Man's past. Indeed, it is no doubt in part due to Johnson's book that by 1988 it was clear that the age of close literary reading had actually ended and that cultural studies was the future.

DECONSTRUCTING OTHERWISE: GAYATRI CHAKRAVORTY SPIVAK

Barbara Johnson's approach to deconstruction was, of course, modeled on critical practices at Yale that stressed a formalist appropriation of deconstruction, something that was most pronounced in the case of J. Hillis Miller who was in search of ever more abstruse concepts of figuration, such as metalepsis or anacoluthon, in order to advance the idea that literary texts used tropes in order to construct meanings in ways that push logic to the breaking point. This was a view widely held by New Critics like Cleanth Brooks who, back in the 1940s and '50s, saw in poets like Donne and Herbert numerous logical paradoxes that forced the construction of double readings in which one interpretive construction contradicted the other. Miller's idea that "the deconstructive critic seeks to find, by this process of retracing, the element in the system studied which is alogical, the thread in the text in question that will unravel it all, or the loose stone which will pull down the whole building" was a natural extension of the New Criticism, which by the late 1960s had, independently of Derrida, come to the conclusion that rather than apply a method of one's own to a text, one should look for the text's own metacritical statements that would do the textual dismantling on their own. For such critics—and not surprisingly for Miller as well—the favored metacritical poet was Wallace Stevens. Because Stevens's work was so critically self-reflexive in calling itself into question, it was not hard for Miller, an admirer of Stevens, to adopt the following sort of doctrine: "Deconstruction is not a dismantling of the structure of a text, but a demonstration that it has already dismantled itself."[98] This view is a variant of what Paul de Man was able to achieve in terms of showing how aporetic textual structures self-deconstruct by counterpointing contradictory narrative structures. Derrida's emphasis upon philological close reading, textual structure, and logical mind bending obviously struck a chord with some formalists who seized deconstruction as a higher order of the old New Criticism.

Although it was at Yale that Derrida was most positively received, his most important early work, *Of Grammatology*, was introduced and translated by Gayatri Chakravorty Spivak, who, at the time, was a professor of English and comparative literature at the University of Iowa. The significance of Spivak's involvement is that she was not, in essence, a New Critic and had no particular interest in advancing what was an Anglo-American tradition of literary exegesis. Yet the fact that Spivak became closely associated with the name Derrida by way of her translation of what was, back in the 1970s, still an enormously esoteric text meant that many were thinking of her as someone whose critical orientation was akin to critics at Yale.[99] At the very least, she appeared to be presenting herself in her translator's introduction to *Of Grammatology* as if her allegiance to Derrida meant that she ought to be considered a deconstructionist, and in essays like "Finding Feminist Readings: Dante, Yeats" (1980) one can see much familiarity with Yale School practices. However, by the early 1980s, it was clear that whatever allegiances Spivak had with deconstruction, she was more critically aligned with socially oriented theories like Marxism, feminism, and what would later become known as postcolonialism.

Of course, when Derrida argued that there can be no one deconstruction, he was quite sensitive to the fact that significant conceptual breakthroughs are likely to be differently appropriated and that this difference is itself endemic to what a term like "deconstruction" is going to mean over a number of years. The differences in deconstruction's propriation (its inter-pretations, uses, transformations, redeployments) is essentially a conflict of propriations that can assert itself as a *polemos*, or struggle among deconstruc-tions. Rodolphe Gasché's attempts to set deconstruction in a rigorous philo-sophical camp apart from the less schooled uses of deconstruction by literary critics would be a case in point where such a struggle becomes marked.[100] The belief that critical theory ought to be considered a suite of "isms" that are re-ducible to orthodox doctrines and methodologies encourages students and faculty to identify themselves with a particular school of thought within which a polemos, or struggle, exists with respect to a conflict of how certain ideas or doctrines are being used: repeated, interpreted, applied, revised, and transformed. Spivak, who in a certain sense always remains faithful to the work of Derrida, has refused to allow herself to be claimed by any critical school in particular. As translator and introducer of *Of Grammatology*, she has participated in the dissemination of deconstruction in the United Kingdom and America without allowing herself to be appropriated or co-opted by de-construction. That is, just as she doesn't allow herself to be claimed by de-construction, she doesn't claim deconstruction for herself either. Hence, in her essay, "Ghostwriting" (1995), she strongly critiques Derrida's *Specters of Marx* (1993) for what she believes to be his disappointing unfamiliarity with Marx, his undertheorized understanding of the International, and his avoid-ance of transposing his thoughts into some Third World contexts not entire-ly foreign to his experiences in Algeria.[101] And yet, despite such critique, she accepts her appropriation by deconstruction, even as she does or does not ap-propriate it in her own writings.

What sets Spivak's work apart from the vast majority of critical writing, then, is its relation to propriations that are, at best, partial, temporary, and only provisionally identificationary. Hence her essays may or may not take up deconstruction. And even if they do, there is no guarantee that this critical ap-propriation is going to be sustained. Spivak therefore will never have to make the kind of decision that befell Johnson when she confronted an either/or choice between Yale School deconstructionism and cultural critique. For, un-like most Anglo-American critics, Spivak has developed a critical orientation that is multiply situated among an array of critical options that can be taken up alongside one another without bothering too much about the war, or *pole-mos*, that concerns critical differences. This is why, for example, it was not problematic for Spivak in the late 1980s to invoke the strategic use of essentialism, despite the fact that her deconstructivist orientations point us in a very different direction. What may look like theoretical sloppiness or incoherence is, in fact, an unusual orientation toward critical propriations that might best be explained with the following analogy. In a military action, one mobilizes a large number of different units—each using somewhat different equipment, tactics, regimens, expertise—and points them in a general direction to accomplish multiple tasks, the overall objective being to defeat and take over enemy emplacements. In the same sense, an essay mobilizes numerous arguments or approaches with the idea that if some of these strategies fall short of their goal, others will succeed. Not all of these arguments have to be methodologically compatible, and it is enough if certain arguments advance only a little bit, while others advance much further. The point, of course, is that instead of an eclectic theory soup, one develops an array of differently configured theoretical units, or systems, so that the whole critical enterprise never rests on one line of argumentation but is positioned in multiple sites along a borderline of argumentative contestation.

Strategically, this mode of advancing multiply situated positions, arguments, theories, and examples, departs from the kind of defensive interlocking approach developed by someone like Paul de Man for whom each "critical move" has to be sequentially covered and protected by other critical moves. De Man's chess board strategy depends upon an all-or-nothing wager: should there be any gaps or weak links in the defensive argumentative chain, the whole project is invalidated. In the earlier part of his career, Derrida had also been writing in this manner and produced essays that were hyperdefensive in their ability to overwhelm any objection with lengthy qualifying remarks and sidebars. Only much later in his career did Derrida begin to think in terms of having written enough texts to make up a considerable archive, or "Derridabase," whose reserve forces could be "called up" to do service whenever needed.

Although Derrida is capable of mobilizing various discourses, there is, however, never any doubt that they are appropriated in advance in the name of deconstruction and, even more importantly, are mutually reinforcing. Nothing is allowed to be sacrificed or to not hit its mark in this struggle to argue a point, because Derrida identifies himself (his integrity, honor, legitimacy, his right to be heard) and is himself identified (as father of deconstruction) with a movement whose fate must never suffer on account of him. In essays like "Limited Inc." and most especially "Biodegradables" and

"Marx & Sons," Derrida has even shown a loss of temper that reveals quite a bit about his personal investment in deconstruction as an intellectual movement whose legitimacy is not to be called into question. In fact, in "Marx & Sons" he even lashes out against Spivak in what I take to be a rather apparent misunderstanding of "Ghostwriting": the view that because she criticizes Derrida, she must be situating herself wholly in opposition to him. In fact, she has advanced her critiques, which are entirely in line with her previous writings, not in order to embarrass Derrida, but in order to show where his critical emplacements are vulnerable to attack. A reading of her work in general should quickly reveal that such attacks are not egotistically motivated, but that they concern a sense of multiple orientation within which the social meaning of various issues can be revalorized. In the process of such revalorization, Spivak's own orientation to deconstruction and to Derrida undergoes changes and reveals a certain conflictedness that I would suppose Spivak accepts as part of her position as a critic who is multiply articulated in social terms.

We will come back to Spivak's critiques of Derrida, though by way of an essay whose structure reveals some general characteristics of her writings. In "Feminism and Critical Theory" (1986), we are told at the outset that "I cannot speak of feminism in general. I speak of what I do as a woman within literary criticism." This is obviously a pragmatic point of view that distances Spivak from an idealized conception of what it means to be a feminist. Rather than positing herself as a general subject, she emphasizes her particularity, or singularity, as a person. However, when pushed to define what it means to be a woman, Spivak responds: "My own definition of a woman is very simple: it rests on the word 'man.'" Anticipating criticism, she immediately cautions, "You might say at this point, defining the word 'woman' as resting on the word 'man' is a reactionary position. Should I not carve out an independent definition for myself as a woman?" Here a universal horizon of understanding has been opened up in terms of the woman/man dichotomy central to anthropology, Lacanian psychoanalysis, and sociology. This, in turn, leads to a "deconstructive lesson":

> No rigorous definition of anything is ultimately possible, so that if one wants to, one could go deconstructing the opposition between man and woman, and finally show that it is a binary opposition that displaces itself. Therefore, "as a deconstructivist," I cannot recommend that kind

of dichotomy at all, yet, I feel that definitions are necessary in order to keep us going, to allow us to take a stand.

She then comes back to her initial point about "woman" being defined in terms of "man" and says, "I construct my definition as a woman not in terms of a woman's putative essence but in terms of words currently in use. 'Man' is such a word in common usage."[102] At issue here is more than one argument or position: (1) there is a deconstructive lesson that is presumed whose effect is to invalidate the dichotomy of woman/man, but (2) there is also the argument that the word "woman" cannot be textually dissociated from the word "man," and that the word "man" is an anchorage point for grasping the definition of "woman." Of importance is that Spivak is only partially invested in either of these two arguments. As if to drop this matter entirely, she moves on to remarks on literature that seem rather unrelated. Of course, it is this habit of dropping arguments in midstream that characterizes something typical in Spivak's work that has annoyed many readers, namely, a seemingly haphazard picking up and laying aside that has the effect of a theoretical inoperability, dysfunctionality, or, at the very least, incompletion. To put it simply, she never finishes what she starts. But this unfinished rough cutting and, as Derrida suggests, rough shodding, concerns precisely what I identify as partial propriations, namely, the taking up of a piece of an argumentative line rather than its complete trajectory for the very reason that the critical move being made is instrumental within an array of other moves, none of which one identifies with or rejects completely, but all of which one identifies with or rejects in part.

To continue, Spivak tells us that in literary study the truth of a human situation is played out in the "itinerary of not being able to find it," and that "the problem of human discourse is generally seen as articulating itself in the place of, in terms of, three shifting 'concepts': language, world, and consciousness." Exactly what any of this has to do with not being able to speak of feminism in general, or defining oneself as "woman" by way of "man" is left unsettled. After discussing "text" for a while, Spivak then turns to a Marxist understanding of the world as text that includes Freud, a discussion that will broach the topic of "alienation in Marx, and the idea of normality and health in Freud." Woman will return like a repressed concept from within the Marxist discussion that, instead of focusing on alienation, as proposed, actually turns to the question of use and exchange value: "Woman in the traditional social situation produces more than she is getting in terms of her subsistence."[103]

We are still only considering the opening matter of this essay, and in later sections we will be asked to consider not only woman but matters of class and race. These are all very disparate topics, though at some point a reader does notice a unifying horizon with respect to questions of equivalence. For example, in terms of Freud: "Pain does not operate in the same way in men and women."[104] This belongs to an array of observations that converge along a borderline of contestation having to do with the "value" of woman in relation to man, that value being multiply situated. Hence Spivak looks at "the repeated agenda of the situational production of [value and of the] concepts [that result] and our complicity in such a production." She insists, "This aspect of deconstruction will not allow the establishment of a hegemonic 'global theory' of feminism."[105] Thus values that are situationally produced have to be thought of in terms of particular modes of production that are not generally applicable, since a mode of production is situated in a particular here and now that may or may not have any relationship with something that is occurring elsewhere. To come back to the initial question of Spivak's definition of "woman," it would appear that if she takes up a definition that is objectionable in terms of its relation to the term "man," it is because without that term questions of equivalence and value could not be posed. No doubt, there is a Saussurean conception of value at work that remains understated, one that may intrude without Spivak's having pledged allegiance to it. However, there are other conceptions of value at work, as well: Hegelian, Marxist, and Derridean. In a telling remark about Derrida, Spivak argues:

> Rather than deconstruction simply opening a way for feminists, the figure and discourse of woman opened the way for Derrida as well. His incipient discourse of woman surfaced in *Spurs* [first published as "La Question du Style" in 1975], which also articulates the thematics of "interest" crucial to political deconstruction. This study marks his move from the critical deconstruction of phallocentrism to "affirmative" deconstruction [Derrida's phrase]. It is at this point that Derrida's work seems to become less interesting for Marxism. The early Derrida can certainly be shown to be useful for feminist practice, but why is it that when he writes under the sign of woman, as it were, that his work be-

comes solipsistic and marginal? What is it in the history of that sign that allows this to happen?[106]

Spivak will delay the answer for some pages, but when she comes back to it she argues that Derrida idealizes woman as the indeterminate by way of her opposition to the tyranny of that which is proper (determinate). This celebration of the indeterminate situates woman as absent, unnamed, and sexually undefined, all of which Spivak finds politically problematic. Spivak's point is less that Derrida's critique of the proper is wrong than that the critique is not accompanied by multiply (i.e., internationally) situated political frames of reference within which the value of this indeterminacy is differently produced. Why is Derrida more solipsistic and marginal when he speaks as a woman? Spivak's answer is that Derrida's feminine subject is politically situated as a bourgeois woman, who by definition is more solipsistic and marginal than the bourgeois male. In making that critique, Spivak does not simply dismiss Derrida as mystified but argues that deconstruction is only a partial success. Indeed, her point is similar to that of the Tel Quel critics, namely, that Derrida lost his political edge at that moment he departed from a value-oriented semiotics that took its cue from Marxism.

"Feminism and Critical Theory" is among the more readily accessible pieces that Spivak published in the mid 80s and exemplifies how she attacks issues from a wide number of differently situated critiques in order to make a point that is general (more or less the case) rather than universal (always the case), that point being the question of how value is constituted and, in many cases, reified by way of establishing a concept whose purpose is to fix value. The construction of value, of course, is one of Derrida's major interests in *Of Grammatology,* and Spivak respects Derrida's deconstruction of prejudicial dichotomies upon which value distinctions have been upheld; yet she has also been in disagreement with deconstruction's postponement of a Marxist encounter, promised by Derrida in the early '70s but somehow never quite instantiated, except rather obliquely in *Specters of Marx* (1990). In "Limits and Openings of Marx in Derrida" (1993), Spivak supplies the Marxist analysis that would make deconstruction more politically and economically viable; this reiterates the kind of project that has also been undertaken by Ernesto Laclau, namely, to do for Derrida what Derrida has not done for himself: to marry deconstruction and Marxism.[107] As we will see, other Marxist-oriented critics proposed an alternative deconstruction that is inherently presupposed, as well, in Spivak's work, namely, a deconstruction that operates by means of a critique of the subject position. Before we examine this very popular alternative at some length, it is necessary to look at some British developments in the 1970s that lead up to this different articulation of theory.

BRITISH DEVELOPMENTS: THE INFLUENCE OF *SCREEN*

By the late 1980s feminism had not only triumphed in the American academy, but it had enabled allied social movements in the study of race, ethnicity, and gender to become very prominent. African American studies, which in the early 1980s was still largely ignored in the academy, started exerting considerable influence in the late 1980s. Latino studies, Native American studies, and Asian American studies were emerging as well. In addition, postcolonial studies gained considerably in stature and by the mid-1990s exemplified the leading model of comparative literary and cultural analysis.

It needs to be stated from the outset that deconstruction has in some respects been very closely affiliated with the emergence of these socially determined critical movements. After all, Derrida's *Margins of Philosophy* (1972) founds the contemporary discourse on marginalization that has been so central to feminism, postcolonialism, and queer theory. Also, Derrida's thinking in the early '60s about the Other in a post-Sartrean sense has also become foundational for contemporary thinking on self-other relations. Furthermore, Derrida's deconstruction of hierarchical oppositions has been of major importance for the critique of prejudicial values and hence for underrepresented peoples and their social issues; and Derrida's early and pathbreaking work on a critique of patriarchy ("Plato's Pharmacy") and notions of sexual difference ("Spurs") made considerable contributions to further work by feminists. Last, Derrida's early work had already transgressed disciplinary lines in such a way that it became possible to work across textual domains that not so long ago were kept separate. Reading philosophy as literature or literature as the law, for example, enable certain kinds of textual analysis that open up new possibilities that otherwise would be suppressed. Given that cultural studies, New Historicism, and postcolonial studies are largely determined by such textual crossing-over points to a certain indebtedness to deconstruction and its theoretical allies among the Tel Quel critics.

Yet, because Derrida withdrew from the Marxist arena in the early 1970s and was relegated to what we might call the dog-house of language, a theoretical and critical set of approaches developed in the mid-'70s that would more or less eclipse, or write out, deconstruction, even as these elaborations kept a seat open for deconstruction should someone wish to exercise that option. Indeed, by the early 1990s there was large-scale agreement on a number of theoretical points that defined the parameters of this particular elaboration. And while these doctrines may seem to have developed in many places over quite some time, almost all can be traced to the work of a single group active in the 1970s that has never been very well known in America. I am referring to critics associated with the British journal *Screen*.

A landmark study that brought many of these theoretical developments together was a critical overview, *Language and Materialism: Developments in Semiology and the Theory of the Subject* (1977), by Rosalind Coward and John Ellis. Because their theorizations were far ahead of the state of cultural study at the time, Coward and Ellis did not receive considerable acknowledgment, although the study has nevertheless been quite influential. Looking back, one notices that their book does recognize the theoretical cornerstones for various socially inspired critical practices to come. Like critics in the Birmingham School, the *Screen* critics had been reading French structuralism before they turned to Marx by way of Louis Althusser's example. The *Screen* critics agreed with the Birmingham School's culturalist view that, in Stuart Hall's words, "One could only 'live' and experience one's conditions *in and through* the categories, classifications and frameworks of the culture"[108] Still, some of the *Screen* critics were of the view that the Birmingham School was theoretically restricted in terms of a Marxist "economic determinism." For this reason, Coward and Ellis pursued the alternative of a semiological theory modeled on that of French structuralism and gravitated to not only Althusser but to Kristeva, Barthes, Lévi-Strauss, Lacan, and Derrida. Conspicuously absent in Coward and Ellis's book, however, is mention of figures such as Stuart Hall, Raymond Williams, Colin MacCabe, or Terry Eagleton. Also conspicuously absent is Michel Foucault, who would become of immense significance to American critics in the 1980s and '90s.

Be that as it may, Coward and Ellis staked out the following points that would become dogmatic for much cultural and social analysis in the following two decades: (1) the idea that social subjects are constructed; (2) that subjects have to be analyzed in terms of subject-positions; (3) that subjects are interpellated into ideology; (4) that subjectivity needs to be reformulated from a materialist point of view; (5) that the concept of the Other is crucial to social analysis; (6) that performance takes priority over representation, and (7) that a revolutionary subject needs to accompany revolutionary ideas.

Whereas we usually associate social constructivism with the writings of Michel Foucault, it is instructive to see that in the mid-'70s Coward and Ellis were citing Claude Lévi-Strauss: "Thus Lévi-Strauss's structuralism shows us that the human subject is not homogeneous and in control of himself, he is constructed by a structure whose very existence escapes his gaze. . . . To see the subject as subjected, constructed by the symbol, is the most radical moment of this structuralism."[109] The idea, taken from structuralism, that a subject is constructed as opposed to being deconstructed will be of immense importance to the history of deconstruction's failed encounters with Anglo-American cultural and social criticisms, since the constructivist line of argument requires the very subject (or self) that deconstruction (but also structuralism) demystifies and annihilates. Also, Coward and Ellis were careful to position themselves within the politics of Marxist theory in a way that deconstruction did not at this time. Nevertheless, they faulted Marx for talking only about how production of the social is dialectically determined by economic production, since this "fails to show how the human subject is constructed, a construction which is specified by ideological practice."[110]

In the Marxist framework, Coward and Ellis replace the term "construction" with "production": "Production of representations necessarily entails the production of subjects for these representations." However, there are also times when both "construction" and "production" are replaced by the Lacanian locution, "*formation* of the subject": "We assert that it is only psychoanalysis which has gone any way to analyzing the formation of the subject which receives its specific subjectivity in the work of ideology."[111] As it turns out, Lacan himself never fleshed out the formation of the subject in terms of the work of ideology—nor did Althusser, though he saw the connection and wrote about it to Lacan in the late '60s with little in the way of response but some appreciative asides. In fact, not until Slavoj Žižek published *The Sublime Object of Ideology* (1989)did anything approaching a full-scale Lacanian theory of ideology see the light of day. Yet, the *Screen* critics saw the potential and devoted themselves to this kind of project via their interest in film, something that Žižek has in common with them.

Anticipating the work of Ernesto Laclau and Chantal Mouffe in the 1980s, Coward and Ellis also spoke of an *articulation* of ideology in terms of "the construction of the relation between the subject and the social relations." The immediate context was the work of Althusser, which, in some respects, they found inadequate: "Althusser closes off the possibility of the subject being constructed in contradiction." Coward and Ellis will elaborate on contradiction in terms of examining contradictory subject-positions. Taking Althusser's point that ideology is a necessary social practice that situates the subject so that it can act, Coward and Ellis conclude: "Ideology is always more than ideas; it is a material force in that it *constructs* subjects in specific relation to the social relations."[112] Later we read that "ideology should rather be seen as . . . a force which operates to produce a certain subject with a certain meaning, in other words, to institute an articulation." In Coward and Ellis, then, the concept of "construction" was broad enough to include a very wide number of possibilities, among them, that subjects can construct themselves by self-consciously performing practices of signification against the grain of ideological representations and structures: "Until Marxism can produce a revolutionary subject, revolutionary change will be impossible."[113]

Given much of what Coward and Ellis write, this is a striking comment for two reasons. First, it suggests that, at the very least, Marxism has not produced a revolutionary subject that is capable of bringing change to bourgeois Western societies and that other alternatives need to be considered. Second, we are being confronted with the theoretical contradiction that after having embraced structuralist and Marxist understandings of the subject that did away with the bourgeois concept of the individual that what is still required is a truly revolutionary agent—a newly born self. By the 1980s, not only women but other minorities would lay claim to such subjecthood. Such subjects were not, in the end, altogether different from Marx's idea of a proletariat or oppressed class, though they differed to the extent that they had much more individuality and less conformity. Minorities were good candidates for the revolutionary subject, because the less they could be structured in terms of stereotypical ideological constructions, the more they could be said to live a conflict of subject-positions articulated in terms of social contradictions. Hence, instead of valorizing those who simply theorized the ideological constructedness of the social subject, academia began privileging those who lived social contradictions on account of their particular situation as subjects whose position in society was atypical or conflicted. Already by 1980, figures such as

Edward Said and Gayatri Spivak became emissaries of the revolutionary hy-phenated-subject in process. More generally, the revolutionary subject was constructed in terms of sexuality and body politics (since these can be constructed by *anyone*). By the late 1980s, some academics who had always been identified as "straight" suddenly proclaimed themselves to be "queer." Also symptomatic was that by the mid-'80s, critics such as Donna Haraway were announcing newly constructed subjects like the "Cyborg" that was supposedly always already posthuman and, as such, a revolutionary subject in material process who carried contradiction (human versus nonhuman) to its extremes.

Here a link to deconstruction becomes perceptible, since it was always the assumption of Coward and Ellis that at the furthest edge of social practice would be found the destabilization, or deconstruction, of contradiction through the movements of opposed subject-positions. However, the model for this deconstruction was not so much Derrida but Julia Kristeva whose semiotic theories explored relations between signification and the body (chora, the mother, abjection, expulsion, etc.), particularly in terms of a negativity, or refusal, that does violence to the norms of language. Whereas emphasis with Derrida fell on a cerebral dismantling of contradictions (by way of *différance*, undecidability, deferral), with Kristeva the dismantling was a visceral expression at the interface of soma and the chora (a level of expression closest to the Freudian drives) that refused, or negated, language as a mode of production whose basis was that of the distinctive feature (or binary opposition) that at a higher level of structuring resembled contradiction. French literary writers such as Céline, Lautréamont, and Mallarmé were said to show a problematization of the subject that was constituted within processes of signification.

Coward and Ellis were already quite aware that, instead of taking Kristeva's line of reasoning (whereby the subject is phenomenologically deconstituted into a complex series of psychological, linguistic, and social registers), it would be more practical for the sake of social change to think of the subject in terms of identity issues and consider that in terms of a struggle with ready-made ideological identifications. In this way, Coward and Ellis posit an alternative deconstruction of the subject that takes distance from both Derrida and Kristeva. It is an alternative understanding of a deconstruction of the subject that will gain a prominent number of adherents in the 1980s and '90s. Coward and Ellis explain, "The production of the subject, and therefore its ideological positions, can now be shown in the place of objective contradictions."[114] Hence, by negating and dismantling the contradictions posed by ideology, the subject not only discovers its various subject-positions but learns to perform them as well as construct new ones for itself.

The constructivist side of this project was an invitation to literary scholars, because for Coward and Ellis art is the practice of language within an ideology whose purpose is to construct (i.e., invent, postulate, or fictionalize) the subject (and its positions) as well as reality.[115] According to the authors, crucial to the study of art is the relation between identity and sign, subject and representation. Eventually, Coward and Ellis argue that a subject-position is the consequence of ideological practices that enable subjects to act within the social totality, a view that quickly devolves into the familiar concept of social role.[116] Hence for them "ideology" will be defined as "the way in which the individual actively lives his or her role within the social totality." Indeed, this is a falling away from the view that "ideology is a system of representations which entail certain *subject-positions*. As these have their conditions of existence in certain social practices, it can operate to reinforce those practices."[117] Obviously, as Kristeva indicates, it is in refusing to reinforce those practices that one revolts. Especially when such a revolutionary subject is Other (say, queer or someone who is colonized), he or she cannot by definition successfully reinforce those practices upon which ideological identification is based. Hence in cultural studies Otherness becomes a significant marker for resistance and revolution, something that was apparent back in the 1970s when French intellectuals—among them, Foucault, Kristeva, Irigaray, Deleuze, and Derrida—displayed interest in madness as a form of social revolt.

In looking specifically at deconstruction, Coward and Ellis fault Derrida for being "unable to account for language as a social practice, that is, meaningful communication between two subjects." It is a statement that entirely overlooks Derrida's work on speech act theory in "Signature, Event, Context" where this question was elaborated at length. In an uncharacteristically muddled statement, Coward and Ellis argue:

> The opposition materialism/idealism is not an absolute opposition as seems to be implied in Derrida's work. Materialism can be found as an "abundance" and "excess" which is repressed in the positing of the transcendental signified. The positionality seen by Lacan as a necessary constraining factor involves a materialist analysis of its construction. It is not a retreat from the problem of meaning which underlies Derrida's

own position of *différance* as movement without matter, in which every-thing is finally unknowable. This is ultimately idealist. Idealist thought appropriates the constraining factor that Lacan analyses, and fixes it as a point of origin, thus affirming "presence and identity," and repressing the process of construction. That is why this process can be found in certain idealist philosophers or writers as an "excess."[118]

The argument seems to be that materialism—i.e., constructivism—is not so much opposed by idealism as it is internalized by way of repression. Derrida is not retreating from meaning when he encounters *différance*; rather, he is ex-ploring what idealism suppresses in the founding of supposedly uncontradic-tory origins. Lacan, who is deemed to be of more help than Derrida, unlocks this repression in terms of studying the formation of the subject within signi-fying contradictions whose subject-positions are paradoxical and hence impos-sible: "woman as castrated," "phallic mother," "the subject who is supposed to know," etc. By pointing out these contradictions, Lacan can articulate the var-ious formations of the subject that require critique. This is considered more useful than Derrida's evacuation of the subject as a *philosopheme*. Despite this, Coward and Ellis leave a place open for deconstructive analysis, since it is their view that social discourses require deconstruction when their value structures are embedded in such a way that prejudicial power differentials are surrepti-tiously kept in place.

In 1985 another coauthored book, Ernesto Laclau and Chantal Mouffe's *Hegemony and Socialist Strategy*, will play the deconstructive card in a discus-sion of a full-scale theory of discourse and sociopolitical power structures. Gayatri Spivak will similarly continue to introduce deconstructive interven-tions into theoretical elaborations that have their first full-scale presentation in Coward and Ellis's book. Yet these forays into a deconstructive mode are tethered not to Derrida but to that alternative deconstruction of the subject that Coward and Ellis broached in the mid-1970s—a disaggregation of the subject into a multiplicity of subjectivized and objectified differences that maintained a theoretical link to questions of economic, social, and political conflicts. It is this alternative deconstruction of the subject within (1) a con-structivist framework of the subject as a self-fashioning agency and (2) an in-terpellative framework of the subject as subjected to the Subject of ideology that will eventually become a dominant paradigm for feminism, postcolonial-ism, and race studies.

ECLIPSING DECONSTRUCTION: HISTORY OF SUBJECT-POSITIONS I

The search for a deconstructive alternative to a Derridean dismantling of the subject goes back, of course, to Jameson's complaint that Derrida was far too textual in orientation. Hence, as we have seen, critics such as Coward and Ellis became interested in looking for a more socially grounded Marxist alternative, which they found in Althusser. However, by the early 1980s, American critics had found an ally in Michel Foucault, who, in their opinion, was far more useful in terms of analyzing problems relating to the social constructedness of identity and how these constructions could be analytically taken apart in order to expose their politically motivated articulations. Hence the search was on for a different kind of deconstruction than the one Derrida had been pursuing, namely, a disaggregation of the subject as a social formation or identitarian construction, which would have as one of its results an analysis of the subject in terms of a distribution of subject-positions. In considering this attempt at an alternative form of deconstruction, I want to focus on the many *faux bonds* that characterize its genealogical development over some thirty years from obscurity to widespread popularity, since it is these failed interlocutions that typify the advent of a theoretically messy history that, as we will see, is as counterproductive as it is inevitable, given how theory has been and is being practiced in our day and age.

Considering the centrality of Michel Foucault's definition of subject-positions for some of those who were seeking an alternative deconstruction of the subject, it is most appropriate to begin this discussion with his *Archaeology of Knowledge* (1969). Foucault speaks of subject-positions as being "defined by the situation that it is possible for him [the subject] to occupy in relation to various domains or groups of objects." Thus the "interrogating subject" would be in a different "position of the subject" than a "listening subject" or a "seeing subject." In addition, Foucault considered "positions that the subject can occupy in the information networks," that is, as "emitter or receiver" of information, including projects, decisions, case histories, etc. This theory of subject-position resembles Roman Jakobson's well-known distinction between addresser/addressee. But Foucault also noted the disparity between systems of notation, description, registration, or integration and systems of observation and intervention (hospitals, methods of inspection, autopsy, etc.). It is across these fields of writing that the subject is differently positioned.[119] Unlike Derrida, who at about the same time not only critiqued the idea of positionality as *Setzung* but also the metaphysical fallacy of marrying a subject to a position, Foucault was perfectly at ease in adopting a rhetorical addresser/addressee model in which subjects necessarily occupy determinate positions for a short time. Foucault, therefore, was not willing to divorce the idea of position from psychological, subjective, moral, or voluntaristic determinations, which is to say, from its humanist foundations. Indeed, there are points in Foucault's analysis when he even says that a subject-position is simply to be considered a social or situational role.

Although Foucault's *Archaeology* is certainly one of the most important source texts for the concept of subject-positions, if not, retroactively, *the* most important source text (given Foucault's popularity), it has to be acknowledged that Foucault was not wholly its originator. And therein lies a tale, because the fact is that the notion of there being subject-positions has multiple origins, among them, a text written by Louis Althusser.[120] Back in 1966, Louis Althusser had proposed the idea of a collective theoretical project to Alain Badiou, Etienne Balibar, Yves Duroux, and Pierre Macherey, and starting in September of that year Althusser began writing some four hundred pages of notes that were never to be published in his lifetime. In *Louis Althusser: Ecrits sur la psychanalyse* (1993), three extended notes from the unpublished fascicle were redacted and published under the title "Trois Notes Sur la Théorie des Discours." It is here that Althusser outlines what is perhaps his most radical formulations on the topics of interpellation, ideology, and the social subject, formulations that he would water down somewhat in subsequent publications. Althusser argued that if one compares the "different forms of existing discourses," such as "unconscious discourse, ideological discourse, aesthetic discourse, and scientific discourse," one will notice *"un effet commun"*: "all discourses produce an effect of subjectivity."

Hence:

Every discourse has a *subject* as a necessary correlate which is *one* of the effects, if not the major effect, of its operationality. [. . .] If we compare the different subject effects produced by the different forms of discourse, we must state 1) that the relation of subjects to respective discourses is not the same, 2) to put it another way, the subject position [*position du sujet*] "produced" or "induced" by the discourse, vis-à-vis other discourses, changes. Hence the ideological subject takes part in person, *being present* in ideological discourse *in person*, since it is itself a signifier determined by this discourse. We note that the subject of scientific discourse is absent in person within scientific discourse, and that no signifier designates it. . . . The subject of aesthetic discourse can be said to be present in aesthetic discourse by *persons who come in between* (always in the plural). The subject of the unconscious discourse occupies a different position [le sujet . . . occupe une position différente] than all of its precedents: it is "represented" in the chain of signifiers by a signifier that "holds its place," and which is its "place holder"; it is absent, then, in the discourse of the unconscious by means of "lieutenance" [lieu-tenance as place-holding and "lieutenantship"].[121]

Shortly following these remarks, Althusser comes back to the idea of a "subject position" when he comments: "The differential nature of the subject-effect, and the place (position) that it occupies vis-à-vis the discourse considered as the proper subject that it 'produced' as effect, must be related to *differences of structure* assignable within the structures of the discourses considered."[122]

These passages are significant if for no other reason than that Althusser did *not* talk about subject-positions in "Ideology and Ideological State Apparatuses" (1969), a text (referred to as "ISA") whose influence on left-of-center Anglo-American cultural criticism has been enormous, to say the least. Indeed, a close look at the "Three Notes" of 1966 and "ISA" of 1969 will reveal a number of parallel passages that demonstrate not just a general simplification and amplification of the "Notes" but a recontextualization of earlier insights concerning the interpellation and positioning of the subject in terms of "relations of production" and their "reproduction." Given that "in a class society the relations of production are relations of exploitation, and therefore relations between antagonistic classes," what was earlier deemed a discursive subject-effect qua subject-position is revised in such a way that the subject is viewed as a "subjected being, who submits to a higher authority by way of ideological interpellation." In place of the notion of a "subject-position" we have the more classical Marxist conception of class antagonism.[123]

Althusser's earlier formulation of subject-positions was clearly more structuralist in orientation and was very compatible with Jacques Lacan's emergent theory of four discourses—defined by rotating the subject through four prescribed subject-positions within a carefully constructed logical formula that corresponds to Lacan's earlier Z diagram of the 1950s. The four discourses include, discourse of the master, discourse of the hysteric, discourse of the obsessional, and discourse of the analyst (as Other). Each discourse not only produces different subject-effects but is characterized by different positions and hence relations of the subject. An argument could be made that given the friendship between Althusser and Lacan, Lacan was attempting to supply Althusser with a model for explaining (1) the interpellation of the subject, (2) subject-positions, (3) subjection of the subject to the signifier, and (4) the modes of unconscious production that constitute different discourses.

Whether this was really Lacan's intent is impossible to determine. However, *Séminare XVII: L'envers de la psychanalyse* (1969–70) comes so close to fulfilling Althusser's open-ended notes of 1966 that it may as well have been an intentional contribution to structuralist Marxism. After all, Lacan was extremely sensitive to the differences of structure, noted by Althusser, and considered how these differences were "articulated," to use a favorite word of Althusser's, in order to produce subjects whose meanings are dependent upon their positions in relation to signs, objects, and others. That these positions are always assignable and interpretable in terms of power relations is, of course, yet another feature that reveals Lacan's compatibility with French Marxian theory of the late '60s. That said, Lacan almost never explicitly refers to the subject as an entity that might have a position. Instead, he prefers to speak of a *relation du sujet*, probably because he resists the depersonalization of the subject that an analytic of positioning would introduce. Moreover, Lacan was concerned with the interpellative capacity of an Other (the unconscious) to hail the subject in such a way that the subject would experience itself as split between its own desire and the Other's demand. This, for Lacan, was a matter of relation, not merely one of position.

Coward and Ellis, we should recall, said nothing about any of these highly relevant texts, in part because some of these texts were not in print, but also in part because they probably did not make the effort to intensively quiz those who knew of Althusser's and Lacan's unpublished presentations in which important background materials to the emerging idea of subject-positions were set forth. There is also the mystery of where Coward and Ellis got the subject-positions idea from, if not from Foucault. Their work suggests that the source is, in fact, Althusser, which would suggest that they did know more about his teachings than was generally available in print. Indeed, their accounts of Lacan seem to be more informed by Althusser's "Freud et Lacan" (1964) than upon knowledge of what was taught in *Seminar XVII* of 1969–70 (available in *dactylographe*).

To get a further sense of how the question of subject-positions relates to Althusser in the absence of its presentation in the published writings, it is instructive to see Ernesto Laclau's *Politics and Ideology in Marxist Theory* (1977), because noticeably absent is the phrase "subject-positions" in the very places that it is crying out for mention. For example, in a suggestive section on Althusser's concept of interpellation, Laclau argues that the unifying principle of ideology is the "subject" it interpellates. He cautions, however, that we must bear in mind that there are "different types of interpellation (political, religious, familial, etc.), which coexist while being articulated within an ideological discourse in a relative unity."[124] This parallels Althusser's own remarks rather closely in the "Three Notes" concerning the different discourses and how each has a different "subject effect" and hence a different positioning of the subject. However, rather than emphasize the discourse as signifying apparatus, as Althusser did in the "Three Notes," Laclau repeats Althusser's emphasis upon interpellation, which is dominant in parts of "ISA." Indeed, Laclau's theoretical attachment to Althusser was probably what prevented him from discovering the notion of subject-positions in 1977, given that Althusser revised out its advent in "ISA," for the sake of encouraging an analysis of modes of production and class struggle.

Taking all these materials into account, it is evident that (1) Foucault and Althusser were not talking about the same thing when they each spoke of a positioning of the subject, given that Foucault was talking about the institutionalization of discourse as an instrument of knowledge production and reception, whereas Althusser was talking about interpellation, subjection, and ideology; (2) that Foucault nevertheless "supplies" the missing term in Althusser that Althusser himself provided in his unpublished "Three Notes" of 1966; (3) that, as we shall see, this supplementation via Foucault will result in an intense interest in the 1980s and '90s in the idea of "subject-positions"; and (4) that because Althusser and Foucault were tentative and open ended in their formulations (if not outright conflicted), the definition of the term would remain in suspension for someone else to complete.

Moreover, if Lacan's four discourses complemented Althusser's formulations of 1966, they were somewhat out of phase with Althusser's "ISA," in which a more orthodox Marxism that stresses positioning in terms of class antagonisms is reintroduced. Here, of course, the work of Slavoj Žižek in the 1990s becomes of great interest insofar as he realigned Althusser with Lacan in ways that reflected Althusser's own more structuralist leanings in the mid-

'60s that were in sympathy with Lacan's teachings. Hence, in books such as *The Sublime Object of Ideology* (1989), Zizek not only breathes new life into Lacan's teachings, which by the late 1980s were falling on hard times, but has kept alive a certain understanding of subject-positions that has its nexus in the Althusser/Lacan relation.

As if this isn't enough of a theoretical fraying, there is yet a fourth major figure to be introduced who also wrote a text on subject-positioning relevant to Foucault's *Archaeology of Knowledge*. In the interview, *Positions* (June 17, 1971), Derrida was pressured to take a clearly determined *position* with respect to dialectical materialism. Although the term "subject-positions" does not arise, Derrida, who was close to Althusser in the 1960s, was nevertheless deconstructing the basis upon which such a notion could be founded:

> Are we agreed also that there is no effective and efficient position, no veritable force of rupture, without a minute, rigorous, extended analysis, an analysis that is as differentiated and as scientific as possible? Analysis of the greatest number of possible givens, and of the most diverse givens (general economy)? And that it is necessary to uproot this notion of taking a position from every determination that, in the last analysis, remains psychologistic, subjectivistic, moral and voluntaristic?

Immediately after these remarks, Derrida speaks of spacing as opposed to positioning. Spacing, he says, "is the impossibility for an identity to be closed on itself . . ." and, "the irreducibility of spacing is the irreducibility of the Other." It is this irreducibility that qualifies how the other is marked (as Derrida puts it) in spacing that Houdebine has related to the concept of taking up a position. "I would even say that the alterity of the other *inscribes* in this relationship that which in no case can be 'posed.' "[125] Given Derrida's long excursus on Emmanuel Lévinas in "Violence and Metaphysics" (1962/67), one has some reason to suspect that these passages show the influence Lévinas had upon the early Derrida. Derrida exceeds Lévinas, however, when he writes, "inscription, as I would define it in this respect, is not a simple position: it is rather that by means of which every position is of itself confounded (*différance*): inscription, mark, text and not only thesis or theme— inscription of the thesis." Hence the mark that marks a relation to the other is that space where positioning is occulted insofar as an other cannot be revealed or known in and as that place. To this, Derrida counterpoints a speculative Hegelian view of *Setzung* (positioning): "The position of the other, in Hegelian dialectics, is always, finally, to pose oneself, by oneself as the other of the Idea, as other-than-oneself in one's finite determination, with the aim of repatriating and reappropriating oneself, of returning close to oneself in the infinite richness of one's determination." This view, according to Derrida, counterpoints that of Lévinas and thereby poses a double reading of positioning that has now been put in position for a meticulous deconstruction. However, the demonstration exceeds Derrida's scope, and he cuts short the discussion with his interlocutors: "I take my leave. Thank you both."[126]

Apparently, this dismantling of the possibility of subject-positioning, or *Setzung*, fell on deaf ears, since we can find no consequence of Derrida's critique in the work of those who will redeploy the term "subject-positions" within their own theoretical frames of reference, as if no one had ever called the term into question as committing the metaphysical fallacy of attaching a position to a subject for the sake of making that subject present to itself and to others. Recall that in Althusser the difference between science and ideology is that in science the subject is absent, but in ideology the subject appears in person. Which is to say, that from its inception, the concept of subject-positions in Althusser is determined by a metaphysics of presence and absence. That this metaphysics haunts the entire genealogy of the subject-positions concept will become self-evident. Moreover, that Derrida's critique has fallen on deaf ears also suggests that even those who have been most eager to employ deconstruction in the name of demystifying ideology do not want to hear this critique when it takes their own theoretical formulations to task. Hence, when the topic of subject-positions is taken up by various figures in the 1980s, it is Derrida's critique in *Positions* that is conspicuously eclipsed.

ECLIPSING DECONSTRUCTION: HISTORY OF SUBJECT-POSITIONS II

By the mid-1980s, not only Laclau but many other social and cultural critics saw the usefulness of exchanging a concept of the positivist subject for a plural articulation that went under the name "subject-positions." It is interesting that all of these later attempts to invent an adequate theory of subject-positions avoid mentioning the intellectual history we have surveyed. Up until the 1980s, of course, this intellectual history had in and of itself been a history of the *faux bond*, or failed encounter, given that, for example, Althusser, Foucault, Lacan, and Derrida never directly addressed one another but simply laid out different theoretical positions, which in and of themselves were not always self-consistent. Althusser, as we saw, suppressed the idea of subject-positions as it was formulated in "Three Notes." Foucault took a number of stands on what a subject-position might be (discourse effect, rhetorical position, social role, etc.). And Derrida, for his part, only sketched out an abstract of what a critique of positioning the subject might be, never following through on the Hegel/Lévinas conflict and how that might transform our understanding of these matters. The Lacan/Althusser connection is exceptional in that we actually have something like a dialogue, however tentative on Althusser's part and unacknowledged on Lacan's behalf.

In the 1980s, the book that brought the idea of subject-positions to the fore was *Hegemony and Socialist Strategy* (1985) by Ernesto Laclau and Chantal Mouffe. Whereas Laclau did not make any mention of Michel Foucault in *Politics and Ideology in Marxist Theory*, he and Mouffe now refered to Foucault's *Archaeology of Knowledge*. However, it has to be said that Laclau and Mouffe approached Foucault rather gingerly by alluding to his remarks on subject-positions without immediately disclosing the source. In fact, Laclau and Mouffe took pains to *revise* Foucault by emphasizing Foucault's idea of the dispersion of discourse in order to avoid notions of subjecthood, such as point of view and role. It is especially when Laclau and Mouffe first introduce the concept of subject-positions after a lengthy discussion of "dispersion" that we see more clearly why they have been so reluctant to embrace Foucault's remarks on this topic:

> The material character of discourse cannot be unified in the experience or consciousness of a founding subject; on the contrary, diverse subject-positions appear dispersed within a discursive formation. . . .Articulation is now a discursive practice which does not have a plane of constitution prior to, or outside, the dispersion of the articulated elements.[127]

Foucault's notion of subject-positions presupposes a single subject who can occupy different roles or perspectives and who can reflect on them even if he or she cannot reconcile them. Also, Foucault does not give as much free reign to the differential and disarticulating capacity of discursive practices as Laclau and Mouffe. Rather Foucault has a tendency to think in terms of the operational regularities of diverse systems and their compatibilities or resistances. Like Coward and Ellis, Laclau and Mouffe are often assuming a subject or subjectivity in process that is the effect of signification understood as the constellation of complex and only partially realized articulations that are each in a different state of evolution or decay. Hence Laclau and Mouffe try to avoid totalizing concepts, such as subject, enunciator, enunciated, message, and context: "There is no social identity fully protected from a discursive exterior that deforms it and prevents it becoming fully sutured."[128] The subject is always an incomplete articulation that can be deformed at any time by yet another interpellation that, in the Lacanian language adopted by the *Screen* critics, has a suturing capacity. Foucault's text, in contrast, emphasizes the disparities of viewpoints within a synchronic structure and never reaches the point where it can begin to think in terms of Laclau and Mouffe's notions of articulation and hegemony: the social negotiation of these perspectives in terms of power relations.

Some three years later, in the anthology *Marxism and the Interpretation of Culture* (1988), Stuart Hall and Chantal Mouffe published conference papers that, according to the editors' introductory remarks, were probably given prior to 1985 but revised later. The papers reveal continuations and disparities that will only become more vexed as we approach the 1990s when a sort of free-for-all breaks loose around the term "subject-positions." In "The Toad in the Garden: Thatcherism Among the Theorists" (1983/88), Stuart Hall writes:

> It is clear that the discourses of the New Right have been engaged precisely in this work of the production of new subject-positions and the transformation of subjectivities. Of course, there might be an essential Thatcherite subject hiding or concealed in each of us, struggling to get out. But it seems more probable that Thatcherism has been able to constitute new subject-positions from which its discourses about the world make sense, or to appropriate to itself existing, already formed interpellations These have arisen through some process, central to the mechanism of ideology itself, by which new positions have interrupted and partially displaced older ones; or else new discourses have emerged that secure real points of identification.[129]

Unlike Laclau and Mouffe, Hall's view of subject-positions is aligned much more closely with Foucault's formulations. However, instead of framing the concept in terms of various institutional practices (reportage, visual observation, diagnosis, mathematical modeling), Hall considers them to be *political* positions, which is to say, no different than *argumentative* positions that people take up in places such as the House of Commons. Hall questions how Thatcherism managed to gain the support of people whose social positions one would have thought could not be compatible with the idea of embracing Thatcherism. How did Thatcherism manage to open up the possibility for political identifications and ideological allegiances that formerly would have been unthinkable? Stripped bare of theoretical exposition, Hall looks at contradictions between political allegiances and economic station and asks how the New Right managed to model a social identity that could encourage people's political allegiance despite the fact that their own best economic and social interests lie elsewhere. Although Hall is certainly entitled to understand subject-positioning in this way, we have to ask why he never bothers to clarify his theoretical departures from Foucault and the *Screen* critics.

Chantal Mouffe's "Hegemony and New Political Subjects: Toward a New Concept of Democracy" (1988) is more odd, because not only is it at variance with Stuart Hall, it is also at odds with the work she coauthored with Laclau. Unlike Hall, she does not see the subject-position as an argumentative perspective that is politically positioned but as a constellation of "multiple *possible* constructions." The implication is that this subject is a *virtual* subject, not a politically concreted subject. Unlike the view she coauthored with Laclau, Mouffe herself opts for a more "imaginary" understanding of the subject in the Lacanian sense. She is also a bit closer to Coward and Ellis when she entertains the idea of subject-position in terms of social role and constructions of self-identity (i.e., self-fashioning):

> Within every society, each social agent is inscribed in a multiplicity of social relations—not only social relations of production but also the social relations, among others, of sex, race, nationality, and vicinity. All these social relations determine positionalities or subject-positions and every social agent is therefore the locus of many subject-positions and cannot be reduced to only one. Thus, someone inscribed in the relations of production as a worker is also a man or a woman, white or black, Catholic or Protestant, French or German, and so on. A person's subjectivity is not constructed only on the basis of his or her position in the relations of production. Furthermore, each social position, each

subject-position, is itself the locus of multiple possible constructions, according to the different discourses that can construct that position. Thus the subjectivity of a given social agent is always precariously and provisionally fixed or, to use the Lacanian term, sutured at the intersection of various discourses.[130]

In this passage, subject-position is a synonym for social position, whereas in Hall it is a synonym for political position. But Mouffe also uses subject-position as a synonym for social relations based on received ideas (constructions) of social identity: gender, religion, nationality, and race. In Mouffe's article, the concept of subject-positions is more fluid and has more applications than in the book she coauthored with Laclau. Her own account touches more on the subjectivity of the subject in process than does her work with Laclau where emphasis falls upon articulation and dispersion of positions that are, in essence, external to the subject. Hall's account reifies those external articulations by turning them into arguments that are invented within the rhetoric of party politics. That none of these differences are critically examined by Hall, Mouffe, or Laclau and Mouffe is peculiar if for no other reason than because there seems to be no interest in working through what are, in fact, quite different understandings of a key critical concept.

This is even more striking in the case of Gayatri Chakravorty Spivak when she speaks of subject-positions in "Imperialism and Sexual Difference" (1986): "The clearing of a subject-position in order to speak or write is unavoidable. . . .The dominant subject-position gives itself as it constructs the subordinate as other. The curious 'objectified' subject-position of this other is what . . . I call the position of the 'native informant.' " Elsewhere in the article we happen across the terms "reading-subject's perspective," "subject-constitution," "subject-status," and "subject-effects" (Althusser's term), which are not defined, though they all seem to be metonyms that inflect the term "subject-position" in ways that maintain a certain disaggregation of agency. Then, too, "subject position" is used in a manner close to Stuart Hall's politically situated subject and also to Foucault's idea of the rhetorical positioning of the subject in terms of power relations between dominator and dominated. Yet, it also is being used to speak of groups rather than individuals. The "other" is not one; rather, the other is a class or group of persons who are rhetorically situated by cultural norms.[131]

In *The Post-Colonial Critic* (1990), Spivak says:

The ways in which history has been narrativised always secures *a certain kind of subject-position* which is predicated on marginalizing certain areas. The importance of deconstruction is its interest in such strategic exclusions. [. . .] You know that you can't just keep with one side of a binary opposition, you can't form constantly regressive positions here in terms of the subject-position, because then what you're ignoring is the other side. . . . And that's where the historical research into the narrativisation and institutionalization of the *subject-position* becomes very important.[132]

Apparently, subject-position is a social category of the group and is closer to Hall's understanding of political position than to Coward and Ellis's position of subjecthood within the individual that is in conflict with other positions of subjecthood. Again, Spivak's idea of subject-position appears to be connected to Derrida's understanding of binary opposition, if not to deconstruction, generally. Whereas the earlier pulverization of "subject-position" into "subject-effects," "subject-status," "subject-constitution," and so on had worked against binaryism, Spivak now leans toward a more oppositional or bifurcated understanding of positions. It is the model that Derrida himself rejects in the letter that ends *Positions*. Here Spivak's own texts are exemplary of missed theoretical interlocutions with themselves, a misfiring that I think is intentional in Spivak, since it is her tendency to subvert self-reflexivity and auto-affectivity.

To add to this fraying of the subject-position concept, Diana Fuss in *Essentially Speaking* (1989) mistakes Spivak's account as a repetition of Michel Foucault's definition of subject-positions in *The Archaeology of Knowledge*. She grafts Spivak onto Foucault if not eventually onto her own conception of the subject, which turns out to be a dead ringer for the bourgeois individual!

> What are the various positions a reading subject may occupy? How are these positions constructed? Are there possible distributions of subject-positions located in the text itself? Can a reader refuse to take up a subject-position the text constructs for him/her? Does the text construct the reading subject or does the reading subject construct the text?

After these questions, Fuss cross-cuts to a remark by Spivak on "clearing a subject-position in order to speak or write."[133] Fuss uses this quote to support her idealist assumption that there is always a fully formed revolutionary individual *who exists apart* from these subject-positions and who can inhabit them and *manipulate* them at will. Of course, the idea that one could simply come on the scene in order to clear away a position is totally at odds with Foucault, who would say that we can only occupy those positions articulated by a system of discourses that are socially produced and institutionalized. In other words, another mutation has occurred in the discourse on subject-positions by way of reintroducing a bourgeois conception of the self. Hence we find Fuss's fascination with Spivak's locution, "I-slots," which she recuperates against the grain of Spivak's view.

In *The Post-Colonial Critic*, Spivak speaks of "differentiatedness." She says, "Like everyone else I am absolutely plural" and, "I think we should also look at the West as differentiated. I'm really not that moved by arguments for homogenization on both sides."[134] The implicit criticism of Fuss is, of course, highly evident and touches on a related problem that Fuss glosses over, namely, the question of hybridity. Fuss would like to legitimize the claim that instead of having to choose between theoretical alternatives, such as homogeneity/heterogeneity or essentialism/antiessentialism, we might draw from both alternatives without reconciling them. Such " 'hybrid' instances in feminist theory," as she calls them, can be justified by means of occupying contrary, if not contradictory, subject-positions, something that she notices in Spivak's work where the subject is multiply interpellated. However, whereas Spivak uses a deconstructive theoretical praxis that disintergrates the concept of the subject, Fuss assumes a pragmatic constructivist viewpoint that instrumentalizes and thereby manipulates hybridity at will. Whereas Spivak remains close to a materialist praxis akin to that advanced by Coward and Ellis in the 1970s, Fuss embraces the return of the subject as idealist agency, which characterizes a dominant trend within American feminism of the 1980s that privileged activism, empowerment, and hence a traditional conception of the Self as historical mover and shaker. Fuss's concept of hybridity is akin to poetic license: the license of the subject to take up whatever positions it wants in the service of its own subjective desires and political interests. Fuss's reading of subject-positions, therefore, reflects the most commonplace use of the term in the American academy: the subject in marginal position where resistance becomes thinkable, the subject as speaker of counterdiscourse and producer of countercultural practices, or, more simply, the subject in position of political opposition.

In closing the circuit, somewhat arbitrarily, we will note that in 1989 Derrida gave an interview to Jean-Luc Nancy in an article entitled "Eating Well." By this time in Derrida's itinerary, the filiations with Lévinas have become even stronger than they were in the 1960s. As if to pick up some strands from *Positions*, Derrida speaks of the positioning of the subject in ways that suggest an interlocution, as well, with Foucault:

> If we still wish to speak of the subject—the juridical, ethical, political, psychological subject, etc.—and of what makes its semantics communicate with that of the subject of a proposition (distinct from qualities, attributes viewed as substance, phenomena, etc.) or with a theme or the thesis (the subject of a discourse or of a book), it is first of all necessary to submit to the test of questioning the essential predicates of which all subjects are the subject.

Derrida then remarks that the subject is characterized by self-presence, "which implies therefore a certain interpretation of temporality: identity of self, positionality, property, personality, ego, consciousness, will, intentionality, freedom, humanity, etc." It is when this presence to self is questioned that all of these traits lose stability and orientation. When something is addressed to the one in the place of the subject who is no longer constituted in or as that place (subject/position), one is then to be thought of as "the 'who' of the other" that can "only appear absolutely *as such* by disappearing as other." Derrida adds: "The enormity involved in questions of the subject, as in the questions of right, ethics, and politics, always lead back to this place."[135] This, of course, restates *Positions* by way of arguing that the "who" of the subject is never in the place of the subject's position, as if the "who" has always already absconded or disappeared from that place where the "who" would be required to be fully present and accounted for.

If we look over this intellectual history—and, of course, this is but a part of a more inclusive history that could be told—we must ask ourselves whether it is entirely fruitful to think of these many positionings as a constellation of open-ended theoretical forays, or whether we should think of them as part of a network of failed interlocutions that make up a very unsatisfactory range of unresolved readings. We can, of course, side with Rosi Braidotti's idea that a postphilosophical molecular movement of terms within a colloid of conceptual relationships might be preferable to an essentialist understanding of thought as a teleology of interlocking positions. Or we might embrace Gilles Deleuze and Felix Guattari's notion of philosophy as a rhizomatic structure. After all, why shouldn't theory move laterally or lattice-like, rather than unilaterally forward in a march along progressive way stations? Why should the terminology of theory endlessly converge on itself in an identitarian manner? And why shouldn't terms disperse or disseminate more or less indiscriminately as the term "subject-positions" has? For doesn't the dissemination of a term make it more aspectual, plural, motivated, and useful? And doesn't each use of such a term delimit a "position" that marks a rupture or break in which something new is learned? Shouldn't one think, therefore, in terms of a mobilization of multiple terms that are and aren't the same, say, "subject-position," "subject-effect," "subject-constitution," "subject-status"? Finally, shouldn't all master-narratives and grand theories be held suspect?

With respect to the case of "subject-positions," we are, in fact, considering a rather technical term that in order to be of much use needs something more than a shouting match of different views and definitions that fail to undertake a systematic investigation and evaluation of work done by various colleagues at various times. If theory becomes so insular that dialogue is excluded as a precondition for doing a theoretical analysis, one has to wonder if we are not being condemned to an interminability of under-theorized positions that quickly degrade into an uncritical morass of differences that are as incoherent as they are arbitrary. If researchers are seriously interested in theorizing social critiques that are going to have any compelling consistency, shouldn't they be willing to learn from one another rather than engage in behaviors of avoidance that I have been calling the *faux bond*? It is here that Hans-Georg Gadamer's understanding of hermeneutical listening or receptivity becomes relevant within an institution that has become so compartmentalized and impatient to effect a "race to theory" (as Barbara Christian has called it) that theorists, both major and minor, speak at cross-purposes rather than in ways that might be theoretically constructive.

In "Conversation and Shared Understanding" (1931), Gadamer rightly points out that in excluding the other from critical conversation, one excludes the other *in his or her positive function* as an interlocutor whose substantive agreement and shared understanding is *essential* to the truth claims of an argument insofar as those truth claims cannot be legitimately made in the absence of a horizon of mutual agreement that is both constitutive within the process of theorizing and as yet to come as the theory is apprehended and judged by others (Gadamer's model, of course, is Plato's *Dialogues*).[136] Here Gadamer provides an Apollonian counterweight to what one might call a wildcat hermeneutics. Indeed, Gadamer's sobriety is required if "theory" is to have a compelling force in our profession, since without the sobriety of what he calls "logos," theory becomes nothing more than ad hoc thinking done solipsistically in the absence of a positive function of the interlocutor.

As I have shown, the theory of subject-positions is an excellent example of wildcat hermeneutics done in the absence of this positive function. As such, this alternative form of a deconstruction of the subject could be characterized as a series of failed critical encounters that would define a so-called theory mess, a process of theorization in the absence of classical hermeneutical controls, among them, the positive function of an informed community of scholarly agreement. It is in this sense that the alternative deconstruction of the subject is itself but the eclipsing of deconstruction(s) that might well be far more viable.

LURCHING TO THE RIGHT

While cultural studies was coming into its own by way of alternative deconstruction and other less friendly means, conservative academics warned of the demise of Western democratic values in higher education, claiming deconstruction was one of the leading causes of this intellectual crisis. Because the wholesale rejection of newer critical trends in the humanities (textual, cultural, social) was predicated on the so-called antics of Derrida and his supposedly vast following of academic lackeys, conservative academics earned the ridicule of those who have noticed the bad faith with which such judgments were, and still are, promoted. There is no excusing the likes of David Lehman, Allan Bloom, Dinesh D'Souza, Alicia Ostriker, and others, who have maintained a studious ignorance of theory in order to take a holier-than-thou attitude to recent developments in the humanities.

Problematic, however, is that if polemicists on the right have engaged in a smear campaign, they have also called attention to aspects of the history that I am trying to tell that might otherwise have been overlooked. For example, it is obvious that during the years in which critical theory emerged as an influential force in the humanities we have seen what conservative scholars have rightly called a "dumbing down" of undergraduates and what the National Association of Scholars has statistically proven to be a dip in academic standards and expectations. It is a contradiction that over the past thirty years high-altitude philosophical understandings of humanist problems have been increasingly accompanied by low-altitude critical thinking in the undergraduate curriculum. However, arguments by Allan Bloom, Roger Shattuck, and others that the introduction of theory *caused* the vitiation of undergraduate standards is a logical leap that is inherently false.

The idea that nihilistic and relativist critical theories are responsible for the vitiation of higher education is, of course, the main thesis of Allan Bloom's *The Closing of the American Mind* (1987). The book's subtitle, *How Higher Education Has Failed Democracy and Impoverished the Souls of Today's Students*, more or less summarizes the main argument, which is as narrow minded as it was captivating to conservatives. Provided one can bracket this polemic—and I realize that for some this may be impossible—one will notice that Bloom makes some points that merit comment. For example, Bloom notices that the university of the 1980s was very much a reflection of political struggles of the 1960s and adroitly cites a presidential address by David Easton to the American Political Science Association in 1966 wherein Easton spoke of "a post-behaviorism in which the great achievements of social science would be put in the service of right values [as opposed to empirical fact]."[137]

As Bloom pointed out, the priority of "right values" would become a major concern in the 1980s, so much so that social science would be dictated more by ideology than empirical fact. Again in recalling the 1960s, Bloom notes that the "new moral experience" would be forged by "indignation and rage" and that such a passion is "the most inimical to reason and hence to the university." Bloom concludes that "anger, to sustain itself, requires an unshakable conviction that one is right" and therefore does not easily admit to argument by reason. Of course, Bloom's own diatribe against higher education falls prey to the same principle. Even if we grant this point, Bloom's account foreshadows the nasty ideological and methodological factionalism that would come to pass in the 1990s within departments of the humanities, a factionalism that on some campuses broke down the capacity to carry out everyday business and put units into receivership for several years running. When faculty forge political relations with one another on the basis of sustaining indignant anger at various social injustices, some of which they see mirrored in the actions of their colleagues, an academic department can become very unpleasant. This would be corroborated by Edward Said in 1999 in a plea for intellectual coherence and decency published in the Modern Language Association's newsletter.

Far less accurate is Bloom's idea that students during the '60s had turned their anger on tradition and had decided en masse that figures such as Shakespeare and Milton were no longer relevant. In fact, most graduate students were not protesting study of the major canon. For during the '60s nothing was more clear cut than the disconnection between traditional education in the classroom and nontraditional education outside the classroom. Bloom makes a faulty cause-and-effect argument when he claims that because students lost interest in studying the "old books," the professoriate scrambled to radicalize the humanities by jettisoning the old standbys for the sake of embracing politically relevant subjects. He thinks this went so far that the humanities have actually been scuttled and that the only relevant field after the auto-da-fé is social science. In fact, the modern languages still hire faculty according to the old canonical divisions of literary history and have often appended new areas (i.e., postcolonialism, feminism, queer theory) as subspecialities. Over the past twenty-five years, these subspecialties have changed with the ups and downs of fashionability, while the old literary historical categories have remained fixed.

If Bloom, like his conservative colleagues, has overstated the case for the demise of the traditional canons of study, there is nevertheless some truth to what he has argued. Some English departments, which are among the largest departments in the humanities, started abandoning major parts of their overall missions in the 1970s. For example, even in the 1960s there was a general understanding that the field of English operated under the big umbrella of "History of the English Language" and that this would include not only coursework in philology (under the aegis of Old and Middle English), grammar, rhetoric, and composition but also coursework in literature, since literature represented the innovative cutting edge of English as a language in historical process.

Cracks in the English edifice started appearing after the 1960s as freshman competency levels in writing kept dropping and basic college composition courses started becoming courses in remedial writing. Ever since the 1970s, faculty in the U.S. have been hired with specialties in composition in order to take over the remedial problem and hence disencumber the professoriate. Under the composition specialists' direction, most of the writing ped-agogy was then turned over to graduate students in English departments, who were asked, in essence, to make up for years of educational neglect in just one semester. To add insult to injury, these graduate students were, and still are, only paid a fraction of what even an assistant professor would earn for teach-ing the same courses. This "plantation system" of labor underscores the con-tempt with which tenured faculty and administrators regard the remedial sit-uation. With the onerous job of teaching composition safely out of research professors' way, most English departments started abandoning the require-ment that undergraduates pass a course of English grammar in order to re-ceive a B.A. Although linguistics programs that mushroomed to fill this void were supposedly to take over this kind of course offering, many did not. Also, because the focus of the English curriculum turned to criticism and theory, an interest in the history of the English language seemed redundant, since it was the point of literary criticism to replace historicism and philology. Hence the requirement that English majors know the history of the language also faded away.

That left literature and literary criticism in the spotlight. However, by the 1980s the profession saw the teaching of canonical literary works attacked by feminists and other minorities who took issue with the predominance of teaching the works of white male authors. Initially, this meant that Christine de Pisan, Jane Austen, the Bronte Sisters, George Eliot, Emily Dickinson, and Virginia Woolf were supposed to become more prominent, though by the end of the 1980s "canon busting" meant that the high literature of even "white women" had to give way to ethnic and popular writings that were as yet not so well known, mainly, because their status as literature had been in question (i.e., Zora Neale Hurston's writings) or had never been established (i.e., the work of Amy Tan). Hence, in the thirty years following the counterculture movement of the 1960s, many English departments had to substantially re-orient themselves in order to embrace "social causes." Traditional liberal arts faculty felt disenfranchised and outraged.

Throughout the 1980s and '90s, there have been considerable editorials and op-ed pieces in *The Chronicle of Higher Education* and *New York Review of Books*, to name but two venues, that complained bitterly about the death of the traditional curriculum and what has often been referred to as "political correctness." During the early '80s, Denis Donoghue published an article in *The New Republic* that spoke on behalf of a silent majority of English professors who had been bullied into silence by the angry voices of the politically and critically enlightened. He pointed out that canonical bellwethers such as the *Norton Anthology of Literature by Women* were not, in his terms, based on "critical" principles—by which he obviously meant *literary* critical criteria—but upon political and social merit: "The literary merit of the items chosen is not a major consideration for the editors. They are concerned to document the range of experience—and the resultant constraints and anxieties—peculiar to women." Again, "the *Anthology* would make a good textbook in a course in sociology called 'Women and Their Fate.' It is flagrantly misleading as a selection of literature by women"[138] Donoghue's point was that in the hands of the feminists, literature was viewed primarily as a social document and only secondarily as an art form. In cases where social significance was strong but art was entirely lacking, texts were included by Sandra Gilbert and Susan Gubar; in cases where the artistic element was strong but social significance was low, literary texts were excluded. It is not surprising that by the 1990s literary criticism, whether New Critical, reader response oriented, psychoanalytical, semiotic, speech act oriented, or deconstructionist, would all become irrelevant to a large constituency of socially-oriented readers whose main interest was to study literature as a social text for purposes of political activism within and outside the university. Literature had been demoted to being a handmaiden to forms of social contestation and political activism that were usually confined to consciousness raising in the classroom. The hope was that if one could politically indoctrinate students over a number of years in college, one might be able to change our world for the better.

Donoghue and others saw this coming. They not only worried that the shift to "ethnocriticism" would introduce a political dimension in the classroom that would preempt traditional forms of literary study, but they suspected that letting critical theory into the curriculum was tantamount to letting the proverbial fox into the hen house. Theory, they said, was problematic if for no other reason than that it was replacing the study of primary texts. In "How to Rescue Literature" (1980) Roger Shattuck warned, "What we should beware of is the temptation to subordinate literature to the claims of any extra-literary discipline to superior authority or knowledge." Like Donoghue, Shattuck insisted that literature "does not belong to any domain outside the domain of art, and we are shirking our responsibilities if we look the other way while self-styled 'literary' critics deliver literature into the hands of one or another branch of the social sciences"[139]

Shattuck's attack on the theory establishment had little impact, not only because of the headlong push to privilege social issues at a time when the Reagan-Bush administration was trying to undo the New Deal and other socially progressive legislation of the past, but because belletrists such as Shattuck failed to acknowledge that critical theory had raised a number of methodological issues that cast considerable suspicion on the philosophical adequacy of traditional scholarship. Deconstruction, for example, invalidated many traditional scholarly assumptions about method in a systematic and irrefutable manner. Donoghue's attack on sociopolitical literary study fell short for a similar reason—*the feminists were obviously right*, because it was self-evident that gender discrimination had been constitutive of English studies in the past and that raising the question of gender—and soon thereafter questions about sexual orientation, race, and ethnicity—forced one to revise a rather large number of critical assumptions about a wide number of topics. Therefore, in terms of both method and bias, the traditionalists had no credible defense for maintaining the paradigm of English studies as it had been constituted in the two decades following the end of World War Two.

This didn't mean that critical theory was introduced into the academy without resistance. The introduction of theory in the '70s was problematic in that there was no wide-spread foundation of philosophical knowledge to base it upon. Hence faculty and students were thrown into totally unfamiliar waters and forced to sink or swim. The sudden arrival of extremely sophisticated and learned French theories (deconstruction, among them) only exacerbated the problem that faculty in the humanities were not prepared to intelligently engage postphenomenological philosophies, let alone, the intricate and elusive thinking of highly difficult and original thinkers such as Jacques Lacan, Gilles Deleuze, Luce Irigaray, Julia Kristeva, and others. The Parisian intellectuals, being elitist and snobbish, made no concessions to British or American audiences. When Lacan came to speak at MIT, he purposely scandalized the audience by asking why for such big animals, elephants leave such small turds. He then proceeded to give a lecture no one could follow. Lévi-Strauss, who was considered a major figure to be reckoned with in the 1970s, wrote such impenetrable analyses of kinship structures that many readers simply gave up. Kristeva's theoretical writings were so difficult to follow that it wasn't until the 1980s that feminists discovered Kristeva really wasn't on their side, if being on their side meant accepting lesbian sexuality as legitimate. Given the apparent difficulties of grasping theory, it is small wonder that when theory was introduced into the classroom, many faculty did not quite know what they were looking at and eventually gravitated to political and moral issues, perhaps out of exasperation, given that these issues put matters in a them-or-us frame of mind that made matters immediately comprehensible, relevant, and manageable.

It is in this context, rather than the one that Bloom provides, that his following comment makes the most sense:

> This left the social sciences as the battleground, both the point of attack and the only place where any kind of stand was made. . . . The social sciences were of interest to everyone who had a program, who might care about prosperity, peace or war, equality, racial or sexual discrimination. *This interest could be to get the facts—or to make the facts fit their agenda and influence the public.*[140]

By putting theory in a political rather than hermeneutical frame, teachers of critical theory, themselves often scrambling to understand the theory texts, could lift what they needed into what they perceived to be a politically effective agenda. Confronted with bewilderingly difficult theoretical texts and a *Bildung* that was quite alien, the turn to politics greatly simplified the task of assimilating and directing the ideas that were being developed in the theoretical works. If one could reduce deconstruction to a "reverse and displace" technique whereby a political hierarchy is overturned and a new value substituted for an old one, then the difficulties of entertaining all the critical questions opened by a text such as *Of Grammatology* can be easily set aside. If one could just invoke Kristeva's concept of abjection as if it were a social or political fact rather than a very precarious and, in many ways, dubious theory based on questionable readings of psychoanalysis, one could save oneself an enormous labor. In short, the political turn is, at least in part, a simplifying move and one that has the added advantage of making instructors and students feel empowered as social subjects. For in place of just studying theory, one is suddenly under the impression that one is changing the world for the better.[141]

As Allan Bloom rightly noted, especially in fields where methods of interpretation dominate methods for establishing fact, there is enormous temptation to change the facts in order to flatter or satisfy the theories:

Reward, punishment, money, praise, blame, sense of guilt and desire to do good all swirl around [the disciplines], dizzying their practitioners. Everyone wants the story told by social science to fit their wishes and their needs. Hobbes said that if the fact that two and two makes four were to become a matter of political relevance, there would be a faction to deny it.[142]

If one disagrees with Bloom, it is harder to disagree with the political experience of someone like Hobbes. In politics, people use or abuse facts in order to serve their own interests. Bloom, for his part, notices a hermeneutic circle at work in the social sciences whereby the closer one gets to just the facts, the further one is from any credible explanation or account for them and that the further one gets from the facts, the more one is likely to make an account fit one's ideological wishes and needs. Unfortunately, Bloom sees the ideological side of this spectrum as crack-pot social science. And this is not unproblematic, for it is necessarily the case that if a hermeneutical circle is at work, one will be fated to an ideological interpretation of some sort. After all, as Jürgen Habermas and Michel Foucault pointed out, even the concept of objectivity historically reflects a certain enlightenment ideology.

In eliding the vicissitudes of assimilating critical theory within institutions that usually see theory as always already implied in the curriculum or as an elective to be studied by those with an interest in intellectual history, Bloom came to the cynical and mistaken conclusion that theory is little more than a concerted attempt to undermine Western civilization by substituting relativism and constructivism for time honored judgments and knowledge of a priori truths. In a statement freighted with conservative paranoia about barbarians at the gates of Western democracy, Bloom called deconstruction "the last, predictable, stage in the suppression of reason and the denial of the possibility of truth in the name of philosophy." Falling back on the bogus articles written by Bate and Wellek, Bloom only exposes himself to the suspicion that he has probably never read Derrida, even while insisting that in deconstruction

the interpreter's creative activity is more important than the text; there is no text, only interpretation. Thus the one thing most necessary for us, the knowledge of what these texts have to tell us, is turned over to the subjective, creative selves of these interpreters, who say that there is both no text and no reality to which the texts refer. A cheapened interpretation of Nietzsche liberates us from the objective imperatives of the texts that might have liberated us from our increasingly low and narrow horizon. Everything has tended to soften the demands made on us by the tradition; this simply dissolves it. This fad will pass, as it has already in Paris. But it appeals to our worst instincts and shows where our temptations lie.[143]

Bloom's functionalist account of deconstruction is that it is a philosophy that justifies an abandoning of the "facts" of social science for the sake of giving free ideological rein over interpretation. Hence deconstruction liberates ideologues from objectivity and reinstates a condition typical of the student uprisings of the 1960s in which historians, economists, and psychologists were being asked to teach their various analytical accounts to better reflect politically correct views held by their student constituencies. Now that these students are themselves deans and chairs of university departments, Bloom thinks it is not surprising that they embrace deconstruction as a prerequisite to doing social analysis. Of course, reductive as Bloom's statements are, they nevertheless get at a point that we have already seen in some detail with respect to the theory of subject-positions—that there has been a concerted effort to turn a blind eye to the facts in order to give free ideological rein to one's own formulations and that this has consequences for the legitimacy of theory even within a theoretical framework.

In *Illiberal Education* (1990) Dinesh D'Souza amplified Bloom's polemic by connecting it with documentation of actual social movements within our universities. As in the case of Bloom, D'Souza has been delegitimized by faculty on the left as a polemical purveyor of lies. It is true that D'Souza is sometimes inaccurate. For example, Paul de Man did not have a "Nazi record," as D'Souza tells us, though de Man was fascist in the context of a Belgian politics that wanted to keep itself separate from Nazism.[144] Such gaffs remind us that disregard for fact is not a monopoly held by critics on the left. Yet D'-Souza also puts his finger on major issues in ways that most academics would rather not consider:

> The real problem is not reader-response theory or deconstructionism per se; rather it is the extent to which they serve the ends of a political movement that has propelled them to the forefront of the victim's rev-

olution on campus. In other words, Stanley Fish's politics are less significant than the politics which have created Stanley Fish.[145]

Clearly, there is considerable ignorance in the waffling of different theorists and theories in such a statement. But D'Souza's fundamental point is not without basis: "It is the ideology which the *au courant* critics serve which explains their popularity across various disciplines."[146] If that is the case, then it would appear that critical theories lose their distinctiveness as specific analytics and quickly devolve into terminological and formulaic reservoirs of "critical thinking" that can be arbitrarily applied to an ideological line of argument. This, again, would serve the immediate need to simplify theory for the masses of students and faculty in need of a quick fix; moreover, it would cast counterintuitive critical thinking into familiar frameworks that are purposive and make us feel good about ourselves as politically engaged intellectuals when, in fact, we are sequestered on college campuses and kept out of public debate.

If a theoretical body of work such as Derrida's is used by various social constituencies in order to prop up their ideological agendas, then we have to consider how this political appropriation inflects deconstruction and provides it with a teleology or function that is supplementary. "By reducing truth to bias, and knowledge to ideology—in short, by politicizing scholarship—some minority activists believe they can win greater rewards."[147] If deconstruction or any other theory is managed in such a way that it serves this function, then its meaning becomes tied to issues of legitimation, social competition, cultural contestation, economic opposition, and so on. D'Souza makes the point quite well when he quotes Jane Tompkins: "The net result of this epistemological revolution is to repoliticize literature and literary criticism. When discourse is responsible for reality and not merely a reflection of it, then whose discourse prevails makes all the difference."[148] Whereas humanists have either bought into or been bullied into an unstated social contract that makes it taboo for academics to say out loud that knowledge has been subordinated in importance to the politics of revising reality to fit one's politically correct vision of the world, D'Souza openly identified the state of affairs in academia for what it often was—illiberal political bulldozing.

As for D'Souza's understanding of deconstruction, it conforms almost exactly to that of Bate and Wellek and supports Allan Bloom's thesis that politically deconstruction fills the need to debunk traditional truths by insisting truth is socially relative: "By reducing all truth to the level of opinion they spurn the legitimacy of any distinctions between truth and error." That deconstruction is extraordinarily scrupulous in its attempts not to collapse into a mindless relativism is, of course, paramount for someone such as Derrida, whose reputation as a philosopher requires that he avoid this fate at all costs. However, this is less the immediate issue—despite D'Souza's opinions about what deconstruction really is or isn't—than the question of what it means for deconstruction to be appropriated by social activists as if it were one of a number of critical modes of access for doing precisely what D'Souza says—undoing distinctions between truth and error that enable various social groups to devalue and debunk traditions that are core to liberal democracy. When Derrida said that there is more than one deconstruction, we might well wonder if the kind of deconstruction that was the product of distortion and redefinition for political reasons of the most pragmatic kind would be something Derrida would welcome. Indeed, it is in terms of D'Souza's investigation into what it means for institutions to abandon traditional principles in the name of ideas inspired by theories from the left that one begins to realize what is at stake when critical theories are used by social constituencies in order to relativize opinions and views in such a way that gross injustices are done to students and professors for the sake of a "political correctness" movement; take, for example, administrative censorship of students and professors that abrogates First Amendment rights and its justification by figures such as Stanley Fish who brashly sound off that "there is no such thing as free speech and a good thing too." Here, of course, D'Souza's locution "illiberal education" hits home with examples culled from newspapers and personal accounts from major university campuses around the country in which gross social injustices have occurred in the name of political policies that point to a larger political network of relations in the community of the university that scholarly and departmental politics do not want to face.

More broadly, this raises the problem that when critical theories are waffled into a politics of direct action—say, censorship—their determinability (or methodological controllability) as texts can easily be vitiated. In *Feminist Accused of Sexual Harassment* (1997), Jane Gallop noticed the obvious problem of what happens when feminist theory is politically appropriated by students and administrators in ways that are turned against those very faculty who were the progenitors of that theory. In Gallop's case, her college administration had misinterpreted questions of feminist transference (in the psychoanalytical sense) and had presumed "power differentials" that had taken the assumption of feminist power *for* women students and transformed it into feminist power *over* women students.[149] In Gallop's view, this was an abuse of the victim/oppressor model, which was not supposed to have led to notions such as "feminist sexual harasser." Gallop's story of having been formally accused of sexual misconduct points to the fact that theories are not in essence political in the sense that many people assume, given that the politics of a text is not actualized until someone uses it for the sake of making policy, reprimand, coalition, and so on. Indeed, when critical theories are translated into policy, there is no guarantee that the theories will not be heavily distorted, if not entirely cannibalized, for the sake of a motivated constituency that simply wants to have a rationale or to borrow prestige in order to get what it wants.

In that sense, the theories are like free radicals that can get enlisted in any number of different political perspectives. Consider, for example, that realism has been the darling of fascist, communist, and democratic politics. Essentialist conceptions of "human being" can be taken up just as easily by right- and left-wing ideologues. In D'Souza's book, emphasis falls not upon critical theories as competing individual perspectives but on the politicized social groups that valorize and mobilize these perspectives for the sake of pragmatic political aims having to do with the gaining of cultural, social, and political power. Of significance for deconstruction, I should think, is that this is no longer what one could call a philosophical or even theoretical understanding, which is to say, an understanding that would respect the protocols of philosophical thinking, given that philosophy's aims have been suppressed and overridden by a performative and pragmatic set of protocols that concern the acquisition of social and political rewards. It is at moments such as this that one recognizes how different deconstruction could be in the classroom (where one simply tries to explain what it is), the essay (where deconstruction is interpreted, critiqued, etc.), and the politics of faculty and student movements (where deconstruction has an ideological function, perhaps quite separate from its appearances in the classroom or scholarship).

Here it is useful to recall Habermas's distinction between (1) establishing communicative actions that lead to communicative understanding or constative agreement among interlocutors and (2) strategic or performative actions that employ rationales that may well be systematically distorted communications whose aim is to procure political advantages and rewards. As Habermas points out, this difference is often ambiguous, since strategic political actions may well try to cloak themselves as communicative actions in order to give themselves more social and political legitimacy than they really deserve. One might add that when theories from the human sciences are transposed into the sphere of political activism, they no longer belong to an open-minded sphere of intellectual inquiry but are turned into dogmatic propositions or principles about social and political states of affairs around which everyone is supposed to be polarized in a them-or-us conflict. Among the effects of this transposition is a dogmatic a priori labelling of actions as either politically correct or not. As Jane Gallop's tale of being a feminist accused of sexual harrassment shows us, the dogmatic implementation of even feminist theory can end up creating an illiberal social and political sphere within which theoretical conjecture is foreclosed and dogmatic stigmatizing is privileged, much to the detriment of even distinguished feminists like Gallop.

SOCIAL ACTS AND EXCITABLE SPEECH

By 1992 the nightmare predicted by Allan Bloom came to pass. Cary Nelson, Lawrence Grossberg, and Paula Treichler published a massive anthology entitled *Cultural Studies* that claimed the center of the language and literature profession for social studies. The anthology included essays on popular music, AIDS, technoculture, widow burning in India, the Hungarian uprising of 1956, postmodern guilt, negative images of black women, missionary stories, *Rambo*, and *Hustler* magazine. Many similar collections would soon follow. Whereas in the 1980s critics such as Fredric Jameson had stressed political readings of cultural phenomena that were predicated on textual analyses indebted to French structuralism and the Frankfurt School, cultural-studies critics such as Andrew Ross, Kobena Mercer, John Fiske, Michelle Wallace, Meaghan Morris, and Paul Gilroy were shifting the focus to "social studies." Unlike text-based critiques such as Jameson's *The Political Unconscious* (1981), which theorize the social by privileging the mediation of symbolic structures, social studies reintroduced the very anthropology that text-based critiques rejected: *the study of people and events in terms of immediate social practices.*

A strong example of the social-studies approach in *Cultural Studies* is Jan Zita Grover's piece on AIDS where we encounter the following:

A significant number of people I've known with AIDS and HIV infec-
tion have talked about their very jarring sense of no longer feeling
themselves as an integrated self, but instead as a container for the virus.
I've sat with people who just stare at their arms and say, "I know what's
going on there."[150]

Here, of course, the subjects speak for themselves. There is hardly any theoretical mediation or *écriture* to come in between subject and object.

In an article by Henry Giroux, we read, "I want to look briefly at how
the concept of difference has been used by conservatives, liberals, and radicals
in ways which either produce relations of subordination or undermine its possibility for developing a radical politics of democracy."[151] The focus here is on
direct use of the concept of difference, not the philosophical concept of difference itself. Simon Frith, however, writes, "It also follows that music-mak-
ing is, perhaps above all, an expression and celebration of *sociability*."[152] In
this case, music is a social act, not an aesthetic object, and certainly not to be
privileged as a score. Last, John Fiske writes, "As [Pierre] Bourdieu (1977)
points out, practices can circulate and reproduce culture *without their meanings passing through discourse or consciousness*."[153]

A commonality of these quotations is the emphasis on pragmatism—on
direct actions that people undertake in order to affect the social. However pri-
vate, self-reflection by the AIDS patient is a public political act, an intervention in the social. For Giroux, if difference is not conceptually problematic in
terms of symbolic systems, it is problematic in the way it is used by politicians
as a social action that bears on social relations of justice, rights, and equality.
For Frith, music is a political act that, like the political manipulation of difference, will impact on social subjects in a collective way. Hence the content
or style of the music is less inherently significant than its social function; the
assumption is that potentially any content or style will do as long as it can
function socially. Last, Fisk's statement encapsulates the hallmark of the social-studies mentality: social practices (actions) are thought to be capable of
existing independently of any given symbolic structure.

Taken together, these symptomatic statements are at the antipodes of
French structuralism, which teaches that actions are only socially significant
when they are given meaning by a symbolic structure that is always already in
place. It's odd that after decades of convincing themselves that meanings are
semiotically mediated (through symbolic forms, archetypes, kinship struc-

tures, rhetorical tropes, bureaucratic discursive practices, or cultural texts) faculty in the languages and literatures put up little resistance to a completely contrary paradigm that insisted upon the primacy of the social acts themselves and the secondariness of the ways in which they are represented or mediated. Instead of justifying such a paradigm shift, Grossberg, Nelson, and Treichler's *Cultural Studies* assumed the view that the primacy of social acts was the only correct way of thinking about the world. Hence, after an intensive critical dismantling of the metaphysics of agency in the 1970s and '80s, cultural studies had the audacity to ignore all these concerns for the sake of reinstating the autonomous individual of social studies from our high-school curriculum. However, the new social studies did breathe new life into this autonomous individual by introducing the idea that the social subject has no essence (the view is reminiscent of existentialism) and is, in fact, a social construction. Hence, despite maintaining an idealist conception of agency that imagines the radical independence of the voluntarist subject as a political agency, social-studies critics also insisted that agency is self-fashioned and that such a subject is an expression of representations and social acts that are, in the end, politically and historically determined by socioeconomics.

Of course, most people considered the practice of self-fashioning mainly to be a willed action whose social significance was ideologically transparent in a world made up of individual subjects whose actions reflect social relations that have become structurally embedded over the course of time through social and economic competition, which, in turn, have established the society's processes and values. Unlike French structuralism, Anglo-American forms of social studies are behavioristic in that they look at the social behavior of individuals who belong to groups (i.e., men, women, immigrants, ethnic minorities) in order to situate human activities within a polemic of values and stereotypes (i.e., beliefs, attitudes, prejudices, master narratives) tied to specific social and political interests. In this sense, social studies is often concerned with "lifestyle," the way of life as a politically negotiated ensemble of social acts that are based on individual and collective practices. When an activist like Jan Zita Grover argues that "too many culture critics see AIDS only in terms of its representations, analyzing the films, television programs, and outpourings of the press as an index to 'what AIDS means,' 'how AIDS means,' while ignoring the relationship between these representations and the lived experience of people coping with AIDS," she is concerned with the function of representations of gay life as social acts that have a direct effect on the real-life circumstances of people with AIDS. Hence, when Grover speaks of a news media blackout that withholds information about gay organizations that struggled to help persons who had AIDS, she speaks of it as a deliberate social action whose function (and, by extrapolation, intent) was to stigmatize a community or lifestyle by reporting only negative information, as if there could be nothing positive that one might say about a gay lifestyle or community.[154] Here, of course, the battle lines are drawn. Indeed, whereas orthodox Marxists had once invoked class struggle as the best political means of transforming society, social-studies critics have noticed that there are other identitarian social formations that can also have revolutionary potential: race, sexual orientation, and ethnicity among them. As Grover's article demonstrates, AIDS has become one of the social flashpoints for delimiting a social struggle that cannot be reduced simply to the old-fashioned model of class warfare.

In using the term "social studies" to define what I consider a dominant strain of cultural studies in the U.S. and the U.K., I want to call attention to a major shift away from the kind of cultural study that was initiated by critics like Roland Barthes in *Mythologies* (1956) or Jean Baudrillard in his *Système des objets* (1969) where emphasis fell upon the taxonomies of semiotics, linguistics, and rhetoric. Crucial to the shift away from what one might call a structural-linguistic approach to cultural studies has been a transition from representation (showing) to performance (doing). This is already quite evident in the ways in which social studies appropriated the concept of self-fashioning, though one can see the shift elsewhere too. If one examines, for example, Louis Marin's magesterial study of kingly representation in the age of Louis XIV, *Portrait du Roi* (1981), one will see that the emphasis falls on the semiotics of unrepresentability as a semiotics of power that has to be shown in terms of inimical self-fashioning. However, if one looks at Stephen Greenblatt's analyses of self-fashioning, I think one will notice a shift in which the emphasis falls less upon self-fashioning as representation (symbolization) than as social act (a performance that has social consequences for others). For example, Greenblatt's work on Martin Guerre, to be examined later, really emphasizes the performative over the representative. This is not to say that Greenblatt has overlooked the mediation of texts and symbols or that Marin occluded the performative in terms of royal actions. Rather at issue is the dominance of representation in Marin and of performance in Greenblatt. My point is that the New Historicism took some influential steps toward the direction of social studies in the early 1980s, something that reflects a significant shift from Marin's '70s-oriented semiotic analyses.

By the 1990s, even the New Historicist domestications and transformations of Continental theory had been increasingly replaced by the surfacing of a full-blown social studies mentality that exaggerated the earlier and more subtle emphases upon the performative. Hence Toni Morrison in her Nobel Prize lecture of 1993 pointed out that "oppressive language does more than represent violence, it is violence."[155] This strong preference for substituting performance for representation implies an understanding of culture that is not declarative but activist, an idea of culture that requires the conceptual analysis, moral adjudication, and social prescription of social acts in the name of promoting a politics whose intent it is to question, renegotiate, and transform mainstream values and forms of everyday life. Central to this social-studies orientation is, of course, the imperative to distinguish what is socially good from what is socially bad and to hold social subjects accountable for their social expression not as mere representations but as social acts that have direct consequences on the lives of others. Given this perspective, to teach a college course, therefore, in modern literature that fails to offer a wide distribution of different social perspectives and backgrounds—i.e., racial, ethnic, gendered—is not merely a failure in accurate representation (or "underrepresentation") but, much more egregiously, a social act that can be construed as being hostile to social diversity and hence to certain student constituencies, if not all progressive students. Such a view holds that a course lacking socially diverse voices would not simply represent bigotry because it would actually enact bigotry, meaning that its instructor could be labeled a bigot.

A philosophical assumption central to such an activist view is that being is a function of doing. Pragmatic in inspiration, such a conflation has precedent in American philosophy. One of the more influential French critics to have habilitated this idea (if not the respectability of pragmatic social study within the languages and literatures generally) is Michel de Certeau. In *Arts de faire* (1980) he argued for the anthropological view that, like tools, proverbs and other discourses are marked in terms of their usages and that they present to analysis the imprints of acts that reflect a process of *enunciation*. In speaking of his visit to an American museum in which a small nineteenth-century settlement had been preserved in tact, de Certeau pointed out that what one is seeing in all the implements and structures is the material embodiment of a way of life that is communicated as a complex ensemble of social acts that are enunciative. They signify the operations of which they are the themselves the objects, operations relative to their situations and conceptualizable "as conjunctural modalizations of practice and the enunciated." De Certeau said further that this comprises a social historicity in which representational systems and industrial processes are not to be seen as normative, but "as tools manipulated by their users."[156] In other words, the material conditions of life are to be seen as instruments or carriers of social enunciative acts that inevitably reveal a struggle between conforming to social norms and resisting them. Whereas a museum curator may just see in these objects a preservation of the way things used to be, de Certeau sees in them a preservation of a contentious social history of performances that have left their marks in the things themselves. For him what things are (their being) is a function of what their former owners did with them (their doing).

The idea that something is what it does is more often applied to people and runs the risk of ad hominem argumentation. This is more likely to surface in departmental meetings than in print. But when it is on good behavior, social-studies approaches tend to conflate performance with representation in order to make the case that material documentation is evidence that social acts have taken place and that we can know people on the basis of the social acts for which they have been responsible. In the anthology *Cultural Studies*, Catherine Hall published "Missionary Stories," an essay that accumulates historical facts about missionaries in Jamaica in order to interpellate them within a complex set of enunciative social actions that are definitive for establishing the identity of the missionaries as a group or type of people: "If gender hierarchy was inscribed at the heart of the missionary enterprise so was that of race."[157] In Hall's account this is not simply a description or representation of what the missionaries thought; rather it is the identification of a factual social practice of differentiation whose enunciation had consequences for their addressees: women and slaves. The documents left behind by the missionaries are thus treated in terms of having agency, since they are treated as acts that have consequences rather than as ideas that belong to a system of thinking already so distanced from us that they appear curious. By focusing on the concept of social praxis, Hall defines the essence of a community of missionaries who settled in Jamaica in terms of describing what they did as agents of action. Hence, they are presented to us as a direct reflection of their social history. In looking at history this way, a social-studies approach restricts itself almost entirely to a politics of social action and how this concerns historical circumstances and social conflicts between privileged and unprivileged groups. Fundamental to such a view is that *everything* one thinks and does is political and that every act should be considered as potentially having the kind of agency that has social consequences in terms of self/other relations.

Although the idea that everything is always already political can reinflect history in ways that highlight social contestation in terms of everyday life, something that more traditional history failed to do, there is the glaring limitation of a certain literality in which what people are is a direct reflection of what they did: the transparency between doing and being. It is in this context that a rereading of Jean-Paul Sartre's *Being and Nothingness* (1943) could be instructive, because his slant is precisely the opposite, namely, that being and doing are never entirely synchronous and that, in many cases, they are quite out of phase. We may recall that Sartre's *pour soi* (the for-itself) is the doer while his *en soi* (the in-itself) is the one who is. For Sartre these are really two horizons of consciousness that are often in dialectical tension, the for-itself struggling to secure itself as an in-itself by means of freely acting as an autonomous agent in the world at large. The problem for Sartre is that once the for-itself succeeds in securing its desired aims in terms of identity, status, way of life, and so forth, it recoils at the feeling of being trapped in the structure of its own making, the in-itself. Yet, without that security, the for-itself feels anxiety and dread, because it feels adrift and never knows what is coming next. Alternatively, the in-itself is always already constituted and presents the subject with its own transcendence by means of confronting it with lack; hence, it calls the for-itself into action in order to satisfy whatever it is the in-itself appears to be missing. However, once the for-itself appears to have succeeded in satisfying this lack, the in-itself reveals itself once more as elusively incomplete, hence alienating the for-itself once more. As being, the in-itself shows itself to doing as a project to be completed or satisfied. But just as the for-itself recoils from the in-itself at the moment of successful accomplishment, the in-itself recoils from the for-itself at the moment of being satisfied. In other words, these two horizons within consciousness are inherently allergic to one another because each knows that the congruence of the for-itself with the in-itself is death: nothingness. To be, therefore, means that doing and being must never literally coincide.

Being and Nothingness takes this noncoincidence of the for-itself and in-itself as the basis for arguing that people do many things that they do not really believe in or may feel very ambivalent about. People act in bad faith, which is less an exception in everyday life than the norm. At the very least, this suggests that what people do and what they really mean by what they do is hardly transparent to us and perhaps not even extremely transparent to them. Actions are not only ambiguously or contradictorally situated within consciousness but are always part of a very complex phenomenology of incompletion that cannot be reduced to what de Certeau calls "enunciation," since that demands the kind of logical distinctions and systematicity that we do not enjoy internally. Then, too, there is the inability of social-studies critics to acknowledge the possibility of the unconscious and the phenomena that psychoanalysis has amply documented during the past one hundred years.

Since they are pragmatists, social-studies critics waive such problems aside by demonstrating that even if we can't know what someone meant to say or do, this does not matter, since we can define that saying or doing retroactively by adjudicating its *function*, that is, by experientially taking either pleasure or offense in the saying or doing—by adjudicating it to be benign or hostile to an other. In short, we don't have to worry about what someone really thinks; all we have to care about is the social function of what he or she performs, since the significance of thinking only matters in terms of its being socially acted out in ways that have consequences for others. Hence one's first priority is in defining the act rather than the person. Moreover, since the act is empirically recoverable in the material evidence and can be judged according to how it functions, we can suspend judgement about the person long enough to retroactively identify him or her with the social act(s).

If Catherine Hall's work reveals a nuanced application of this principle, there is also the more reductive approach to be considered that identifies a remark as, say, having a racist function in order to tar and feather the speaker as a racist. This may have the advantage of instituting some unambiguous political definition as to who is morally acceptable and who is not, but it does lose sight of the consciousness of the offender, which is a concern to the extent that people, and not the actions themselves, have intentionality. When Toni Morrison argues that oppressive language is violence, she is making the subtle error of imagining that actions (i.e., statements) are free agents doing harmful things to people. I would counter that, in fact, hate speech is an intentional act that cannot be divorced from the psychology and phenomenology of its authors. In and of itself it cannot be violence; it can only be a representation of someone's intention, however defined or muddled, to do violence to someone else. Consider, for example, the experience of Alice

Kaplan in *French Lessons* (1993) when she writes of her interviews and relations with Maurice Bardèche, an avowed French anti-Semite and supporter of Faurisson and other Holocaust deniers.[158] There is no doubt that he is a racist and that his social acts are extremely despicable. Labeling him a racist and having done with it, however, is not sufficient. One needs to gain some insight into how someone like Bardèche is capable of treating Kaplan, a Jew, in a very personal and genial manner, even to the point of making her feel as if she were family, and who then sends her a chilling letter in which his anti-Semitism sadistically comes out. An extreme ambivalence that is capable of generating rather contrary actions toward Jews requires thought, for it is a tiny but significant piece of a larger puzzle concerning social interrelations: How is it that people are capable of separating very different intentionalities with respect to others? And how does that relate to racism in general as a social practice kept in reserve within people who, for all outward appearances, can will themselves to appear quite liberal and friendly to minorities? It is here that the tendency toward conflating doing with being reveals limitations, because the state of being of consciousness is often far more varied and complex than the doing.

Some social-studies critics avoid such problems by analyzing the social act as the expression of social systems. Hence Tony Bennett speaks of the social as "a particular surface of social management." For him, and many other social-studies critics:

> Culture [is] a historically produced surface of social regulation whose distinctiveness is to be identified and accounted for in terms of (1) the specific types of attributes and forms of conduct that are established as its targets, (2) the techniques that are proposed for the maintenance or transformation of such attributes or forms of conduct, (3) the assembly of such techniques into particular programs of government, and (4) the inscription of such programs into the operative procedures of specific cultural technologies.[159]

In other words, the social act is now seen as transparent forms of conduct, techniques of maintaining or changing the form, assembling these forms into programs, and writing these programs out as templates for action. However, as Franz Kafka noticed, bureaucracies are even more difficult to fathom than even the most elusive individuals. This is one of the curious lessons of the lengthy studies written by Holocaust deniers. According to them, close scrutiny of the documentation we have makes the events seem less and less plausible, because the details reveal a lack of consistency, reasonableness, efficiency, and, ultimately, sanity on the part of the persecutors. Hence the deniers seize the opportunity to begin asking whether any of this could have been at all plausible. The answer, of course, is that implausible as the events may have been and odd as the documentation may be, these events occurred, even if there was considerable opacity between the actions and the agents of action.

Like many intellectual movements over the past thirty years, the turn toward social studies has made allies of critics with rather different intellectual credentials. Among them is Judith Butler, whose early publications displayed an intense interest in Continental philosophers like Hegel and Sartre. Her book *Gender Trouble* (1989) even returned to the familiar stomping grounds of Claude Lévi-Strauss, namely, the distinction between nature and culture, in an attempt to disassemble the dichotomy. In *Excitable Speech* (1997), however, Butler engages the field of activist social studies, a shift in orientation that is rather striking, given some of her previous work. Among the challenges that a reader might well expect is for Butler to somehow marry pragmatic social studies with some of the French approaches she has engaged in the past, deconstruction among them. In fact, there clearly are some attempts in the book to do just this, but apparently the social studies model proves itself to be too narrow to accommodate anything more than some brief forays, and rather timid ones at that.

Problematic is that however one twists and turns the paradigm, social studies remains committed to an Enlightenment sender/receiver model of communication that, as in the case of Condillac, Locke, and others of their time, is predicated on the presence of direct face-to-face communication. *Excitable Speech* engages what is perhaps the most highly charged instance of such face-to-face encounters: face-to-face insult and injury. It is here, of course, that the social studies idea of representations being performative is most self-evidently uncontrovertible, if not paradigmatic, for a definition of all social acts. Butler, however, wants to wriggle out of this blatant metaphysics of what Derrida once called "voice" in order to maintain that the initiator of hate speech is never to be considered the original or authentic locus of speaking, because that person is repeating ("citing") a ritualized discourse of injurious conduct whose history is so well known that it is a cliché. Indeed, Butler may well be alluding to Derrida's remarks on iteration in "Limited Inc.," which, as in the case of Butler's text, explores hate speech, though in the more nuanced form of an ad hominem polemic. Whereas in Butler the iteration of the hate monger is seen to establish a bond with an invisible community of like-minded haters—many of them long dead—in Derrida the iteration of excitable speech results in a confrontation that is, at the same time, a failed or missed encounter. In other words, excitable speech does and doesn't work as a performative speech act in ways that can be carefully dissected and worked over, all to the cost of John Searle, Derrida's antagonist. Unlike Derrida, for whom the iteration of hate speech results in multiple injuries that are both savage and comical, cruel and yet funny, but, most importantly, furious and yet still good natured enough to be playful, Butler examines examples of hate speech like cross-burnings that are univocal: no *faux bond* here.

When Butler takes up Catherine MacKinnon's complaint that the United States Congress perpetrated a pornographic logic wherein the testimony of Anita Hill was purposely misrecognized as the very opposite of what it was intending to establish—that she was not consenting to Clarence Thomas's advances—the reversal is established as absolute, univocal, and hence morally objectified in such a way that it can be unilaterally condemned by politically progressive academics. Still, Butler opens the door to thinking of such a repetition—that is, the repetition of a pornographic trope in which "no" means "yes"—as having a certain resonance with prior acts of verbal violation. In the case of overt hate speech, she imagines that the speaker is merely citing from a prepared and conventional script of racist lingo that is far beyond the ken of the injurer, and that this repetition conjures up in the victim a collective memory of beatings, shootings, lynchings, and gassings, whose "force" is highly incommensurate with the simplicity of name-calling, cross-burning, and the like. However, whereas in Derrida the iteration of a speech act results in deformations and displacements that break with past usages and resonances, in Butler the citation is really univocal with the past. Hence, whereas for Derrida reproduction, citation, iterability, interpretation, parasitism, and translation would put the speech act of something like hate speech (the speech of the ad hominem) into question, for Butler iteration returns over and over again to a primal scene of hate that appears to be compulsively reinvoked from generation to generation and is even reproduced within the American judicial system. Moreover, in the court system she detects the collusion of a *use* (performative)/*mention* (representational) distinction whose difference doesn't disarticulate the act of hate—but repeats it. That is, according to Butler, the mention/use distinction works in favor of racists (who are protected because their slurs are merely representations as mentionings) and against homosexuals (whose representations of sexuality are considered uses). For Butler the battle lines are clearly drawn: a highly delimited confrontation is taking place with respect to how social acts are being adjudicated. But in Derrida's "Limited Inc.," it is this confrontation between addresser and addressee that is at issue. For Derrida iteration is problematic, because it results in an ensemble of texts that are not really reproductions of one another. Can one identify a singular intention that runs through all of them? Or is this intention (*vouloir-dire*)—literally, the wish or impulse to stay, for whatever reason—dissociated and even conflicted?

Butler never approaches the hate speeches of Hitler, but if she had, she would have had to recognize that they are not entirely settled on their intent, though the overall direction of that intent is never in question. What were the various aims of Hitler's intent? Did he hate all his antagonists the same and in the same way? Are his various acts of hate speech entirely univocal? And if so, why didn't it become clear to politicians in places like America and Britain in the 1930s that Hitler was dangerous? Or did this become clear? Consider, for example, Charlie Chaplin's *The Great Dictator* (1940) in which the Holocaust is presciently recognized. Why and how, then, did the European community miscalculate so dreadfully? Wasn't this a failure to distinguish between use and mention, a failure that points to the impossibility of absolutely separating them? In the French press during the 1930s, it is quite evident that many people were reading Hitler's intentions rather differently. Was this a sham? Is one going to opt for a vast conspiracy theory of dissimulation, of feined shock at what the Nazis were prosecuting? There ought to be questions, too, about the history of Hitler's hate. Did it have a telos? Was it just a reproduction (i.e., citation) of Viennese hate speech, as some have suggested? Were there ruptures in this history? And was the Holocaust one of these? Then, too, what precisely did Hitler think he was confronting in his speeches? Is there even a confrontation?

Absurd as that question sounds, Jean-Francois Lyotard's *The Differend* (1983) substantiates a strong case for saying no: that in some senses a confrontation never occurred, because the speech acts of hate eliminated the addressees of hate in advance as subjects that could be encountered as subjects of redress and counterargumentation. What characterizes such hate speech was precisely the absence of a typical Lockean speech situation within which an other talks back or countermands. To what extent did Hitler's early victories at the outset of World War Two instantiate that lack of confrontation as an experience of capitulation? Perhaps these are indecent questions. And perhaps Daniel Goldhagen was right in thinking that Germany was of a single intention and that its hate speech was the prelude to a collective desire to kill all the Jews. Perhaps. But in not asking these questions could we not be fooling ourselves into simplifying the realities of something like hate speech, something that could be problematic in an age of terrorism, Internet hate networks, and so on? In short, isn't Butler's social-studies turn highly inadequate to the task at hand?

To return: in *Excitable Speech* one encounters a metaphysics of speech acts, not its overcoming. Is this tantamount to saying that Butler's work is mystified? For those convinced by the critiques developed in French theory during the '60s and '70s, one would have to make that argument. My point is that there is a rather major conceptual difference that is at odds between that part of Butler's work that is influenced by Continental philosophy and that part of her work that makes common cause with the metaphysics of American pragmatism and social studies. Among the most glaring of these metaphysical traits, hallmarks of the social studies venue, is the question of the addressee as countersigner for the truth of the social act—the injured individual, the community that empathizes and makes common cause with the supposed authenticity of the experience of this injury, and, ultimately, the politics of courtroom adjudication of what is harassment and what is not, what is prosecutable hate speech and what is protected speech, and so on.

Then, there is the question of the presence of bodies—the social studies predeliction for the physical entity or material thing: "A statement may be made that, on the basis of a grammatical analysis alone, appears to be no threat. But the threat emerges precisely through the act that the body performs in the speaking [sic] the act." Or, "The act of threat and the threatened act are, of course, distinct, but they are related as a chiasmus. Although not identical, they are both bodily acts: the first act, the threat, only makes sense in terms of the act that it prefigures."[160] We will return to bodies that matter shortly, but from a deconstructive vantage point, not a reified one. Yet first consider the problematic of the name. For Butler, the name is always a matter of interpellation, and even in those instances when she tries to argue that interpellation need not be vocative, that one can be interpellated in script, the reigning paradigm remains the "Hey! You!" of the cop on the beat, because the operative principle is that we are the addressee of an address that has consequences, whether we like it or not. Moreover, this appeal or call is univocal in its force as a determinate social act, however we wish to interpret it for ourselves, since its functional significance is socially consequential. Certainly, this is not to say that Butler cannot imagine another way of considering the name—she is familiar with deconstruction—but that given the limitations of an activist social-studies paradigm, this would undermine her project.

Finally, and most importantly for us, there is the issue of the social relation. Social studies presupposes conceptions of social relatedness that deconstruction puts into question. For example, the addresser/addressee model imagines a social relation is established the moment the one speaks to the other. Interpellation, for example, would be that hailing through which the social bond or relation is instantiated by way of selection, recognition, obligation, exchange, and so on. Moreover, the social act is never anything else but the instantiation of a social relation or, if one prefers, a social-political relation. In social studies, hate speech defines the social relation in terms of self/other, privileged/underprivileged, superior/inferior, and so on. Hence hate speech functions as an easy social delimiter for people who are in need of boundaries to orient themselves socially, which is to say, hierarchically. If there is any doubt about this, there is the observable excitable speech of children wherein an effort is apparently made to find out where one is and who one is in a certain social order where the difference between superiority and inferiority is everywhere marked (adult/child, smart/dumb, liked/not liked, etc.). That verbal aggression can function as a mode of social cognition is something that probably most children are likely to discover for themselves at some point or other and it would be naïve to think that this isn't going to carry over into adult life.

However, it is not just the link between aggression and cognition that is problematic but the sense of having arrived at an objectified social relation when, in fact, that social relation is only partially, and probably incorrectly, realized. Here, again, social studies fails us, because we encounter the Derridean problematic of the failed encounter, or missed relation. And this takes me back, yet again, to Nazi Germany, this time in terms of the body politic. Everyone knows that Hitler, Goebbels, and the others were not Aryan types and that whatever interpellations and social relations they thought they had forged with the myth of Aryanism was a farce as plain as day. Here the materiality of the body belies the fantasy of the social relation. In fact, of most interest is that in order to imagine the social relation, one has to actively suppress the materiality of the body, to purposely suspend disbelief in what is being asserted. Now the materiality, or presence of the body, in the German body politic is a complex and vexed issue that has by no means been adequately dealt with. However, in the absence of even a schematic analysis, let me at least point out that the status of a body like that of Goebbels is precisely that of a nonappearing body, or invisible body: the Aryan body that Goebbels never had.

Here, too, we could have an opportunity to talk about the white sheets of the Klan. What I'm getting at is that we're dealing with an absence of the body, or of a body to come, which is not this body right here before you that preaches hate. And that it is in the instability—or deconstruction, if you wish—of the presence/absence of the body (of the presence of the person who delivers speeches of hate) that hate speech is transmitted in order to found a social relation that is imaginary—a phantasm. It is here that the social cognition of aggression defaults into a miasma of phantasy about the social relation at that very moment the social relation is constituted on a bed of violence. Now what does this suggest? That the bodies of Hitler, Goebbels, and Goering were the material trait of their absence as Aryan bodies to come, that they were the material trait of the specter of their other, the Aryan. The social relation to this other is a phantasy and a phantasm, an artificial construction that holds in place the promise of a body to come, a being to be. Therefore, what one sees in the here and now does not count and is to be disregarded. The social relation to *this* actual body with the club foot, in other words, is moot. But then of what kind of social relation are we speaking in which the body is there and not there at the same time? The answer is that of a relation/nonrelation, a body of the nonbody, of the body to come, of the specter of Aryanism, materialism/antimaterialism. This, then, is the illogic of racism, the function of an *illogical relation* that posits itself as the only valid objectifiable relation there is.

Of course, we are not anywhere close to social studies anymore, where one can only posit the face-to-face relation of self and other in their full presence as antagonists. Nor can social studies do anything other than posit the logic of a social act insofar as the moralizing imperative of social studies requires a simple binary logic of good and evil. It cannot instantiate the illogic

of a social and visible suspension of disbelief, a suspension that actually occurred during the Nazi period on a vast collective scale, a suspension of disbelief that not only disregarded the physical disconnection between the Aryan
ideals of Nazism and the realities of who the leaders of Nazism were but, alternatively and at the same time, disregarded the intentions of Nazism, an active suspension of belief in which many world powers were involved for the
simple reason that they could not imagine or believe what they were hearing.
This, then, would constitute some analytical fragments of a familiar history
that would challenge the social-studies foundations of *Excitable Speech*, which
is to say, the foundations of social studies itself, which, in my view, are far too
restricted—something that Butler herself suggests in her book.

That said, it is important to note that the wide chasm between social
studies and deconstruction narrows when one considers that deconstruction
is itself a critique of the social relation and that, as Butler may be indicating,
there is a way of reading deconstruction as a social study of another sort. In
that case, my evaluation would be that Butler's reading is still too charitable
to the more pragmatic strains of American cultural/social study.

VICIOUS DUALISMS

Anyone who is familiar with the basic tenets of a postmodern worldview cannot help but wonder how it is possible for there to be an institutional coexis-
tence between (1) a social studies paradigm that stresses the authenticity of the
social act as performed by empirical agencies and (2) a cultural paradigm of
virtuality that argues, in effect, that reality is so highly mediated by representations of all sorts that one cannot any longer speak of social acts of any political significance that aren't highly mediated, if not entirely transformed, by
technologies of representation. While a social critic like Axel Honneth might
argue that it is possible to say that we live in a world where at times the social
subject is to be characterized in a social-studies sense and at other times the
social subject can be characterized in the virtual or postmodern sense, the fact
is that when taken as worldviews such paradigms become polarized because
they simply do not mesh.

This conflict of worldviews leads one into a dead end of vicious duality,
which becomes evident the moment we encounter a one-sided presentation.

Once more, consider *Excitable Speech* in which Judith Butler talks about the Clarence Thomas hearings in the U.S. Congress and the testimony of Anita Hill. Butler never addresses the virtuality or mediatedness of that testimony within the medium of broadcast television, which applied techniques of representation familiar to sports fans: play-by-play commentary, short biographies of the participants, instant replays, score keeping, and the highlighting of the pornographic potential of Hill's testimony by repeatedly privileging it—a technique typical of a Sadean text. Butler never questions the "reality" of the Thomas hearings, even though for most of the general public it was derealized in the media and, as such, as quickly forgotten as the Super Bowl. Because of Butler's activist allegiances, she cannot allow that these Congressional hearings be considered merely virtual or that the political be viewed as merely a hollow spectacle or seduction in Baudrillard's sense of a fraudulently concealed surplus meaning of sexuality that lures the viewer. Because social studies is so focused on issues of wrong, damage, and victimhood, Butler cannot say the hearings were referenceless and that no concrete social acts were taking place, because this would efface the victim.

Yet, the postmodern critic would object: What does it mean to insist upon the performativity of such social acts in the absence of acknowledging a representational circus as powerful as the print and television media, given that this circus affected Congressional leaders who found themselves on a prime-time television venue with exceptionally high ratings? After all, how one appears in the virtual space of the television screen translates into faxed responses and e-mail messages during the performance itself. Manipulating Anita Hill's image by providing "media spin" is directly correlative to this, because if she were allowed to win the hearts and minds of viewers, how would these politicians look in comparison? And, not insignificantly, what would happen to the politics of appointing Thomas? Or voting patterns in the next Congressional elections? Given such issues, is it possible to disentangle the literal self-present social act from its mediation and televised construction, as Butler does?

However, if we structure a debate in this way, we fall into a fallacy of critical thinking endemic to much cultural study, namely, the construction of a vicious dualism whereby a circulation between two terms or paradigms occurs. Whichever term or paradigm we choose, its opposite is waiting in the wings to invalidate and replace it. Hence we have no other option but to circulate from one position to the other and back, something that we will see in the context of New Historicism, postcolonialism, and gender studies. In terms of the example above, this is a movement between a paradigm of representation (that is to say, of the virtual) and of performance (that is to say, of the social act) with no synthesis or resolution, given that they are fundamentally two separate intellectual worldviews that when brought into relation form a vicious dualism.[161]

In the demonstrations that follow, I will look at vicious dualisms in the work of Stephen Greenblatt, Anne McClintock, and, again, Judith Butler, whose *Gender Trouble* (1989) has been so influential that it cannot be ignored. At issue will be three dualisms of considerable prominence: (1) The inability to decide whether language is the performative expression of an experience, or whether experience is the representational expression of language; (2) the inability to decide whether the subject constructs itself by self-consciously using cultural discourses, or whether the subject is constructed by those various cultural discourses in advance of its coming into being as a subject; and (3) the inability to decide whether identity rests upon traits that are essentially manifest, or whether identity rests upon inessential traits that are made to appear as if they were timeless, universally present and, hence, essential. Of interest here will be the structure and repetition of dualistic impasses and their debilitating prevalence across a wide spectrum of cultural study.

No doubt, the distinction between representation and performance that is so crucial to social studies has a history that achieves a turning point in the late '70s and early '80s, when critics started to imagine putting agency back into what was called "poststructuralism." New Historicists like Stephen Greenblatt were, in fact, reactionary critics eager to modify Michel Foucault's work in such a way that his repudiation of anthropocentrism—the reduction of all information to the experience of "man"—was sidestepped in favor of reintroducing agency in terms of performativity, something that Foucault himself was thought to have accomplished in his work on sexuality in the late '70s. The reintroduction of agency was particularly high on the American critical agenda, because of a general agreement with critics like Jameson in *The Prison-House of Language* that the absence of agency in structuralism and poststructuralism was not only counterintuitive but politically counterproductive, since only agencies can get things done. Central to Greenblatt's work in the early '80s was an attempt to finesse the question of agency by advancing a concept of "self-fashioning," which drew inspiration from Foucault's work on "practices of the self." Unlike Foucault, for whom the social subject was an effect of praxis, Greenblatt maintained a bipolar understanding of the self as alternately representational and performative. In a well known essay on the historical account of Martin Guerre, "Psychoanalysis and Renaissance Culture" (1986), Greenblatt wrote that "the social fabrication of identity is, I have argued, particularly marked in [Renaissance] drama where, after all, identity is fashioned out of public discourse, and even soliloquies tend to take the form of rhetorical declamations."

In the case of Edmund Spenser, whose work is undramatic,

> psychic experience is not manifested in the representation of a particular individual's inner life but rather in the representation of the hero's externalized struggle to secure clear title to his allegorical attributes and hence to his name. [. . .] For Spenser the psyche can only be conceived as a dangerous, factionalized social world . . . just such a world as Spenser the administrator inhabited in Ireland.

The self, in other words, is a social construction that draws various social elements together by way of, say, an allegorical interface that stands for the subject's conflictual and heterogeneous attributes. Identity, therefore, is a schematism that results from a cultural appropriation of traits. Hence in the *Faery Queene*, "Red Cross's own identity—his name—is only revealed to him when he too has undergone the trials that belong to the signs he wears."[162] Similarly, in the case of Martin Guerre, one man claims to be another who has been long missing in order to take possession of the missing man's wife and property. He does so by self-fashioning himself through appropriating the signs of being a particular social subject with a particular identity.

This understanding of social identity is modelled directly on structuralism. What made New Historicists different is that they put the self back into "self-fashioning." Hence Greenblatt invokes an actual historical figure, Arnaud de Tilh, who self-consciously tried to rob a gullible French household by pretending to be someone he was not. Moreover, Greenblatt is interested in how this "construction" gets socially negotiated (this is, we recall from social studies, a social act) in a court of law. Having argued for representationality (i.e., structure) by saying the subject is the effect of an "accumulation of institutional decisions and communal pressures," Greenblatt also wants to argue for performativity (really, agency) in terms of a self-willed subject who fashions himself in his own right for the purpose of *self-interest*. What results is the clash between (1) the impostor's self-willed act to dissimulate Martin Guerre and seize his property, and (2) the court's right and even legal duty to put this man to death for overstepping his bounds as an agency or social subject. What we have, then, are self-conscious social agents struggling to see whose will may be affirmed. Moreover, despite the fact that Greenblatt would like us to imagine the story of Martin Guerre as disassembled in terms of "multiple, complex, refractory stories" or "practices, strategies, representations, fantasies, negotiations, and exchanges," the "case of Martin Guerre" does, in the end, gather all these pluralized accounts into a case history about a conflict of social acts or performances.

In Greenblatt's work it is the consistency of an irresolution between whether agency is a prime mover of social actions or a secondary effect of cultural representations that forms a theoretical impasse, because at one moment we see the subject as agency coherently fashioning himself in a deliberate manner, and at another moment we see the subject as constructed, negotiated, or produced by split off practices, strategies, representations, and fantasies that make up a heterogeneous field known as "the social." That the one perspective serves as a corrective to the other means that throughout an essay like "Psychoanalysis and Renaissance Culture" we experience a fugitive see-sawing from one perspective to the other across the logical abyss that marks their mutual contradiction.

In the 1980s and '90s, such polarized dualistic thinking often turned out to be structurally central to many cultural/historical analyses and, moreover, appeared to be symptomatic of a general inability within the languages and literatures to decide or resolve major conceptual problems. Consider Anne McClintock's *Imperial Leather* (1995). It studies how a vast imperium of discourses—that of British Imperialism— delimits contradictory or uneven liaisons between "imperial and anti-imperial power; money and sexuality; violence and desire; labor and resistance."[163] In her chapter on Hannah Cullwick, "Imperial Leather: Race, Cross Dressing, and the Cult of Domesticity," McClintock presents a traditional historical account of a woman who had been cross-dressing in the Victorian period as a man, a slave, an upper-class woman, and so on. Her photographic archive of these various performances become the topic of McClintock's analysis, which, in a manner reminiscent of Greenblatt, see-saws between a view of the subject as self-fashioner and the subject as culturally fashioned. Does the female subject manipulate the discourse regimes available to her within British Imperialism, or is she the effect of these discourse regimes?

Who or what is the agent of her agency? That her self-fashionings are part of an elaborate sexual relationship with Arthur Munby, her barrister lover, complicates matters in that we can see a correspondence between a sexual relationship between man and woman defined in terms of sadism and masochism and its relation to other social power relationships, including that of colonizer and colonized. In other words, Cullwick is structurally situated at the nexus of social discourses and expressions of power concerning the master polarity central to postcolonial criticism: subjection/subversion. It is a dualism that determines Cullwick's subjecthood, even as she manipulates it to determine her subjecthood for herself.

As in Greenblatt, the accounts in McClintock hinge on a structural ambiguity of power that cannot be resolved: the subject as both active and passive, doer and done-to, master and slave. That McClintock seizes upon sado-masochistic sexual relations as emblematic of how British Imperialism is socially and culturally configured may reflect how well s/m relations relate to the impasse of New Historical methodology into which the reader is being drawn. Despite the wealth of cultural, social, and political discourses that McClintock can marshal from virtually all corners of the globe, the fact remains that her theoretical understanding of the discourse/subject relation is limited to a fundamental critical incapacity to decide whether subjects can actively and subversively fashion themselves by making use of various culturally constructed discourses, or whether they are passively situated in society in such a way that they are either interpellated by these cultural discourses or otherwise semiotically constructed by them in ways that suggest subjection. The inability to decide for or against agency in terms of subjection/subversion is an unproductive indecisiveness—it is the antithesis of what Derrida would call "undecidability"—and hems in any theoretical advance beyond a dualism of which one polarity always forces one to embrace its opposite in compensation for what it lacks.

Such indecisiveness is quite different from Derridean undecidability in that undecidability is a *productive* rupturing of boundaries that deconstructs dualisms, while *indecision* is an unproductive impasse that limits research to alternatives that are contradictory and that can only be appeased by a compulsive swinging back and forth that resolves nothing. So far we have seen two major indecisions: the inability to decide whether language is the expression of an experience or vice versa, and the inability to decide whether agency constructs or is constructed. To this we can now add the inability to decide the dualism of essentialism/antiessentialism. Without going into an excursus on a debate that has been raging since the 1970s, let me just say that, owing to her fate as a reader who cannot evade the impasse of compulsive indecision, McClintock falls apart when this dualism arises:

> I remain unconvinced, however, by arguments that race is a mere affect of floating signifiers as well as by claims that "there must be some essence which precedes and/or transcends the fact of objective conditions." . . I am in agreement with Paul Gilroy's cogent argument that "the polarization between essentialist and anti-essentialist theories of black identity has become unhelpful. Exploring the historical instability of the discourse on race . . . by no means entails a spin into the vertigo of undecidability.' "[164]

In other words, McClintock is unable to accept the essentialist argument, the antiessentialist argument, or the argument for undecidability. Not being able to occupy *any* of these positions, she drops the topic in total indecision. At least the sentences that follow what I have quoted veer off the point:

> To dispute the notion that race is a fixed and transcendent essence, unchanged through the ages, does not mean that "all talk of 'race' must cease," nor does it mean that the baroque inventions of racial difference had no tangible or terrible effects. On the contrary, it is precisely the inventedness [sic] of historical hierarchies that renders attention to social power and violence so much more urgent.[165]

These sentences change the topic. Instead of thinking about the theoretical choices of essentialism, antiessentialism, or undecidability, McClintock changes horses in midstream and addresses those who talk about the sorts of social consequences these positions have had. Just because people have essentialized race doesn't mean we now have to not talk about it; just because one takes a constructivist position doesn't mean such constructions haven't had a terrible effect. Then, in the non sequitur that follows, McClintock says that the invention of historical hierarchy (is she still talking about race or something else? I can't tell) leads us to pay attention to social power and violence. Not only does this not decide the preceding conundrums, but, if I am not mistaken, we've just been given a red herring in the mystified form of an abstruse tautology that says, in effect, that when society is divided up into masters and slaves we ought to be concerned about abuses of power. It is here, of course, that the indecision of the paragraph is figured in the compulsive repetition of power-dualisms: sadist/masochist, master/slave, colonizer/colonized, active/passive, subversion/subjection, and male/female. In other words, McClintock's analysis is grounded upon an unhappy consciousness of bipolarity, an indecisiveness in which a predialectical opposition holds sway.

To get a sense of just how generally accepted such indecisiveness is, one must turn to Judith Butler's very popular *Gender Trouble* (1989), in which she also fabricates a construct-or-be-constructed dualism: "What sense can we make of a construction that cannot assume a human constructor prior to that construction?"[166] Butler will confront sociology by attacking the conventional idea that "the person" takes "ontological priority to the various roles and functions through which it assumes social visibility and meaning."[167] However, she also queries Foucault's work on sexuality: "To what extent do regulatory practices of gender formation and division constitute identity?" Butler then forges a middle path between Foucault and cultural studies (of which the New Historicism is one) when she asks: "If 'identity' is an *effect* of discursive practices, to what extent is gender identity, constructed as a relationship among sex, gender, sexual practice, and desire, the effect of a regulatory practice that can be identified as compulsory heterosexuality?"[168] In short, if Foucault is right about the subject being constituted as an effect of intersecting discursive regimes, that does not rule out a theory of social domination whereby societies compel conformity to a subjecthood deemed proper by the state. This view is later ratified by Butler when she reveals her thesis: "The univocity of sex, the internal coherence of gender, and the binary framework for both sex and gender are considered throughout as regulatory fictions that consolidate and naturalize the convergent power regimes of masculine and heterosexist oppression." Moreover, this oppression can be

> "contested" and "subverted" once we understand that the body is not "a ready surface awaiting signification, but a set of boundaries, individual and social, politically signified and maintained. No longer believable as an interior 'truth' of dispositions and identity, sex will be shown to be a performatively enacted signification (and hence not 'to be') one that, re-

leased from its naturalized interiority and surface, can occasion the parodic proliferation and subversive play of gendered meanings."[169]

By arguing that we should not assume gender has substance—"There is no gender identity *behind* the expressions of gender"[170]—Butler maintains there is no agency prior to the act that performatively suggests such an agency has preceded it. According to this logic, agency is the vestige of an act that always appears as if it (agency) had existed a priori to the doing. Yet, much later, Butler will give a wink to social studies: "Consider gender, for instance, as *a corporeal* style, an 'act,' as it were, which is both intentional and performative, where 'performative' suggests a dramatic and contingent construction of meaning."[171] Here gender can be viewed as a politically subversive strategy whose aim is to purposely counter the dictates of compulsory heterosexuality. Although Butler wants the concept of performance to denote a pure act that is without agency as such, the slide into intentionality and self-construction requires us to believe that there is a self-willed agency at work, and that this agency is politically and hence strategically motivated to do battle with dominant social codes. Although Butler's text raises one's hopes for a theoretical breakthrough that will forge a new line of thinking, she cannot extricate her analysis from an untenable contradiction that waffles on the question of agency. Butler leaves her readers in a state of indecision that reifies the untenability of a debate that cannot resolve its core question. In this she is theoretically congruent with Greenblatt and McClintock. Nevertheless, Butler's book was received with enormous enthusiasm, since readers with an interest in gay activism and feminism saw it as the best of two worlds—the sophisticated French theoretical scene with its critique of agency and the politically savvy American scene with its aggressive performativity. Thanks to Butler, the American idea of sexually designing and redesigning the self became chic in student circles. It is here that the New Historical emphasis on the self-made man (an American cliché that the folks at *Representations* dressed up to look like something else), the postcolonial emphasis on subjected and subjecting subjects (a Marxist mainstay), and a countercultural ideology of free sex (the banality of sex any way you like it) converged in a supposedly critical understanding of the sex/gender dualism. In fact, that dualism, like all the typical dualisms commonplace to contemporary criticism, is but a vicious logic that cannot determine what comes first, your sexuality or your gender, and therefore quits the scene in the indecision of nonperformativity.

DECONSTRUCTION OF THE SOCIAL RELATION I: HEIDEGGER AND SEX

Given some of the previous sections, it would appear that Derridean decon-struction has been eclipsed, since it appears to have little, if anything, to do with social and cultural study. But consider Greenblatt, McClintock, and Butler yet once more. As in the case of Foucault, they position the concept of the social subject at a place where it will always be encountered as a conflict of certain interpretations of subjecthood. As Deleuze put it in his book, *Foucault* (1986), "What can I do, What do I know?, and Who am I?" are the three questions used to stabilize and position the Foucauldian subject.[172] Unlike Greenblatt and McClintock, Butler even orients her analysis on a subject that is, in essence, none other than herself, a lesbian female subject who performs gender against the grain of "enforced heterosexuality" by asking Foucault's "What can I do, What do I know, and Who am I?" Indeed, Anglo-American women's studies has been largely fated to a logocentric conception of the so-cial relation insofar as it is necessarily oriented in terms of a doing, knowing, and being that requires the positing of a subject to whom the woman ques-tion can be posed: What can woman do, What can woman know, and What is woman? Hence feminists and, by extension, queer theorists negotiate ques-tions of sex and gender from fixed rhetorical positions. Critics whose sexual or racial social identities are essential to their thought "situate" them in a way that is quite restricted, compared to someone such as Derrida.

Consider, for example, that in *The Post Card* we're not sure whether Derrida is gay or straight, or, if one prefers, whether the text is gay or straight. Hence "situatedness" is refused. In *The Ear of the Other* (1982) we are given a forceful account of how Nietzsche's ear concerns the way in which future readers will "listen" to Nietzsche's voice in order to hear what he heard when he read his precursors. With whose ears are they listening? Again, the situat-edness or positionality of this relation is not at all determinate. In fact, the so-cial relation that comes of it can be monstrous, as in the case of National So-cialism's appropriation of Nietzsche. In *Of Spirit* (1987) Derrida showed how Heidegger's acceptance and rejection of the word *Geist* had a lengthy history spanning several decades and that the history of his vacillations comprised a certain social relation whose situatedness is unstable and yet not entirely in-determinate either. Derrida's situatedness with respect to Heidegger is also un-stable. Is Derrida of Heidegger's ilk or not? Does Derrida approve of Heideg-ger or not? This is rather unclear because Derrida does not practice "splitting" in the Kleinian sense: turning all relations into relations of friend and foe. There is a similar problem with the social relation that comprises the friend in *The Politics of Friendship* (1994). One's relationship to one's friend or enemy cannot be stabilized or concretely positioned; therefore, the whole question of what a relation is finds itself in a quandary.

Even more to the point, Derrida's resituation of the social relation in terms of, say, Nietzsche's ear, Derrida's letters, or Heidegger's spirit changes the parameters of even these highly unstable situations to such an extent that one cannot think in terms of a centered problematic, let alone situationism. This is most carefully worked out in *Given Time I: Counterfeit Money* (1991) in which the relation between beggar and bourgeois is entirely evacuated of reliable frameworks, and hence its relevance as social relation is called to account. In this, Derrida differs not only from Butler and Anglo-American feminisms but also from the social-studies texts published in Grossberg, Nelson, and Treichler's *Cultural Studies*, where the pragmatic tripartite question of "What can I do, What do I know, and What am I?" is positioned as a self-evident centering point of orientation.

In considering Derrida's interest in the social relation, it should occur to us that he has purposely tried to analyze such a relation before it gets concretized or positioned in the way Marx imagines in *The Grundrisse*. To put this another way, Derrida does to the social relation what Heidegger did to the concept of the human subject: he steps back to look at those forestructures that precede the reified articulation of such an entity. Seen from this perspective, the social relation is necessarily unsituated or unhinged to a degree that prevents that relation from being entirely fixed, structured, or determined. Derrida's concerns, then, touch on *what comes before the subject*: phenomenologies of social relation such as giving, forgiveness, and promising. Social studies, in contrast, arrives on the scene *after the subject* is already constructed or constituted. This social subject exists in a theoretical space that is rigidly fixed and stands in the way of an onslaught of conflicting views on questions concerning sex/gender identity, none of which can be adequately resolved because of the structural immobility of the subject as a point of theoretical convergence. This, in turn, leads to dichotomization: heterosexual versus homosexual, essentialist versus antiessentialist, sex versus gender, agency versus absence of agency, masochism versus sadism, subjection versus subversion. Structurally, then, such a social subject is akin to Lacan's *point de capiton*, a button that holds the fabric of a politicized discourse together by keeping the antagonisms in tension. In Butler, the fixity of this *point de capiton* displays itself in *Bodies That Matter* (1993), when Nella Larson is structurally positioned in such a way that her subversion of racial identity is entirely congruent with Butler's subversion of sexual identity. Larson is forced to conform to a preexisting structural position that determines her relation as a speaking subject in advance to the tripartite question, "What can I do, What do I know, and What am I?" It is precisely this sort of positionality that Derrida wishes to challenge in ways that go beyond a mere multiplication of the subject in terms of various perspectives that operate under a rubric such as subject-positions.

In "Différence sexuelle, différence ontologique" (1986) Derrida rethinks questions of sexuality and gender. Derrida's seemingly inauspicious starting place is Martin Heidegger's silence in *Being and Time*, his not asking the question of sexual difference when he posed the question of ontological difference. Although this may not seem to be a fruitful place to begin a full-scale analysis of sex and gender, Derrida will show that, in fact, Heidegger's writings are an important source for troubling this ground.

    FIRST MOMENT.   Typical of philosophers in general, Heidegger took the position that sexual difference was irrelevant to the meaning of being and that it had no value or significance as an ontical predicate. Hence *Dasein* has no sex. "The discourse on sexuality would be thus abandoned to the sciences or philosophies of life, to anthropology, to sociology, to biology, perhaps even to religion or ethics."[173] According to Derrida, Heidegger purposely refused the modernist view that all sexuality is political and all politics is sexuality. Heidegger does so because *he refuses to objectify the social relation of Dasein in terms of an identitarianism* that asks itself over and over again, "What can I do, What do I know, and What am I?" Derrida puts the matter this way: by making Dasein neutral, Heidegger eliminated all anthropological, ethical, or metaphysical predeterminations that would lead to "une sorte de rapport à soi," a relation to self of the "What can I do? What do I know? and What am I?" kind.

    SECOND MOMENT.   Heidegger nevertheless admits that Dasein is characterized by a *Geschlechtslosigkeit*, an asexuality. Derrida sees this social relation as marked in the very place where such a relation is being eliminated in advance, since it implicitly appears to know something about sexual difference, given that Heidegger is saying *Geschlechtslosigkeit* is not a part of either of the two presupposed sexes—"keines von beiden Geschlechtern ist." Hence asexuality or nonsexuality is actually derived from sexual difference, which is a difference that is more fundamental and primary. Oddly, even if Dasein isn't reducible to human being, self, consciousness, unconsciousness, subject, or individual, a relation of sexual difference still precedes it, a relation that cannot be entirely stripped of its social significance as *the* fundamental relation to being (i.e., human reproduction).

Heidegger's discussion occurs in *The Metaphysical Foundations of Logic* (1928) in which *Being and Time* is at issue. There Heidegger writes that the neutrality of the term "Dasein" "also indicates that Dasein is neither of the two sexes [*beiden Geschlechtern*]. But here sexlessness [*Geschlechtslosigkeit*] is not the indifference of an empty void, the weak negativity of an indifferent ontic nothing." This neutrality, Heidegger says, is "not the voidness of an abstraction, but precisely the potency of the *origin*, which bears in itself the intrinsic possibility of every concrete factual humanity."[174] Hence in place of imagining a neutered, sexless, or impotent Dasein, Heidegger thinks of Dasein as "the intrinsic possibility for being factically dispersed into bodiliness and thus into sexuality." Again, Dasein is the "not yet of factical dispersion [*Zerstreutheit*]," something that the translators could have translated as "ejaculation." Derrida dryly remarks: "If, as such, Dasein doesn't belong to any of the two sexes, that doesn't mean that the being that it is is deprived of sex(uality)."[175] We must therefore imagine a "pre-differential sexuality" or a "pre-dual" sexuality that does not imply a unitary, homogeneous, or undifferentiated sexuality.

THIRD MOMENT.   The preceding argument concludes that Dasein really has a double origin that is neutral, on the one hand, and sexed, on the other hand. Heidegger brings these two incompatible origins together when he thinks about the "multiplication present in every factically individuated Dasein," for multiplication implies reproduction (as in sexual reproduction), and multiplication also implies a negation or destruction associated with dispersion (or multiplicity in dissemination). It is in this sense that Dasein's essence, in fact, "already contains a primordial bestrewal [*Streuung*]," which Heidegger also calls a *Zerstreuung*, or dissemination. Indeed, this is an elaboration of the thematic of Dasein's thrownness in *Being and Time*. Dasein as the "free projection of Being-constitution" concerns thrownness as a transcendence of Dasein itself, except that now this thrownness has (1) sexual connotations (thrownness, dissemination, dispersion, ejaculation, multiplication) as well as (2) unsexed destructive connotations (break up, dispersion, ruination). When Heidegger discusses the "thrown dissemination of Dasein" as "being-with," the nimbus of a sexual relation becomes even more noticeable, even though "being-with" is also to be seen as a neutralization or negation of sexuality, given that "being-with" is a Platonic (i.e., nonsexual) relation.

FOURTH MOMENT.   Instead of positing a subject upon whom sex and gender will be ascribed—whether the subject as agency is there before the assignation or merely there as an aftereffect of its occurrence doesn't matter—Derrida considers the social relation at a point when *it is as yet an unincorporated and unassimilated connection*, one that cannot be logically integrated into a given situation or structure. Social studies, to the contrary, takes sexuality as a given that, however mysterious one wants to make it, is nevertheless apprehensible in the world as a social fact that can be studied if for no other reason than that it is logically incorporated or bound into human culture and its political operations. In contrast, Derrida is detaching the social relation from a concretized social sphere in order to investigate something other than structural meanings imposed upon the social relation by a cultural system.

No doubt, Heidegger's use of the word "*Geschlecht*" is culturally overdetermined by the fact that this is a colloquial word which is not used by biologists or medical doctors. Which is to say, we can find structural meaning (ideological motivation, cultural precedent, political allegiance) should we wish, something that Derrida does not wish to suppress. After all, it is here that one has to begin thinking of the political associations between sex, race, tribe, kin, kind, genre and how these are to be determined as social relations. Key, however, is that the analysis does not stall at this level of social understanding. Instead, Derrida wants to find out whether there is a social relation *prior* to society as such, where we might locate it, and why it cannot be suppressed. Heidegger, like philosophers before him, wants to neutralize sexual difference in order to embrace universality or commonality, a social norm in and of itself predicated upon asociality, apoliticality, and so on. Given that this strategy is privative, the specter of sexual difference and social relatedness always precedes the coming about of commonality and neutrality. To prohibit this, Heidegger starts to invent a new sexuality for which we have no name or model, a sexuality that is, in essence, the thrownness or scattering of difference. In English, the term "ejaculation" quickly reveals a sexuality close in proximity to this third unprecedented sexuality, though it has to be remembered that thrownness could just as easily refer to female reproduction in terms of giving birth: the laborious throwing of being into the world. Because Heidegger's third sexuality is one that always already arrives before the advent of sexual difference between male and female, it knows no gender. The third sexuality, therefore, is a sexuality without gender. But is it also a sexuality without society, which is to say, an asocial sexuality? Is this new sexuality one that exists outside of the social altogether? As thrownness, this third sexuality still carries the essential trait of the social insofar as thrownness is difference and chance, the chance of being as *Mit-Sein*. That is, already in this chance, the social is posited as a being-alongside or being-with that is predicated on thrownness and difference. Dasein, in this sense, is as yet de-limited, and its sexuality is therefore unfettered and therefore stronger and more powerful than that of a social subject restricted by kind, say, a body politic.

FIFTH MOMENT.   Dasein's sexuality is therefore inherently *different* than a sexuality bounded by gender or kind (say, sexual orientation), even if they both have difference in common. The difficulty, of course, is that here the term "*différance*" isn't identical to itself, since the difference of *Geschlecht* is polarized (i.e., male/female), while the difference of Dasein's thrownness is scattered, disseminated, dispersed. That is, the one understanding of difference is characterized by *dualism*, whereas the other understanding of difference is characterized by *multiplicity* and, it has to be said, *diversity*. Indeed, given that he is such a politically conservative thinker, it is odd to think that Heidegger, of all people, should have stumbled upon an understanding of diversity that is predicated on the elimination of prejudice: the a priori imposition of formal kinds upon social relatedness—gender, race, and ethnicity, among them. Yet Heidegger's invention of a third sexuality is largely about the dismantling of *Geschlecht* for the sake of an understanding of Being-as-Diversity understood as the scattering of difference.

Of importance with respect to social studies, is that, as Barbara Johnson once noticed, this kind of exploration requires us to think of the subject in terms of multiple frames of reference. One has to keep the sexed social subject in mind even as one entertains an *other* understanding of difference that precedes it, which I have termed *Being-in-Diversity*. That the sexed social subject is this Dasein as a Being-in-Diversity is always already in place and, hence, is not to be considered a social construction, cultural option, or "lifestyle." That is, Being-in-Diversity is always ontologically pre-given as an arche-trace that accompanies sexual difference as polarized difference (male/female, homosexuality/heterosexuality). Diversity is not in essence political, even if politics can be a social site where diversity becomes a social issue. Hence diversity is less negotiable and socially constructable than one might assume in the name of social engineering, since our very thrownness into the world as beings entails diversity. At moments like this, of course, we can see how far aspects of Heidegger's philosophy could stray from political thinking that was caught up in the most reductive and rigid understandings of *Geschlecht* as kind.

DECONSTRUCTION OF THE SOCIAL RELATION II: DERRIDA'S ITINERARIES

Derrida has been fortunate insofar as he has had many excellent and dedicated translators, among them, Gayatri Spivak, Barbara Johnson, Alan Bass, Peggy Kamuf, Geoffrey Bennington, John Leavey Jr., Richard Rand, Elizabeth Weber, Ned Lukacher, and Barbara Harlow. In addition, there have been a number of prominent books in English on Derrida, including: Geoffrey Hartman, *Saving the Text* (1981); Rodolphe Gasché, *The Tain of the Mirror* (1986); Gregory Ulmer, *Applied Grammatology* (1985); Christopher Norris, *Jacques Derrida* (1987); Geoffrey Bennington, *Jacques Derrida* (1991); Richard Beardsworth, *Derrida and the Political* (1996); John Caputo, *The Prayers and Tears of Jacques Derrida* (1997); Simon Critchley, *Ethics, Politics, Subjectivity* (1999); and Marian Hobson, *Jacques Derrida, Opening Lines* (1999). To varying degrees such studies have emphasized Derrida as transgressive stylist, philosopher, and ethicist. Bennington's overview of Derrida's work, apparently published with Derrida's approval, divides Derrida's writings into topics: supplementarity, undecidability, the signature, singularity, and so on. The result is a formal approach to Derrida that breaks his writings up into major conceptual discoveries that, like Freud's uncovering of the unconscious or Heidegger's disclosures of Being, should not be ignored by anyone who engages in certain kinds of analytical work within the humanities. This approach is taken up by Hobson, as well, and is repeated in *La Contre-Allée* (1999), a collaborative text by Catherine Malabou and Jacques Derrida that is rather more successful than other books in this mode, since it contains well-selected short extracts by Derrida on a more varied menu of topics like khora, the cape, the post, destruction of the archive, aporia, catastrophe, schibboleth, Heidegger's concealment of Being, and so on. Whereas studies written by Anglo-American critics often attempt to position Derrida's works in terms of a more or less structured or focused project, *La Contre-Allée* stresses vagrancy, drift, and a criss-crossing of interests and conceptual modes, hence the subtitle of the series in which this book appears: "Voyager avec Jacques Derrida."[176]

It is useful to recall that the early reception of Derrida in England and America was largely framed within the context of literary theory and that emphasis fell upon Derrida's understanding of *écriture*. This was reinforced by Gayatri Chakravorty Spivak's preface to *Of Grammatology*. However, texts such as *Of Grammatology* were also very concerned with the question of social relations, something that almost entirely escaped everyone's attention. In contradicting Derrida's impetus to think of his own work as an archipelago, I will also stress a certain coherence in his work that cuts across much of his writing, namely, an implicit and explicit critique of the social relation that fits into the philosophical context developed in recent years by Jean-Luc Nancy and Philippe Lacoue-Labarthe, who have stressed the relation/nonrelation of what one might call "Being-in-the-Social."

For now, consider that in *Of Grammatology* Derrida focused on Rousseau's *On The Origin of Language*, whose thesis was that verbal communication is fundamentally the result of a sexual attraction between men and women that is foundational to the existence of society *as we know it*, which is to say, a society that is founded upon differences of kind. In looking back at *Of Grammatology*, it is instructive to see just how much of contemporary cultural study was actually foreshadowed in that text. Why, for example, was Derrida interested in Rousseau's belief that there were once "families, but there were no nations; there were domestic languages, but there were no popular ones. There were marriages, but there was no love at all. [. . .] Instinct held the place of passion."[177] Was Derrida's concern not fundamentally one with the social and the political? Rousseau argued that with increased familiarity and the capacity to feel the refinements of pleasure in place of instinctual satisfaction of needs, desire was born—and with it, the inclination to converse. This transition from need to desire, in Rousseau's view, comprises the true beginning of sociality and of society. Sexual difference, desire, and language are the basis for the articulation of a *social* relation as opposed to relations of brute force and blind will. Whereas blind will is just a matter of force, the social relation is inherently political, because difference, desire, and language are formally negotiated by groups as well as individuals. In fact, language is the formal negotiation of desire and difference. Rousseau's entire account is based on the presupposition that *speech* is at the origin of communication and sociality, since it is in the presence of speech that the social relation is founded. Oddly, Rousseau never asks why speech supplements brute force, that is, why brute force was never enough to satisfy human relations. And he never posits the question of why a politics of negotiation comes to take the place of blind will. Instead, Rousseau formalizes the presupposition that a binary distinction between need and passion is axiomatic as the frame of reference for explaining the origin of language. "Once languages are constituted," Derrida writes, "the polarity need/passion, and the entire supplementary structure, remain operative within each linguistic system: languages are more or less close to pure passion, that is to say more or less distant from pure need, more or less close to pure language or pure nonlanguage."[178] Moreover, given that Rousseau divides languages geographically into Northern languages inclining more to need and Southern languages inclining more to passion, he introduces the political as a function of geographical differences. It is in terms of this prejudicial theory of geographical differences that Rousseau situates what already by Stendhal's time would be national characteristics and identities that inflect what Rousseau considers the presence of living speech. Long before Edward Said published *Orientalism* (1978), Derrida was wondering about how the geopolitical is inflected by metaphysical presuppositions that have given rise to ideological prejudices of a political nature.

Then, too, Derrida wrote at length on auto-affection in Rousseau's *Confessions* by demonstrating that self-reflexivity cannot escape the phenomenon of supplementation, particularly in the context of writing, which is, of course, essential to Rousseau's self-directed reflections. By a certain absence, writing restores a presence "disappointed of itself in speech. To write is indeed the only way of keeping or recapturing speech since speech denies itself as it gives itself."[179] Rousseau's problem is that he can only have a relation to himself by way of this inauthentic detour through writing. "Thus an economy of signs is organized. It will be equally disappointing, closer yet to the very essence and to the necessity of disappointment." That this economy of signs establishes a social relation by means of putting Rousseau in contact within himself occurs by means of authorship, Rousseau's relation to others, his society, in other words, as that which is not authentically him. "The act of writing would be essentially—and here in an exemplary fashion—the greatest sacrifice aiming at the greatest symbolic reappropriation of presence."[180] The difference between speaking and writing, then, is fundamental to the question of recapturing presence as the self that one is, a recapturing that is frustrated, because mediated, by this difference. In Derrida's famous section on supplementarity, he connects this question of the differential of self-relatedness to the "uniting and dividing" of Rousseau's "proper name." In short, the question of difference immediately concerns the name, "Jean-Jacques Rousseau," as a social relation that abstracts itself from the person, Rousseau. Whereas Louis Althusser at around this time was developing his concept of interpellation and Lacan had published his seminar on the *Che Voi*—both based on the creation of a social relation based on the presence of speech (the "What do you want?" or "Hey! You!")—Derrida was exploring the resistance of the name to such hailing and its refusal, as writing, to be called up in the way Althusser and Lacan imagined. Here, again, Derrida critiques a conception of social relation that is founded on a metaphysics of presence.

In *Writing and Difference* (1967) Derrida undertook yet another different approach to the question of social relation when he wrote at length about an obscure philosopher at the time, Emmanuel Lévinas. The opening to "Violence and Metaphysics" (1962) specifically asks what a philosophical community is and notes that such a community is both one of decision (identity, authority, presence) and questioning (asking the unanswerable, differing with, putting into doubt). A community of the question would be precisely a community that would expect philosophy to open itself to nonphilosophy or, at the very least, to a thinking that lies outside of philosophy's known borders and its disciplinary decisions. A community of the question suggests that philosophy still would have a future, a philosophy to come that would arrive by way of a response to what was asked. The community of the question is, strictly speaking, not within the community that has negotiated and ratified its decisions. This is why Lévinas's questioning is not and cannot be a part of philosophy, even as it requires philosophy to be held accountable and to respond. But if this is so, what kind of social relation are we talking about?

> If the messianic eschatology from which Lévinas draws inspiration seeks neither to assimilate itself into what is called a philosophical truism, nor even to "complete" philosophical truisms, nevertheless it is developed in its discourse neither as a theology, nor as a Jewish mysticism (it can even be understood as the trial of theology and mysticism); neither as a dogmatics, nor as a religion, nor as a morality. In the last analysis it never

bases its authority on Hebraic theses or texts. It seeks to be understood from within a *recourse to experience itself*. Experience itself and that which is most irreducible within experience: the passage and departure toward the other; the other itself as what is most irreducibly other within it: Others.

Derrida calls this messianic eschatology a "hollow space" and an "opening," since it has no category or totality. Such a space is "everything within experience which can no longer be described by traditional concepts, and which resists every philosopheme."[181] Here Derrida is at the opposite end of what anyone might suppose to be a social relation. Yet, for Derrida this irreducibility of the other for which we have no philosopheme—e.g., social relation—is the very essence of what, after Lévinas, Derrida will call obligation and responsibility, two terms which pertain to the social and the political. Starting in the mid-'80s, Derrida increasingly turns to an elaboration of what one might call a negative theology of the social relation that questions philosophemes such as hospitality, forgiveness, the gift, the promise, the secret, and testimony. Already in the 1960s, Derrida had been theorizing Otherness as a question that puts the social relation as we know it into default. This differs substantially from social studies, which invokes the Other in order to reinforce a commonplace understanding of the social relation that is predicated on the opposition of tolerance/hostility: receptivity to versus rejection of others.

In *Glas* (1974) the problematics of auto-affection, social relation, and the proper name were redeployed in the context of reading Jean Genet, whereas problematics relating to the family, to religion, and to collective identity were deployed in the context of reading G. W. F. Hegel. *Glas* is perhaps Derrida's most ambitious text and certainly pathbreaking in its understanding of the social relation as sexual relation. Long before the arrival of queer theory, Derrida elaborated a complex account of sexual orientations that deconstructed the philosophical preconditions of identity and difference that underscored the category distinction between the homo and the hetero. In Hegel's writings on the family, the people, and the state, it is already clear that there is a difference-identity problem, given that the family is structured around fairly absolute differences, and sexual differences in particular. How is a relation based on such differences? What relates? Consider that in Hegel the transition from family to *Volk* can only occur by way of a self-destructive moment. "The family, through marriage, possession, and education, annihilates or relieves itself, 'sacrifices' itself," Hegel says. "And consequently, in the course of a struggle for recognition, the family loses and reflects itself in another consciousness: the people. The family exists in the people only 'relieved' (*aufgehobene*), destroyed, preserved, debased, degraded, raised."[182] In Hegel, apparently, social relations are themselves at odds when one moves from smaller to larger social units, say, from the family to the people. That is, the *relation* has to undergo *Aufhebung*: destruction, transformation, and recovery. Derrida will show that *Aufhebung* is, in fact, a very complex variation of auto-affection, since the history of consciousness's development in its passage from individual to collective social relations is nothing other than "being's return to self," that is, to that essence which one always already was since the very beginning of things.

To the contrary, in Genet the proliferation of identities redoubling upon themselves forecloses the differentiatedness of the Hegelian social order. When Genet names something, the gap between the name and the thing is swallowed up: "Magnified, the recipient [of the name] becomes somewhat the thing of the one who names or surnames him, above all if this is done with the name of a thing." When Genet calls someone "Mimosa," he "arraigns" that person, makes that person a part of himself in a way that leaves the other no freedom, no separate identity, no self. In so doing, the other is deprived of *his own* name and is, in Derrida's word, "decapitalized."

> When Genet gives his characters proper names, kinds of singularities that are capitalized common nouns, what is he doing? What does he give us to read beneath the visible cicatrix of a decapitalization that is forever threatening to open up again. If he calls Mimosa, Querelle, Divine, Green-Eyes, Culafroy, Our-Lady-of-the-Flowers, Divers, and so on, does he violently uproot social identity, a right to absolute proprietorship? Is that the most effective operation, the most significant revolutionary practice?[183]

Genet strips the other of his family name and gives him a common noun in its place that repeats by way of a displacement the name Genet (a common noun). Yet, if difference is negated, Derrida argues that it is accompanied by the production of a singularity that cannot be socially identified and exists, therefore, outside of any social relation. But if that is the case, isn't singularity also an otherness that begins to suggest itself as absolute difference? In both

Hegel and Genet, something irreducible falls outside of the social relation, which then becomes the precondition without which a relation of some sort could not be established—no homosexuality without difference, no hetero-sexuality without identity.

By the time Derrida wrote *The Post Card* (1980), he had already made some very significant incursions into speech act theory, given that speech acts, like performative and illocutionary speech acts, are constitutive of social relations. In "Limited Inc." Derrida demonstrated with hilarious effect the inadequacy of speech act theory to account for a social relation—i.e., prop-erty ownership—as simple as a copyright. What Derrida shows, in his metic-ulous humiliation of John R. Searle, is that the correlation of speech acts to social relations are not as logically straightforward as some would have us be-lieve. In *The Post Card* itself, the issue of auto-affection is raised with respect to Derrida's own autobiographical texts, and emphasis now falls on the ques-tion of *destin-errancies*, the misrouting or unexpected deviation of messages that are posted or telecommunicated. In a lengthy critique of Jacques Lacan, Derrida argues that the social relation, as Lacan articulates it in his "Seminar on the Purloined Letter" from *Ecrits*, is, for all its sophistication, logocentri-cally constructed from the point of view of the letter's circular trajectory wherein a letter always reaches its proper destination. Derrida demonstrates that even in Lacan the letter can be misrouted, if not lost, and that Lacan has overplayed his hand on account of putting too much faith in the structural-ist view that one's identity is structurally determined by social practices of ex-change. Social relations would be structurally determined in this way were it not for the fact that the object of exchange experiences destin-errancies. In other words, the structure upon which a social relation depends is dysfunc-tional and therefore cannot, in fact, account for the social relation. Again, in a dazzling reading of Freud, Derrida shows how the legacy of Freud's thought is a social relation that is retroactively constituted by Freud's heirs. In *Archive Fever* (1995) Derrida will develop this thematic from the perspective of the Freud archives in London.

We have already seen the significance of Derrida's interest in Heidegger's remarks on *Geschlecht* that were made in the late 1920s as an addendum to his remarks on Dasein in *Being and Time*. Also, in the late 1980s Derrida turned his attention to Heidegger's strategic censoring and mentioning of the highly charged metaphysical expression "*Geist*," since invoking or suppressing the term has significance in terms of acknowledging a political relation that Heidegger both admits and disavows. The politics of invoking or suppressing *Geist* provides insight into what may or may not have constituted a social relation for Heidegger, since the term is a kind of password. It is here that Derrida's *Of Spirit* (1989) finds its companion essay in the small book entitled *Schibboleth* (1986), which considers the poems of Paul Celan.

By 1990 Derrida was writing about phantom social relations in the book *Specters of Marx*: "[Deconstruction] does not deprive itself of the means with which to take into account, or to render an account of, the effects of ghosts, of simulacra, of 'synthetic images.' . . ."[184] Derrida's analysis considers an "essential lack of specificity" that is part and parcel of what we call "history" and through which a certain indeterminacy gives rise to *Unfug*, a temporal mischief or unhinging that characterizes a time-out-of-joint. It is through unspecificity that the *future* comes about as a "whatever may be the case concerning x." Through unspecificity, the *past returns* as a reappropriation of "whatever may have been the case concerning x." Unspecificity—say, the condition of East Germans after the fall of the Berlin Wall—gave rise to emancipatory promises of the future accompanied by ghosts of the past: hence, Neo-Nazism in Saxony, Brandenberg, and other German provinces. Derrida calls these sorts of phenomena "conjuries," whose effect is to form an alliance around the specter. The dead, having supposedly lived in a more specific or determinate time, can be conjured to deliver the present out of its historical doldrum, to foster and support a social alliance (for example, a *Volksgemeinschaft*) that looks to a future-anterior for vindication of its will to power. Here, of course, *Specters of Marx* serves as a manual on group psychology as well as on what constitutes a social/political relation. That an inoperative community of the dead has a certain spectral leverage upon the future of the living (as repetition of the past) is an illusory retroactive understanding by the living of how absence begets presence. However, the social psychology of this illusion is itself a mode of historical production that at times may well be the determining force in a particular society that privileges spectral avatars over everything else.

With respect to deconstruction, Derrida has written in *Specters of Marx* that it can be limited to certain traits,

for example, of what is called deconstruction, in the figure that it initially took over the course of these last decades, namely the deconstruction of the metaphysics of the "proper," of logocentrism, linguisticism, phonologism, the demystification or the de-sedimentation of the auto-nomic hegemony of language (a deconstruction in the course of which is elaborated another concept of the text or the trace, of their originary technization, of iterability, of the prosthetic supplement, but also of the proper and of what was given the name exappropriation). Such a de-construction would have been impossible and unthinkable in a pre-Marxist space. Deconstruction has never had any sense or interest, in my view at least, except as a radicalization, which is to say also *in the tradition* of a certain Marxism, in a certain *spirit of Marxism*.[185]

From the perspective of much social and cultural analysis, deconstruc-tion has been problematic in the eyes of many, because it supposedly lacks the revolutionary character of an analytic that can engage the question of agency without forcing it to take a detour into quagmires such as language and semi-ology, blunting revolutionary momentum. Derrida himself, however, has been extremely sensitive to the Marxist idea that if one is going to be think-ing in terms of social and political revolution, one has to rethink (1) the con-cept of the social relation and perform a meticulous and multiply articulated deconstruction of it, (2) conceptions of law and jurisprudence in relation to what we call the "social and the political," and (3) not just the overthrow of institutions, but their reinstauration as institutions that have been drastically transformed in ways that do not reinforce the metaphysical assumptions upon which all prior institutions have been uncritically based. Derrida's mode of ac-cess to these issues, of course, has often been linguistic, since it is in the ma-teriality of language that the social relation is socially and formally constitut-ed, though in recent years he has also considered social performativity in terms of processes of exchange, questions of hospitality, the concept of the friend, and so on. Whereas it would be a stretch to say that Derrida is funda-mentally a Marxist thinker—he is actually much more closely allied with fig-ures such as Freud, Heidegger, Blanchot, and Lévinas—he does work in the spirit of Marxism to the extent that Marx critiqued the social relation in ways that his predecessors would not or could not.

During the 1990s, Derrida published essays, some in monograph form, that have explored notions of what he calls "passion." In particular, *Passions* (1993), "Foi et Savoir" (1994), *Adieu à Emmanuel Lévinas* (1996), and *Demeure* (1997) explore the concepts of passion, secrecy, and testimony as performative speech acts that break the usual conceptual horizons of person-to-person relationships and hence their social determinacy. Some of the stakes of Derrida's studies are, in fact, developed by Jean-Luc Nancy who has asked how "the 'social tie' can be conceived in terms of something other than self-sufficiency"?[186] As what is the self-sufficient tie of a social relation given, and what are the performatives that bind this tie? Derrida's concern has been to deconstruct these performatives in order to show that the assumptions we hold about social ties are, in fact, mystifications whose philosophical roots escape notice or mention. Derrida also wonders about how the social is predicated upon a demand that there be a social tie, something that also piqued Rousseau's interest. What is it that demands we think in terms of friends and enemies as the ground upon which we determine our social relation to others?

In *The Politics of Friendship* (1994) Derrida invokes Michel de Montaigne's citation of Aristotle, "Oh my friends, there is no friend" in order to instantiate the paradox of the *faux bond*, the performativity of a social tie whose negation is essential to its instantiation and constitution. This *faux bond* is inverted in the case of Carl Schmitt, a German theorist of politics and jurisprudence, for whom the enemy is foundational for the establishment of a political order. Is one's enemy ever entirely determinate as an enemy? How is the hostility of the enemy something that is present to itself, say, an entity that one can take hold of? Rather, don't we merely encounter the effects of a hostility that has vanished and that cannot be recovered as something present to itself? Isn't that what makes for uncanny experiences when we meet up with enemies who have committed atrocities? The thing that makes people enemies isn't often apprehensible, because it is absent in the place where we know it to have expressed itself. Even when the enemy is being cruel to us, is this cruelty any more understandable or believable? Does it utterly displace kindness, even some bit of charity or friendliness? Alternatively, isn't a characteristic of the true friend that he or she may challenge us in a way that is not friendly and that might well characterize the actions of an enemy? Consider the remonstrations of the teacher, the probation officer, or the drill sergeant. Aren't they both friendly and hostile? Are they not related essentially to Montaigne's paradox, "Oh my friends, there is no friend"? In general, Derrida wonders to what extent all social ties are bound/unbound by binary distinctions. To what extent is this tie predicated on processes of exchange: giving/not giving, touching/avoiding? What is "singular" in this relation that cannot be anything other than absolute or incommensurable? Such inquiries are quite striking, since they go far beyond generally accepted assumptions of the social that are often taken for granted by social-studies critics.

DERRIDA AND THE POLITICAL

In "Ontology and Equivocation: Derrida's Politics of Sexual Difference" (1995) Elizabeth Grosz points out that Derrida has had a rough political reception in America, because he "does not offer any political solutions for either feminism or any other politics. This has tended to evoke suspicion." She notes that if Derrida is only going to show the "complex and paradoxical nature of any political commitment," academics "commonly and naïvely assume that his work is nonpolitical, apolitical, or, worst of all, allied with the forces of conservatism or even fascism." Grosz is one of the few feminist critics to have openly acknowledged that "what is usually not recognized is that his [Derrida's] work has the effect of rethinking entirely the ways in which politics and theory have been considered." Grosz has noticed that Derrida's complication of the political has interfered with those who "seek to be reassured of the rightness of their positions," who "seek to be sure that, in all contexts and in all situations, they have a position that remains on the 'right' side." She concludes that this moralist political bifurcation is really an attempt to "end politics, to stop contestation, to have an answer which admits of no complications and ramifications. To know, to be right." Such political knowing, then, is a strategy of silencing others in the name of bearing the truth of one's political positions, to assert that one's positions are superior to those positions that differ. In acknowledging the aporias of politics, Derrida sets himself up for attack.

> This may explain why those who have pretensions to any political certainty or of having answers for political issues seem so hostile to what deconstruction may offer in rethinking the political. They see Derrida's work as an alternative that competes with their own positions without having anything commensurable to offer by way of political solutions. All he offers are complications, modes of unsettling.[187]

What Grosz does not mention, however, is that preliminary to this unsettling of the political is what we have already seen in terms of a deconstruction of the social relation. In other words, being a philosopher, Derrida wants to re-examine the ground upon which the political is established, hence debunking assumptions of sociality that are not even intuited as being potentially problematic by critics who are entirely ignorant of a myriad of fundamental questions that could and should be asked.

Among the issues to be raised is that of propriation—in particular, self-apprehension, self-knowledge, self-certainty, retrieval of the self as self-same-subject, but, in other contexts, expropriation (refusal, avoidance, dissimulation, etc.), exchanging (giving/getting), and appropriating (garnering, taking hold of, mastering, but also subjecting oneself to something). In *Spurs* (1976), a lengthy essay on the conceptualization of woman in Nietzsche's philosophy, Derrida considered propriation in terms of how "woman" obeys the strictures of a formalized law of identification, while, at the same time, defying it in terms of a propriation (woman as giver/getter, woman as property/nonproperty, woman as im/proper, etc.) that cannot be calculated or formalized, because its logic exceeds any formal or universalizing process of exchange (sexual, economic [doweries, and the like], familial [kinship patterns, aristocratic marriages], or gendered [cultural equivalences between men/women], to name but a few obvious social relations).

In *Glas* (1974) Derrida started to use the word "singularity" to characterize the particularity of what is disappropriated within the general economy of propriation. Judging from how Derrida developed the term in the 1980s, one could retroactively interpret "woman" in *Spurs* as an instantiation of a singularity that cannot be appropriated to itself as a Subject, since by definition it falls outside of any economy of social relations that could establish it as such. However, it is only in the 1990s that the full significance of Derrida's thinking on singularity comes to the fore, as Peggy Kamuf demonstrates in the essay, "Deconstruction and Feminism" (1997):

> We began by asking what it might mean for feminism to affirm the inappropriable subject. One thing is already clear: it could not mean a simple evacuation or negation of the "I" as instance of the inscription of difference. Rather than that of the subject, however, this instance would be that of a singular force of insistence, a singularity. Singularity is not the subject, which, as we have seen, is but the possibility of a repetition. The singular is not repeatable *as such*, but is precisely the impossible presentation of an "as such." The singular remains in excess

of—before or beyond—representation, the difference between the subject and an unpresentable *I*. The latter [singularity] is finite, determined by the singular events of birth and death, whereas the former [the subject] is infinitely or indefinitely repeatable, having no origin nor end other than in that repetition. The notion of the singular cannot, by definition, be accommodated by any generality.[188]

In contextualizing Derrida's thought within the Anglo-American political scene within the humanities, Kamuf observes that the political in academia is always a struggle for appropriation, the appropriation of an other for the sake of movements of liberation, whether these are inspired by the right or the left. When one says, for example, that "the personal is the political," one is attempting to appropriate singularity as subjecthood.[189] When Kamuf feels herself appropriated in this way, she says she feels "expropriated of 'myself,' 'my life,' 'my person' " because whatever is particular to her is typified and claimed by politicos as so much social property to be claimed in the name of some ideological principle or activist cause. In fact, there is an "uncertain limit, by definition highly divisible and unstable, [that] cannot therefore reliably set off the political from the personal; it cannot fix the point at which the freedom of individual choice and the right to be free from political constraint is posed unconditionally."[190] Jean-Paul Sartre would have agreed with this insofar as he, too, insisted upon the singularity of one's otherness, a uniqueness that in his view was our freedom in the face of all interpersonal and political coercions to force us to posit ourselves as subjects who are completely available and vulnerable to others whose motives are hardly innocent. What separates Derrida from Sartre, however, is the undialectical understanding of this singularity, and its detachment from a metaphysics of presence, which already characterizes Derrida's analysis of propriation in Nietzsche.

Since Derrida wrote *Spurs*, Jean-Luc Nancy has developed the idea of singularity in a book that has been quite influential for the later Derrida, *The Inoperative Community* (1986). Inspired mainly by Georges Bataille, Nancy argues that the metaphysics of an ideal community of presence is based upon the impossibility or failure of experiencing its own immanence, which makes this failure within the community its own truest relation. In the inoperative community, what one has are singularities in the finitude of their being as beings that are not generalizable, universalizable, or unifiable in terms of Being.

In other words, Nancy invokes Heidegger's understanding of an inappropriability of being as if that inappropriability were constitutive of finitude and otherness. But what, then, is the relation of these singularities? Derrida's later writings and his meditations on Emmanuel Lévinas are an attempt to work this out.

In America, feminist theoreticians like Drucilla Cornell were quick to make an application of these ideas to questions concerning women and minorities who are seen in terms of their singularity as Others. Cornell's adaptation of French theory starts from the premise that the metaphysics of an ideal community of presence is predicated upon a logic of identity (homogeneity) that presumes social subjects who are politically appropriable or representable within a rationalist model of exchangablility. Such subjects are fully present to themselves, relating to others in the same way that they relate to themselves. Such a community excludes difference and hence those who are not transparent to the whole. Such communities are totalizing, exclusionary, and closed. According to Cornell, who has her sights set on Hegel's understandings of law and community, Derrida disrupts the closure of ideal conceptions of community by introducing terms like "trace," "*différance*," and "supplement" that have the effect of calling the self-presence of the social subject into question.[191] More importantly, perhaps, Cornell recognizes that "the subject as spirit, the substratum of freedom, is detached from the concrete subjectivity of the embodied living human being." Hence there is a "subjugation of the concrete subject in the name of an imposed unity of the individual."[192] Although Cornell doesn't invoke the term "singularity," it is this "concrete subject" that in Nancy and Derrida would fit its description. Given that for Cornell in "the ideal of a universal, transparent, thoroughly rationalized humanity, the society of rational wills carries within it a violent attitude toward the nonconformist who can always be labeled irrational," the notion of singularity would be, precisely, that finite expression of being in which the general and the rational is not necessarily reproduced.[193] Indeed, for Cornell it is the *difference*, or otherness, of the singularity that disrupts the ideal community of identical subjecthood. She also points out that this rupture with the metaphysics of community is consistent with Derrida's interest in Lévinas's face-to-face relation that is nonencompassable by anything like a Hegelian spirit of community, let alone Heidegger's *Miteinandersein* (being-with-others). In place of the interchangeable subject, Lévinas imagines nonsymmetrical relations between singularities (Others). If Cornell's adaptation of Derrida's (and, implicitly, Nancy's) views runs a risk, it is in terms of smuggling the metaphysics of the Subject back into notions of social relatedness by means of appealing to an alterity politics in which the Subject is marked not only as Other, but as an Other with a preestablished social identity: Jewish, gay, Latino, female, and so on. In short, when singularity becomes too closely identified with subalternity, a certain politics of appropriation, as Kamuf describes it, threatens to turn the tables on deconstruction.

No doubt, this is a move that Homi Bhabha has been good at resisting in his very influential *Location of Culture* (1994) in which he handles the question of propriation somewhat differently than Derrida. A close reading of Bhabha will reveal that he considers propriation not only in terms of Derrida's thinking but also in terms of Jean-Paul Sartre's *Being and Nothingness*, which is rather closer to the thought of someone like Frantz Fanon. Sartre was extremely aware that self-appropriation is not possible as such because consciousness exists in a temporality that indicates a constant change in the way the self (as *for-itself*) objectifies itself as an *in-itself*.[194] Bhabha is sensitive to Sartre's realization that self-construction is a tricky affair, because the for-itself and in-itself are never quite coincidental and, in any case, can never be in complete accord, because desire sees to it that we are never entirely satisfied with what we have become. Bhabha also embraces Althusser's understanding of interpellation, which, as Derrida has remarked, is entirely metaphysical in orientation and therefore problematic for deconstruction, as well as Lacan's theories concerning the subject which imagine propriation in very different ways than those outlined by Slavoj Žižek in his many books and articles.[195] Then, too, there are questions of how individuals or groups in non-Western societies understand or practice what Derrida calls "propriation," an issue that Gayatri Spivak took up in "Can the Subaltern Speak?" (1988) when, among other things, she characterized the subaltern woman as a singularity in Derrida's sense without specifically making that connection. For Bhabha himself, various philosophical models of propriation are in play at the same time, which, if I read him correctly, cannot be dissociated from a politics of situatedness in the world. According to Bhabha, one has to be prepared to accept a number of different propriative formations that do not reflect Drucilla Cornell's utopian view that one must set aside a "rational" or "ideal" community for the sake of a better (that is to say, less metaphysical) society to come. In short, our problem is not that a bad form of propriation (the Subject) has taken precedence over a good form of propriation (singularity). Rather our problem is that multiple propriations are at work at the same time and that this multiplicity situates and defines people differently. Central, of course, to Bhabha's concerns is how national or provincial borderlines are part of this politics of propriation and the extent to which borders and singularities are related. Here, we may reencounter the problematic of subject-positions once more, though this time on a more global scale.

Bhabha's work accords with Derrida's remark in a very significant interview, "Eating Well" (1988), that

> The singularity of the "who" is not the individuality of a thing that would be identical to itself; it is not an atom. It is a singularity that dislocates or divides itself in gathering itself together to answer to the other, whose call somehow precedes its own identification with itself, for to this call I can *only* answer, have already answered, even if I think I am answering "no" (I try to explain this elsewhere, notably in *Ulysse Gramophone*). Here, no doubt, begins the link with the larger questions of ethical, juridical, and political responsibility around which the metaphysic of subjectivity is constituted.[196]

Given what we have seen of Derrida's long-term interest in the social relation and his influence on feminists like Elizabeth Grosz, Peggy Kamuf, Drucilla Cornell, if not to say postcolonial critics like Gayatri Spivak and Homi Bhabha, it is hard to accept the repeated cat-calling from various leftist quarters concerning Derrida's supposed apoliticality or his general irrelevance to questions of culture, society, and politics, charges that are factually wrong, given Derrida's well-known political involvements in Europe.Deconstruction is indeed of vital importance to fields such as cultural studies, race studies, and gender studies in that it critiques those very aspects of social studies that require sustained examination and demystification. Without such critique we will see a continuation of retrograde thinking in the service of progressive ideals that can never be realized, given that this thinking is indebted to philosophical assumptions fundamental to the bourgeois subject, which, as Wendy Brown has noted, is, unfortunately, endemic to the countercultural thinking of the vast majority of humanists concerned with social issues.[197]

RECONCEIVING THE THEORY MESS

In "Some Statements and Truisms About Neologisms, Newisms, Postisms, Parasitisms, and Other Small Seismisms" (1990), Derrida implicitly continued some of his thoughts from "Deconstruction in America" and undermined the idea that theory could be thought of as a unified field or discourse, let alone a stable intellectual ground for propping up the humanities generally. Just as Derrida had once rejected the idea of "one" deconstruction, in "Some Statements and Truisms" he came to reject the idea of theory as a discipline with its "tree of theory" and "stabilized tables" (i.e., genealogies), its known entities and proper names, its taxonomic objectivizations and ready-made doxas. He rejected the laying out of theories as if they were "chessboard pieces"—New Criticism, structuralism, postmodernism, post-Marxism, New Historicism, and so on. He rejected theory as a "merry-go-round" with its endless circulation of general approaches: content analysis, formal analysis, aesthetic analysis, psychological analysis, social analysis, ethical analysis, philosophical analysis, and theological analysis. And, most pertinent to us, he absolutely rejected the concept of theory per se as a field within which one could, from some transcendental or panoptical point of view, compare and evaluate all the different critical formations for the sake of bringing them to justice. Here, more than likely, Derrida was implicitly touching bases with critics like Rosi Braidotti, for whom we are in a postphilosophical moment and for whom theory is not a single entity with a single definition.

Derrida's insistence that "theory" cannot be relegated to a univocal field or intellectual discipline means that a phrase like "the theory mess" is highly problematic for the very simple reason that it strongly implies a field or domain that can be determined from some transcendental perspective to be coherent or not. To claim that theory is in a messy state is to claim, first of all, that there is a singular totalizing "state" of theory and that, second, this state is in disarray. Derrida opposes the view that one ought to think in terms of coherence/incoherence, adequacy/inadequacy, validity/nonvalidity, or truth/error. Taking a Wittgensteinian line that Braidotti might also embrace, Derrida says simply that "theory" is whatever people in the languages and literatures are doing that goes under the theory rubric, and that we should not be surprised to see a myriad of transplanted ideas, hybridized models, parasitical genres, and mismatched relays within so called critical discourses. Theory, Derrida says, is by its very nature a "monstrosity" (the term is his) or, as I have been putting it, a "mess," since what makes theoretical writing interesting are precisely those mistaken conceptual transpositions that end up having a rich lineage as they migrate from one critical site to another, somewhat like viruses.

In fact, Derrida will privilege another metaphor of critical development, which is perhaps more significant from my point of view. He advances the idea that theories are like jetties that are thrown out into rough seas for the sake of creating still backwaters.

> For convenience I'll use . . . the word "jetty," in which I distinguish, on the one hand, the force of the movement which throws something or throws itself (*jette* or *se jette*) forward and backwards at the same time, prior to any subject, object, or project, prior to any rejection or abjection, from, on the other hand, its institutional and protective consolidation, which can be compared to the jetty, the pier in a harbor meant to break the waves and maintain low tide for boats at anchor or for swimmers. Of course, these two functions of the jetty are ideally distinct, but in fact they are difficult to dissociate, if not indissociable.[198]

The jetty is yet another metaphor for the undecidable border (others in the past have included the hymen, the fold, the borderline, and the tympanum). The jetty is bifold in that it is, at once, a destabilizing construction that is thrown out ahead of us into a zone where its effects are not quite certain. After all, what will be the ecological effects of constructing a jetty? What disorder does it produce? Despite these questions, the jetty nevertheless stabilizes and produces order in back of itself. This undecidability between order/disorder is significant, because it speaks to the disorder/order that is created by new ideas, which, like jetties, throw themselves into intellectually troubled waters in order to both disrupt and stabilize. The theory mess is but one aspect of theoretical innovation: the destabilizing jetty that throws itself out somewhere and puts things into disarray. But the mess is undecidably a part of a theory order that has the stabilizing effects of calming the waters, which is to say, theoretical delineations, definitions, rules of order, methodological certainties, in short, theory in its most conservative disciplinary sense.

The point is that an intellectual discipline lies behind the breakwater of an initially destabilizing theory. Derrida's undecidable borderline, the jetty, emphasizes that the difference between the avant-garde and the rear-guard is never entirely distinguishable as a dualism, because the two moments are given both at once even as they are to be held separate. It is in this sense that Derrida will come around to defining deconstruction as the jetty with two names: deconstruction *and* deconstructionism. Deconstruction is the destabilizing name that pertains to the view, "deconstruction is neither a theory nor a philosophy. It is neither a school nor a method. It is not even a discourse, nor an act, nor a practice. It is what happns, what is happening today . . ." Deconstructionism "consists in formalizing certain strategic necessities of the deconstructive jetty and in putting forward—thanks to this formalization—a system of technical rules, teachable methodolgical procedures, a discipline, school phenomena, a kind of knowledge, principles, theorems, which are for the most part principles of interpretation and reading (rather than of writing)."[199] To recall an early essay by Derrida, "Force and Signification" (1967), there is an undecidable limit imagined between force and form in which the difference between conserving and exceeding is called into question in order to imagine theory in which conserving and exceeding are not logically determinable according to the law of contradiction. Hence Derrida has dismantled the kind of hermeneutical distinction Paul Ricoeur once made between event and structure, Derrida's point being that meaning (structure) does not occur before the act (of writing) and that only after this act will meaning come about, if it does at all, by way of retroaction. In other words, there will come a historical moment in which force is given signification and event will be given structure.

Derrida's metaphor of the jetty not only characterizes how ideas break two ways and thereby avoid the vicious dualism of order/disorder, but the jetty also can be thought of as a phenomenological horizon. In his posthumous papers on phenomenology, Jan Patočka commented that a horizon is a unity that makes present to us what was never present in and of itself. It does so not as a pure and simple imposition but as a thetic form that is directly linked to what is intuitively given, the two (the thetic and the intuitively given) forming the unity or oneness of this horizon.[200] This unification of the thetic with the intuitively given is what Edmund Husserl called "judgment" and cannot occur in the absence of the intelligibility of what is being given to thought. For Husserl, "judgment" refers to how we come to understand or determine something to be the thing that it is and to grasp our relation to it. With respect to the history of criticism and theory, we have texts that can be objectified only after they are bounded by a horizonal consciousness that is itself not yet thematic but given as an intuition of a limit that circumscribes a field of relations opened up by the thoughts of others. This, I think, could be another way of describing what Derrida calls "the jetty," since a horizon is always thrown out ahead of one's own thought even as it delimits or constitutes a field.

The jetty, then, could be construed as a hermeneutical metaphor for what lies beyond our immediate field of apprehension, something that might require an interpretive leap into troubled waters. Not only that, but intellectual horizons are often the limit at which a judgment comes about, since they are themselves the limit of apprehension. Hans-Georg Gadamer's well-known concept of the "fusion of horizons" speaks to how the horizons of different interpreters' apprehensions come into a temporary agreement in the course of time. However, such horizons are inevitably broken open again as the effects of historical retroaction (the structural changing of our interpretation of the past by means of historical distance produced by the passage of events in time) take place in terms of revivals, revisions, or forgettings of the past that are, in their own ways, also judgments. For Gadamer this infinite conversation in which horizons fuse and break open is called "tradition."[201] What we are currently lacking are attempts by critics working in the area of theory to project horizons within which theoretical formations are critically recapitulated in ways that are intelligibly related and not simply conflicted or at variance in ways that cannot be adjudicated. Despite Derrida's interest in monstrosity, parasitism, and various hybrids, the fact is that he, too, is indebted to a critical (i.e., perceptual, judgmental) horizon by means of which he adjudicates other critiques. For only by situating or orienting himself in terms of deconstruction (or, deconstruction-isms) can he make judgments, such as: "the problematic of the border and of framing . . . is seriously missing in new historicism," and that the New Historicists should address this "in some of the texts called deconstructionist."[202] At such junctures, the states of theory are delimited such that they can be apprehended, situated, and judged. But given that, what horizon could we imagine that would posit itself as the limit of theory in its present state?

If I have invoked a theory mess from the outset, it is because the theory mess itself is a critical (and judgmental) horizon that threads its way through what otherwise might appear to be merely a jumble of critical constructions and viewpoints. Indeed, the idea of there being a mess concerns differences and the possibility/impossibility of their adjudication. That is, the horizon of there being a mess implies not only the threat of chaos but the possibility of a general and synthetic critique. Thus the theoy mess manifests a negativity that concerns the obliteration of any critical horizon of apprehension, a nihilistic moment in which the jetties break in a deluge of conflicting arguments. Indeed, this may even be expressed as an apocalyptic fear with banner headlines like "The End of Literary Study," "The End of Theory," "The End of 'the Profession,'" "The Death of Deconstruction," which, however fantastic, are horizonal insofar as they can be imagined. The fear that such a nihilistic moment within critical theory is already upon us translates into a disgust and hence eclipse of theory, as if theory were always too glaring, too excessive, too conflicted, too new, too difficult, too corrupt, or too ideological. However, the fact that this fear is a *general concern* already means that within the horizon of the theory mess there is something of a convergence or synthesis in which, if only in fantasy, we have come to an agreed upon judgment at the limits of apprehensibility. In other words, even at its most nihilistic and fantastic, the horizon of the theory mess opens up onto something other than pure negation and dissolution.

This is not to say that we will ever achieve the kind of rational comprehensibility and totality that stands opposed to the negativity of dissolution, for that, too, is just as fantastical a horizon for all of the deconstructive reasons given in the past by Derrida and others. Nevertheless, it too will not simply fade away, because whereas the nihilistic moment engenders fear, the totalizing moment engenders utopian hope in the form of holding out the possibility for the resolution of conflicts. These, then, are the imaginary limits of the horizon I have been trying to follow.

Of course, in addressing the theory mess, I have oriented our horizon in such a way that it speaks to the situations of deconstruction, either directly or in terms of a certain avoidance or refusal to articulate. There, too, the nihilistic moment of a suppression or eclipse of deconstruction has come into play, a destruction or erasure that comes to pass in terms of a general avoidance or refusal to read—a general rejection, passing over, or eclipse that leaves an important body of work out of consideration or contention. To prohibit this from happening has been Derrida's struggle, since he has often been put in the situation of having to protect deconstruction from its eclipse or eradication by uncritical critics. Which is to say, that even Derrida is fated to play with this fantastical apocalyptic mentality, as depicted in "Biodegradables" in a parodic aside:

Now we are in an academic casino. Standing behind the gaming table, holding the card of deconstruction (there is only one card, obviously, "Paul de Man's War"), I alone represent "Deconstruction" all gathered into one for this last throw, this last chance. Oh yes, I almost forgot: it must be the last chance, at the last moment, at dawn. And if I lose, the croupiers will declare "Deconstruction" in ruins, bankrupt. Exit "Deconstruction."[203]

Apparently, any direct critical interlocution with Derrida is viewed by his detractors as some kind of all-or-nothing card game in which the moment Derrida makes an argument, the whole enterprise known as "Deconstruction" is being wagered in a winner-take-all gamble. Naïve as it may be, the fantasy of a "showdown" nevertheless speaks to a nihilistic horizon of critical apprehension against which Derrida must defend himself, if not by way of parody or ridicule, then by way of constructing defenses and mounting counterattacks. Here, of course, deconstruction has been forced to submit to an all-or-nothing polemos, that is, to a highly decidable outcome.

Another dimension of that same horizon, however, is the undecidedness of any wager concerning deconstruction, which is to say, the skeptical refusal of a so-called theory gaming commission to side absolutely either for or against deconstruction. Instead of the threat of Derrida's losing all, there is also the threat of his never being able to win a decisive victory, since his wagers will always result in a "maybe so/maybe not" response, given that this is the general horizon of a deadlock that is instrumental to keeping the so-called game open to innumerable wagers and possible players. Indeed, one could go so far as to claim that what the deadlock of undecidedness keeps open is not just critical debate but, far more importantly, *uncritical* debate, such as Derrida's parody describes. If the theory mess could be redefined as the border or horizon line where the critical and the uncritical converge upon the same debates in terms of what is a matter of *faux* bonding, this should not overlook the fact that enabling a place for unphilosophical and uncritical debate is essential to what Derrida metaphorically calls the "game," since those faculty and students within the humanities who refuse to participate in the serious study of theory are still professionally entitled to speak out on it or to "profess," as evidenced in letters to the editors of tabloids like the *Times Literary Supplement* and *The Chronicle of Higher Education*. Critical deadlock, undecidedness, or quarrelling opens the door for the relatively uncritical colleague

to step in with whatever opinion he or she wishes to advance, since, to recall
Ann duCille's point, the game then appears to be an "anybody-can-play pick-
up game" in which everyone has the right to make a wager. Yet, aren't such
uncritical wagers necessary if there is to be fuller participation in the adventure of critical theory? And don't the uncritical arguments provide us with
some critical orientation as well? For example, Derrida's sarcastic parody exposes the naïve apocalyptic fantasy of some American critics who have prided
themselves on their critical sophistication; whereas, duCille's point about a
depricating "anybody-can-play" attitude reveals much about the uncritical op-
portunism, cynicism, and feelings of superiority with which some academics
justify their work, even as it exposes a democratic ideology in which a professor feels empowered to have as much say about a topic as anyone else, re-
gardless of training and competence.

POSTSCRIPT

In Derrida's recent book *Demeure* (1997), one may notice a small "literary supplement," really a broadside in small print, that is not very related to the main
text. A complaint or lament, it is entitled "Reading 'Beyond the Beginning'
or of Venim in Letters" and is a retort that displays considerable annoyance.
Its justification for being included in *Demeure* occurs via a citation of Ernest
Robert Curtius that reminds Derrida of an insult he received in the *Times Literary Supplement* on May 2, 1997 from a certain J. Drake. Apparently, Mr.
Drake took Derrida to task for his use of Curtius in *Of Grammatology*. Other
letters to the editor at around this time reveal a similarly uncharitable view of
Derrida's scholarship, if not just blind hostility. A certain R. Harris circles
back to the topic of Cambridge's *Doctorat honoris causa*, which, in his view,
should be denied the French on nationalist principles, at the very least. In citing the book, *Derrida for Beginners*, Harris says that the worst thing that could
happen is if students were to venture beyond the beginning, because then they
might actually have to take Derrida seriously.[204] In a French translation of this
piece, the editors, based in Montpellier, ran the title, "The Nero of Philosophy." Apparently, for the editors, deconstruction is just a synonym for cultural assassination. Slander, of course, is but an injunction to censor Derrida
by encouraging the public to not read him. Moreover, this slander has been

widely disseminated by the press, as if the public needs to be warned of there being a dangerous philosophy that could have disastrous effects on contemporary society. If such attacks are numerous, Derrida himself continues to be scandalized by the bad faith and ignorance of his attackers. For example, Derrida is outraged that Mr. Drake, on the one hand, accuses Derrida of being an "intellectual charlatan" and, on the other hand, himself confuses Phaedrus and Phaedo in ways that cannot be accidental. Derrida points out, therefore, that if Mr. Drake would read Plato, he might, first of all, learn to tell the difference. And isn't it disturbing, Derrida continues, that such a person not only appoints himself a cultural guardian who is jealously reserving the right to interpret Curtius, a major philologist and historian, but that such a person can even get published by the *Times Literary Supplement*. As to the author of "The Nero of Philosophy," should he not be counseled to "venture beyond the beginning" of a text and open his mind to the ideas of others?

What Derrida is encountering are the residual effects of a theological mentality that can lay direct claim to the thinking of the Middle Ages in which one imagines philosophy as doctrine or dogma rather than as disinterested critical speculation. What lies beneath the hate mail disguised as gentlemanly debate and critique is a certain hysteria concerning what is apprehended as the heresy of contemporary thought, Derrida being cast in the role of chief heretic and blasphemer. This would be merely funny were it not for the fact that the West has never successfully negotiated modernity as a philosophical repudiation of long-held values and beliefs. The sentiment that deconstruction is evil, immoral, dishonest, malicious, or simply the invention of a charlatan is based on the conviction that it is a resurgence of nihilistic twentieth-century thinking that like some Antichrist is opposed to everything holy and good. Such demonization points to the fact that there is still considerable resentment and opposition to the replacement of a Christian humanist worldview by difficult contemporary philosophies that when stripped of their elaborate arguments seem to merely welcome the death of God, meaning, and man. In other words, the philosophical representatives of modernity with which existentialism and deconstruction are both notoriously identified in the minds of many opponents are seen as contemporary negations of traditional religious and ethical values, negations that are spiritually bankrupt because they do not put anything positive in the place of the values they delegitimize. The word "deconstruction" only reinforces the conviction that contemporary philosophy is merely negative and hence spiritually dead.

Jürgen Habermas is right in suggesting that Western societies today have no adequate means for negotiating conflicting systems of belief, a view that, in this case, reflects rather badly on universities that have, among their many functions, a responsibility to provide the kind of institutional space within which major philosophical antagonisms can be worked though rather than sustained by means of pluralist acceptance. By relegating all critical views to mere perspectival or specialized approaches—i.e., the "approach-approach"— universities work against the historical imperative of intellectuals to confront ideological, critical, philosophical, and theological divisions constructively. Whereas one can sympathize with Derrida's annoyance over intellectual nitwits writing absurdities about him in the *TLS*, if not the *TLS*'s willingness to broadcast such idiocies, there is nevertheless the fact that Derrida is fated to suffer these sorts of attacks for the simple reason that his work is part of a modern intellectual formation that has aggressively set itself apart from, if not openly offended, traditions of thinking that modernism has not been able to supplant or even transform.

Although Derrida can "deconstruct," "fissure," or make a text "tremble," he cannot do it without the reader's or listener's cooperation, which is to say, the willingness of a reader or listener to be open to the possibility that a text *can* be deconstructed, and that this deconstruction necessarily requires a transformation of thinking so major that one cannot simply ignore it as just another approach and continue with whatever traditional convictions one happens to have that wouldn't stand up to Derridean critique. It is here that a certain logocentric horizon of analysis betrays deconstruction, however, in that for deconstruction to be persuasive—to be compelling enough to change our minds and affect our practices of theory—a common horizon or limit has to be reached at which one necessarily has to assent that what Derrida has shown impacts on every other theory to some degree, in which case a change in thinking is self-evidently required, *or* that what Derrida has shown is either untrue or inessential and therefore of little significance. Perhaps it is here that "communicative rationality," as Habermas uses the term, is required to adjudicate what I have earlier referred to as a "theory mess," of which deconstruction is inevitably a part. Indeed, as Derrida's own responses to his critics shows, "communicative rationality" is precisely what is missing when certain voices in the *TLS* demonize deconstruction.

I think it is highly significant that as the 1990s came to a close, a major critical theorist like Edward Said had to acknowledge the existence of a theory mess and its harmful effects on the languages and literatures: "All manner of fragmented, jargonized subjects of discussion now flourish in an ahistorical limbo"; we are now experiencing a "new fragmentation" and "an often reckless abandonment of what could be a common intellectual pursuit in favor of highly specialized, exclusivist, and rebarbative approaches that destroy and undercut the historical as well as social bases of the humanities." Said pleads for a return to historical analysis which requires one to put ideas into logical relation and overall perspective, and he asks his colleagues to abandon exclusivist and rebarbative approaches for the sake of commonality or, in Gadamer's terms, dialogue. Like Derrida, Said calls for "a reinforced sense of intellectual responsibility—responsibility to what in fact we ought to do, namely, the interpretation, analysis, and serious consideration of literature in its historical and social environment." This does not necessarily mean the practice of postcolonial criticism for which Said is so well known. In fact, Said isn't sure what is to be gained or lost if literary and humanistic education is given over to issues like "citizens' rights, new legislation, the restructuring of power, the problems of minorities, and so on." Furthermore, Said casts doubt on involving literary study in "a sociopolitical struggle over such issues as identity, gender difference, postcolonial politics, and theoretical innovation for its own sake," particularly if such issues lead away from the teaching of canonical works ("I have always rather severly limited myself to canonical works of the Western tradition").[205]

Not only does Said ask us to return to the classical protocols of critical thinking—plausible interpretion, systematic analysis, and adequate contextual support—but he is also asking us to return to the Western canon that by now everyone has been encouraged to abandon. This call to order is a plea for curricular coherence and a return to disciplinary roots. However, for such a call to order to work, one cannot simply turn back the clock. Indeed, as I have suggested, the order/disorder distinction is itself inherently problematic and hence inadequate for interrogating the history I have described. We need to realize that the past cannot be reduced to a mess or lack of coherence that one could walk away from merely by asserting some virtues—analytical responsibility, among them—or by changing one's habits—analytical practices, textual choices, or ideological convictions. Rather, we have to work through the critical horizons of the immediate past in order to come to some determinations about the value and legitimacy of work that has, for the most part, been only provisionally accepted as valid and significant.

Some would say that one ought to see the critical messiness of our time as a very creative and productive period for the humanities, and, indeed, there is much to be said for this view. Considerable ground breaking has taken place since the early '70s, and it is quite possible that we are not quite yet at the point where we can see the full extent of what these new developments have meant for the liberal arts. In my view, the time has come for attempts to study and adjudicate what has occurred. In looking at the vicissitudes of deconstruction in the context of contemporary criticism, I have sketched out but one complex of relations that reveals a certain logic of the *faux bond* that has characterized much critical thinking in recent years.

Obviously, there is much more work to be done on criticism in the recent past that is just as pressing. Certainly, the best of this work will fall to a generation of scholars as yet to come who will have abandoned the fantasy, which goes back to the German Idealists if not earlier, that a philosophical theory could be advanced in our time that will transform the world. After all, over the past several decades, this Messianic fantasy can be blamed for a hasty impatience with every new critical theory that, once examined closely, fails the unrealistic expectation of an epistemic revolution that will solve all the crises of our times. Indeed, deconstruction has itself fallen under the sign of such a final solution, which is one of the reasons why many of Derrida's contemporaries have been disappointed with him. Once such unrealistic expectations can be set aside, however, I think critics will be better able to take on a careful accounting of critical theories, an accounting that will have to start with the kind of dedication to reading that has not been in evidence in the history that could be called the eclipsing of deconstruction. Hence I am hopeful that with such an accounting in the future will come the kind of responsible and realistic reading that was not often afforded Derrida in his lifetime. In this, however, Derrida would share much with other thinkers like Heidegger or Lacan whose complete works are not even entirely redacted at this time and whose theoretical consequences will not be generally known until some rather distant future. In that sense, my remarks can only be taken as a preliminary report by a theory watcher of the past three decades.

NOTES

PREFACE

1. Gilles Deleuze and Felix Guattari, *A Thousand Plateaus*, trans. Brian Massumi (Minneapolis: University of Minnesota Press, 1987), 7.

2. Jacques Derrida, "Marx & Sons," in *Ghostly Demarcations*, ed. Michael Sprinker (London: Routledge, 1999), 223. Derrida is attacking Spivak's "Ghostwriting," in *Diacritics* 25, no. 2 (Summer 1995).

3. Jacques Derrida, "Three Questions to Hans-Georg Gadamer," in *Dialogue and Deconstruction*, ed. Diane P. Michelfelder and Richard Palmer (Albany: State University of New York Press, 1989).

4. Jacques Derrida, "Afterword: Toward an Ethic of Discussion," in *Limited Inc.* (Evanston: Northwestern University Press, 1988), 150–51.

5. Edward Said, "Restoring Intellectual Coherence," *MLA Newsletter* (Spring 1999), 3.

6. Christopher Fynsk, "Community and the Limits of Theory," in *Community at Loose Ends*, ed. Maimi Theory Collective (Minneapolis: University of Minnesota Press, 1991), 20.

7. Bill Readings, *The University in Ruins* (Cambridge: Harvard University Press, 1996), 126.

8. Ibid., 187.

9. Edmund Husserl speaks of horizons as constant presumptions that aim beyond the immediate object. See *Experience and Judgment* (Evanston: Northwestern University Press, 1973). Horizonality, however, is often situated in terms of the life world. Ludwig Landgrebe's *The Phenomenology of Edmund Husserl* (Ithaca: Cornell University Press, 1981) defines horizonality in Husserl's *First Philosophy* as that which directs or guides acts of consciousness. "This horizon is known to be open in terms of an indeterminate openness, 'without real boundaries and yet bounded and with variable boundaries,' an openness therefore which for the immediate having of the world cannot be designated as the consciousness of either a finite or an infinite openness." (95) (The quote within the citatation is by Husserl.) This horizon also concerns a "world certitude," which is to say, a

horizon of validation that comes to judge the world as something particular. This only comes about through a historical consciousness, that is, a consciousness aware of temporality in its historical dimensions.

10. Harold Bloom, *Shakespeare: The Invention of the Human* (New York: Riverhead, 1999). Helen Vendler, *The Art of Shakespeare's Sonnets* (Cambridge: Harvard University Press, 1997).

INTRODUCTION

1. Ann duCille, "The Occult of True Black Womanhood," in *Female Subjects in Black and White*, eds. Elizabeth Abel, Barbara Christian, Helene Moglen (Berkeley: University of California Press, 1997), 32. (My italics.)

2. John Searle, "Reiterating the Differences: A Reply to Derrida," *Glyph* 2 (1977).

3. Jacques Derrida, *Limited Inc.* (Evanston: Northwestern University Press, [1977] 1988), 35–36.

BEGINNINGS

4. Jacques Derrida, *Points of Suspension* (Stanford: Stanford University Press, 1995), 122.

5. Elizabeth Roudinesco, *Jacques Lacan and Company* (Chicago: Chicago University Press, 1990), 411.

6. *The Structuralist Controversy*, ed. Jose Harari and Richard Macksey (Johns Hopkins University Press, 1966), 171.

7. Jacques Derrida, *Positions* (Chicago: Chicago University Press, 1981), 58

8. Jacques Derrida, *Speech and Phenomena*, ed. Newton Garver, trans. David B. Allison (Evanston: Northwestern University Press, 1973), xix.

9. Ibid., xxii.

10. Ibid., xxxviii.

11. Paul de Man, *Blindness and Insight* (New York: Oxford University Press, 1971), 102–41.

12. Fredric Jameson, *The Prison-House of Language* (Princeton: Princeton University Press, 1972), 14.

13. Ibid., 175.

14. Jonathan Culler, *Structuralist Poetics* (Ithaca: Cornell University Press, 1975), 132–33.

CO-OPTING DECONSTRUCTION

15. E. D. Hirsch, *Validity in Interpretation* (New Haven: Yale University Press, 1967).

16. Derrida, *Points*, 212.

17. Gayatri Chakravorty Spivak, "Translator's Preface," in *Of Grammatology* (Baltimore: Johns Hopkins University Press, 1976). It is important to note that Spivak's translation appeared late in 1976 and that it didn't start to make an impact until some years later. Moreover, it was commonplace for readers to informally comment that Spivak's introduction was unreadable. Certainly, for readers who were familiar with Derrida's sources and writings this was not the case, though such readers were, at that time, a rather small minority. Unfortunately, Spivak made no attempt to ease readers into Derrida's sources and innovations. For example, she began her preface with some abstruse imitative footwork that mirrored Derrida's critique of prefaces that he advanced in *La dissémination* (Paris: Seuil, 1972), which, back in 1976, was still untranslated and hence not known to the vast majority of Spivak's readers. Spivak also didn't prepare her readers for an appreciation of the later Heidegger and his esoteric conceptions of the trace and the erasure of Being. Nor did she condescend to introduce readers to Freud, de Saussure, or Husserl; rather, she assumed familiarity. Last, she attempted to talk about many works written between 1967 and 1975, not just *Of Grammatology*. This was, again, problematic if one imagines that the purpose of her preface should have been to clarify Derrida's book rather than drown it in a welter of very difficult and, at that time, relatively unknown texts, *Glas* (1974), among them.

THEORY AS POSTPHILOSOPHY:
ROSI BRAIDOTTI, GEOFFREY HARTMAN, ANNETTE KOLODNY

18. Rosi Braidotti, *Patterns of Dissonance* (New York: Oxford University Press, 1991), 2.

19. Geoffrey Hartman, *Saving the Text* (Baltimore: Johns Hopkins University Press, 1981), xv.

20. Hartman, *Saving the Text*, 49, 51.

21. Annette Kolodny "Dancing Through the Minefield," in *Feminisms*, ed. Robyn R. Warhol and Diane P. Herndl (New Brunswick: Rutgers University Press, 1997), 184

22. Kolodny, "Dancing Through the Minefield," 172. (My italics.)

23. Ibid., 176.

24. Ibid., 183, 184.

25. "D'un ton apocalyptique adopté naguère en philosophie" in *Les Fins de l'homme* (Paris: Galilée, 1981); *La Carte postale* (Paris: Flammarion, 1980); "Deux mots pour Joyce" in *Ulysse grammophone* (Paris: Galilée, 1987); *Schibboleth* (Paris: Galilée, 1986). "Des tours de Babel," in *Psyché* (Paris: Galilée, 1986). Despite the publication dates, Derrida wrote and delivered these pieces in the early to mid-1980s.

26. Hélène Cixous, *Rootprints* (New York: Routledge, 1997), 31.

THE MISCONSTRUCTION OF DECONSTRUCTION: GERALD GRAFF AND FRANK LENTRICCHIA

27. William H. Pritchard, "The Hermeneutical Mafia or After Strange Gods at Yale," *Hudson Review* 28 (Winter 1975–76). Murray Krieger, *Theory of Criticism* (Baltimore: Johns Hopkins University Press, 1976).

28. Meyer Abrams, *Critical Inquiry* 3 (1977), 431. See also J. Hillis Miller, "Deconstructing the Deconstructor," *Diacritics* 5 (Summer 1975), 30.

29. Abrams, "The Deconstructive Angel," 429.

30. Ibid., 429, 436. Worried about the spread of deconstruction to Yale, Abrams criticized Paul de Man's affinities with Derridean thinking: "Each deconstructive reading . . . reaches . . . the same moment of an aporia," 435.

31. Gerald Graff, *Literature Against Itself* (Chicago: University of Chicago Press, 1979), 179.

32. Ibid., 193.

33. Garver's introduction in *Speech and Phenomena*, xxviii.

34. Graff, 101.

35. Ibid., 116.

36. Ibid., 101.

37. Frank Lentricchia, *After the New Criticism* (Chicago: Chicago University Press, 1980), 227.

38. Ibid., 241.

39. Ibid., 302.

40. Ibid., 209.

41. Ibid., 182.

DEMONIZING DECONSTRUCTION:
WALTER JACKSON BATE, RENÉ WELLEK, AND DAVID LEHMAN

42. Walter Jackson Bate, "The Crisis in English Studies," *Scholarly Publishing: Journal for Authors and Publishers* 14, no. 3 (April, 1983), 209. The article originally appeared in *The Harvard Magazine* in 1982.

43. Ibid., 208.

44. Ibid., 209.

45. Rene Wellek, "Destroying Literary Studies," *The New Criterion*, 2, no. 4 (December, 1983), 3–7.

46. Graff, *Literature Against Itself,* 61–62.

47. David Lehman, "Deconstructing De Man's Life,"*Newsweek*, 15 February 1988, 63–65.

48. Jacques Derrida, "Like the Sound of the Sea Deep Within a Shell: Paul de Man's War," in *Responses to Paul de Man*, eds. Werner Hamacher, Neil Hertz, and Tom Keenan (Lincoln: University of Nebraska Press: 1988).

49. Terry Eagleton, *Literary Theory: An Introduction* (Oxford: Oxford University Press, 1983), 144–45.

50. Ibid., 146.

51. Ibid., 204.

52. Ibid., 211. (My Italics.)

AMERICA IS DECONSTRUCTION?

53. Jacques Derrida, *Memoires for Paul de Man* (New York: Columbia University Press, 1986), 14.

54. Ibid., 14.

55. Jacques Derrida, "Deconstruction in America," *Journal of the Society for Critical Exchange* 17 (Winter 1985), 2.

56. Ibid.

57. Ibid., 3.

58. Ibid., 4.

59. Ibid., 5.

60. Ibid.

61. Ibid., 6.

62. Ibid., 7.

NON-PLACET

63. Derrida, *Points*, 420–21. Derrida writes at length about this affair, quoting liberally from his attackers.

64. Gilles Deleuze and Felix Guattari, *What Is Philosophy?* (New York: Columbia University Press, 1994), 139. No doubt, there is another way of looking at this, namely, in terms of performing a rhetorical reduction by means of advancing what on the surface appear to be trivial-sounding problems on the order of: if x's head was stuck on y's body, would we be talking about x with y's body or y with x's head? In such examples, focus is on a logical rather than a rhetorical level of thinking. For analytical philosophers, a thinker like Derrida completely violates their sense of epoché, which is antirhetorical to the extreme. The last thing such philosophers want is Derrida's enriching of the rhetorical possibilities, since they think this obscures the logical problems they are trying to delimit. Deleuze and Guattari wonder if such reductionistic thinking can ever be suitable for real-world problems in which rhetorical ambiguity is inevitable. Of course, this debate between the logicians and the rhetoricians has a venerable Medieval intellectual history that falls outside our scope.

65. Derrida, *Points*, 402.

66. Ibid. 402.

67. Ibid., 403.

68. Ibid., 403.

69. Ibid., 406.

70. Ibid.

71. Ibid., 407.

A WORLD APART: DERRIDA AND THE FRANKFURT SCHOOL

72. Fredric Jameson, *Late Marxism: Adorno, or, the Persistence of the Dialectic* (London: Verso, 1990), 5.

73. Ibid., 121.

74. See Mark Poster, *Critical Theory and Poststructuralism* (Ithaca: Cornell University Press, 1989), 17. "The poststructuralists hold no uniform view of the Frankfurt School. Lacan and Barthes rarely, if ever, refer to it directly. . . . Deleuze's *Anti-Oedipus* explicitly opposes . . . the Frankfurt School. As to Derrida, I recall seeing but a single mention of the Frankfurt School or its members in any of his works." In the footnote to this remark, Poster says he recalls seeing only Benjamin mentioned in Derrida in *The Truth in Painting* (Chicago: University of Chicago Press, 1987). But, as we will see, the references to Benjamin are more conspicuous. In a text that appeared after Poster's book, Derrida will acknowledge having considered Adorno in a course on Jewish intellectuals and the Germany psyche, given presumably in the 1980s. See *Force de loi* (Paris: Galilée, 1994). Where Poster is highly off base is in his comment that "Lyotard's writings have been the most explicitly antagonistic to the Germans." In fact, Lyotard wrote a very appreciative essay, "Discussions," on Derrida and Adorno that appeared in *Les fins de l'homme* (Paris: Galilée, 1981).

75. Christoph Menke, *The Sovereignty of Art: Aesthetic Negativity in Adorno and Derrida*, trans. Neil Solomon (Cambridge: MIT Press, 1998), 146. Originally published as *Die Souveränität der Kunst: Äesthetische Erfahrung nach Adorno und Derrida* (Frankfurt, Athenäum Verlag, 1988).The English translator apparently changed Menke's title in order to avoid the obvious problem of introducing the concept of experience in the context of deconstruction where such a concept would be difficult to sustain. Hence Menke's original "aesthetic experience after Adorno and Derrida" becomes "aesthetic negativity in Adorno and Derrida." For Menke, however, negativity is constitutive of aesthetic experience, which he discusses in terms of aesthetic and nonaesthetic cognition.

76. Jacques Derrida, "From Restricted to General Economy," in *Writing and Difference*, trans. Alan Bass (Chicago: Chicago University Press, 1978), 259.

77. Theodor Adorno, *Negative Dialectics*, trans. E.B. Ashton (New York: Continuum, 1973), 153.

78. Fredric Jameson, *Marxism and Form* (Princeton: Princeton University Press, 1971), xiii.

79. Michael Ryan, *Marxism and Deconstruction: A Critical Articulation* (Baltimore: Johns Hopkins University Press, 1982). Speaking of Adorno and Derrida, Ryan notes, "Both philosophers attack the idealist privilege of identity over nonidentity, universality over particularlity, subject over object, spontaneous presence over secondary rhetoric, timeless transcendence over empirical history, content over mode of expression, self-reassuring proximity over threatening alterity,

ontology over the ontic, and so on. The point of each of their critiques is not simply to reverse the hierarchy in each case, but to displace it as well. For Adorno,
this leads to the emergence of a more radically dialectical concept, one given over
to nonidentity. For Derrida, it leads to a questioning of the concept of conceptu-
ality . . . a questioning of the very grounds of metaphysical identitarian conceptualization. . . . The principle target of each is the logos of ratio, the principle of
rational domination through conceptual identity whose operation denies dialectical mediacy and differentiation" (75).

80. Drucilla Cornell, *The Philosophy of the Limit* (New York: Routledge,
1992). Cornell's book is admirable in the way it attempts to bring Derrida into relation with Anglo-American discussions of social justice and the politics of alterity.

81. Jürgen Habermas, *The Philosophical Discourse of Modernity: Twelve
Lectures* (Cambridge: MIT Press, 1987), 181–82.

82. Ibid., 182. "Derrida's grammatologically circumscribed concept of an
archewriting whose traces call forth all the more interpretations the more unfamiliar they become, renews the mystical concept of tradition as an ever *delayed*
event of revelation. Religious authority only maintains its force as long as it con-
ceals its true face and thereby incites the frenzy of deciphering interpreters." Also
note: "The labor of deconstruction lets the refuse heap of interpretations, which
it wants to clear away in order to get at the buried foundations, mount even higher" (183). Perhaps the "refuse heap" has unfortunate evocations for those who remember the abject state of Jews in concentration camps during World War Two.
No matter how hard the Jews labor, their end is the refuse heap.

83. Hugo Ott, *Martin Heidegger: A Political Life*, trans. Allan Blunden
(New York: Harper Collins, 1993), 257.

84. Habermas, *Philosophical Discourse*, 182–83.

85. Philip Watts, *Allegories of the Purge* (Stanford: Stanford University Press,
1998).

86. Jeffrey Mehlman, "Perspectives: On de Man and Le Soir," in *Responses: On Paul de Man's Wartime Journalism*, ed. Werner Hamacher, Neil Hertz, and
Tom Keenan (Lincoln: University of Nebraska Press, 1989). In this article
Mehlman suggests that Derrida is akin to Jean Paulhan, a writer of the Resistance, who delighted in paradoxes and reversals that led him in the postwar period to support the collaborators as resisters and condemn the resisters as collaborators. But one has to wonder whether a formalist analogy of this sort is really
adequate. Céline, for example, wrote in an avant garde style that isn't so far removed from the kind of thing one reads in William Burroughs. In fact, Céline's

Nord even has numerous affinities to Art Spiegelman's *Maus*, despite their apparent differences. But this doesn't make Spiegelman a collaborator or Céline a writer of Holocaust literature.

87. Jacques Derrida, "Like the Sound of the Sea Deep Within a Shell: Paul de Man's War," in *Responses*, 163.

88. Jacques Derrida, "Force of Law," in *Deconstruction and the Possibility of Justice*, ed. Drucilla Cornell, Michel Rosenfeld, and David Gray Carlson (New York: Routledge, 1992), 65–66.

89. Ibid, 66.

1980–1987: A WORLD OF DIFFERENCE

90. Jonathan Culler, *On Deconstruction* (Ithaca: Cornell University, 1982), 64.

91. Ibid., 171.

92. Ibid., 220.

93. Barbara Johnson, *The Critical Difference* (Baltimore: Johns Hopkins University Press, 1980), xi. (My italics.)

94. Barbara Johnson, *A World of Difference* (Baltimore: Johns Hopkins University Press, 1987), 18–19.

95. Ibid., 131.

96. Ibid., 132.

97. Ibid.

DECONSTRUCTING OTHERWISE: GAYATRI CHAKRAVORTY SPIVAK

98. Quoted in Vincent Leitch, *Deconstructive Criticism: An Advanced Introduction* (New York: Columbia University Press, 1983), 195. Lietch is quoting from J. Hillis Miller, "Stevens's Rock and Criticism and Cure II," which was published by the *Georgia Review* in 1976. Leitch's book is one of the first theory guides to deconstruction and is very much rooted in Yale School thinking. For a good critique of Yale's appropriation of Derrida, consult Jeffrey Nealon's *Double Reading* (Ithaca: Cornell University Press, 1995).

99. In her translator's acknowledgements to Jacques Derrida's *Of Grammatology*, Spivak prominently thanks both Paul de Man (for his thorough examina-

tion of the manuscript) and J. Hillis Miller for his help with her preface and for introducing her to Derrida.

100. Rodolphe Gasché, "Deconstruction as Criticism," *Glyph* 6 (1979).

101. Gayatri Chakravorty Spivak, "Ghost Writing," *Diacritics* 25 (1995).

102. Gayatri Chakravorty Spivak, "Feminism and Critical Theory," in *In Other Worlds* (New York: Methuen, 1986). I am quoting from a reprint of the essay in *Contemporary Literary Criticism*, eds. R. C. Davis and R. Schleifer (New York: Longman, 1994), 520–21.

103. Ibid., 521.

104. Ibid., 523.

105. Ibid., 526.

106. Ibid., 527.

107. Gayatri Chakravorty Spivak, *Outside in the Teaching Machine* (New York: Routledge, 1993).

BRITISH DEVELOPMENTS: THE INFLUENCE OF *SCREEN*

108. Stuart Hall, *Critical Dialogues in Cultural Studies*, eds. by David Morley and Kuan-Hsing Chen (London: Routledge: 1996), 81.

109. Rosland Coward and John Ellis, *Language and Materialism* (London: Routledge Kegan Paul, 1977), 20.

110. Ibid., 64.

111. Ibid, 69.

112. Ibid., 73.

113. Ibid., 91.

114. Ibid., 8–9.

115. Ibid., 35.

116. Ibid., 64.

117. Ibid., 67.

118. Ibid., 126.

ECLIPSING DECONSTRUCTION: HISTORY OF SUBJECT-POSITIONS I

119. Michel Foucault, *The Archaeology of Knowledge* (London: Tavistock, 1972), 53.

120. No doubt, the concept of subject-positions could be taken back in time, of course, to include W. E. B. DuBois's "double consciousness," Mikhail Bakhtin's "polyglossia," if not fictional strategies like William Faulkner's multiple narration of the same story in *Absalom, Absalom!* Also, the Ancient Greeks retold stories from different vantage points, the tragic chorus, for example, representing a subject-position other than that of the protagonists. Again, in the larger fragments we have of Sappho's poetry, it is apparent that we are supposed to read the lines in terms of conflicted subject-positions.

121. Louis Althusser, *Ecrits sur la psychanalyse: Freud et Lacan* (Paris: Stock/IMEC, 1993), 131. (My translation.)

122. Ibid., 132.

123. Louis Althusser, "Ideology and Ideological State Apparatuses (Notes Towards an Investigation)," in *Lenin and Philosophy* (New York: Monthly Review Press, 1971), 183, 182.

124. Ernesto Laclau, *Politics and Ideology in Marxist Theory* (London: Verso, 1977), 102.

125. Derrida, *Positions*, 95–96. Originally *Positions* was published as a monograph by Editions du Minuit in 1972, its interviews appearing somewhat prior in other venues.

126. Ibid., 96.

ECLIPSING DECONSTRUCTION: HISTORY OF SUBJECT-POSITIONS II

127. Ernesto Laclau and Chantal Mouffe, *Hegemony and Socialist Strategy* (London: Verso, 1985), 109.

128. Ibid., 111.

129. Stuart Hall, "The Toad in the Garden: Thatcherism Among the Theorists," in *Marxism and the Interpretation of Culture*, eds. Lawrence Grossman and Cary Nelson (Chicago: University of Illinois Press, 1988), 49.

130. Chantal Mouffe, "Hegemony and New Social Subjects," in *Marxism and the Interpretation of Culture*, 90.

131. Gayatri Chakravorty Spivak, "Imperialism and Sexual Difference," *Oxford Literary Review* 8, no. 1 (1986): 225–39.

132. Gayatri Chakravorty Spivak, *The Post-Colonial Critic* (New York: Routledge, 1990), 43.

133. Diana Fuss, *Essentially Speaking* (New York: Routledge, 1989), 32.

134. Spivak, *The Post-Colonial Critic*, 38, 39.

135. Jacques Derrida, "Eating Well," in *Who Comes After the Subject?*, ed. Eduardo Cadava et al. (New York: Routledge, 1991), 109–10.

136. Hans-Georg Gadamer, *Plato's Dialectical Ethics* (New Haven: Yale University Press, 1991).

LURCHING TO THE RIGHT

137. Allan Bloom, *The Closing of the American Mind: How Higher Education Has Failed Democracy and Impoverished the Souls of Today's Students* (New York: Simon and Schuster, 1987), 327.

138. Dennis Donoghue, "A Criticism of One's Own," *The New Republic* (1986). Reprinted in *Men in Feminism*, eds. Alice Jardine and Paul Smith (New York: Methuen, 1987), 147.

139. Roger Shattuck, *The Innocent Eye* (New York: Washington Square Press, 1986), 378.

140. Allan Bloom, *The Closing of the American Mind*, 353–54. (My italics.)

141. There is much I am leaving unsaid about the utopian desire of intellectuals to create a better world versus the condition of being relegated to the college classroom where one is actually rather powerless to effect drastic social change. For example, in an institute on cognitive psychology and analytical philosophy sponsored by the National Endowment for the Humanities (Cornell University, Summer 1998), I discovered that professors in philosophy and psychology had little knowledge of current theoretical developments in language and literature departments; nor did they seem to care. Hence, if, after some two or three decades, professors in the languages and literatures have not been able to broadcast their political messages across departmental/disciplinary lines within fields that are, in many ways, cognate, what does that tell us about their chances of being heard beyond the confines of the university?

142. Bloom, *The Closing of the American Mind*, 354.

143. Ibid., 379–80.

144. Dinesh D'Souza, *Illiberal Education* (New York: Random House, 1991), 191.

145. Ibid., 182.

146. Ibid.

147. Ibid., 185.

148. Ibid., 183.

149. Jane Gallop, *Feminist Accused of Feminist Harassment* (Durham: Duke University Press, 1998), 22.

SOCIAL ACTS AND EXCITABLE SPEECH

150. Jan Zita Grover, "AIDS, Keywords, and Cultural Work," in *Cultural Studies*, eds. Cary Nelson, Paula Treichler, and Lawrence Grossberg (New York: Routledge, 1992), 239.

151. Henry Giroux, "Resisting Difference: Cultural Studies and the Discourse of Cultural Pedagogy," in *Cultural Studies*, 206.

152. Simon Frith, "The Cultural Study of Popular Music," in *Cultural Studies*, 177.

153. John Fiske, "Cultural Studies and the Culture of Everyday Life," in *Cultural Studies*, 159. (My italics.)

154. Grover, "AIDS, Keywords, and Cultural Work," 232.

155. Quoted in Judith Butler, *Excitable Speech* (New York: Routledge, 1997), 16.

156. Michel de Certeau, *Art de faire* (Paris: UGE, 1980), 64.

157. Catherine Hall, "Missionary Stories: Gender and Ethnicity in England in the 1830s and 1840s," in *Cultural Studies*, 259.

158. Alice Kaplan, *French Lessons* (Chicago: Chicago University Press, 1993).

159. Tony Bennett, "Putting Policy Into Cultural Studies," in *Cultural Studies*, 26.

160. Judith Butler, *Excitable Speech* (New York: Routledge, 1997), 11.

VICIOUS DUALISMS

161. The prototype of what I am talking about is the famous hermeneutic circle of Friedrich Schleiermacher in which he detected an inevitable circulation between understanding (getting the facts right) and interpretation (explicating meaning). I prefer to speak of vicious dualisms, because the circularity is without end and simply keeps one fixated within a narrow problematic with only two major alternatives.

162. Stephen Greenblatt, *Learning to Curse* (New York: Routledge, 1990), 144. Originally published in *Literary Theory/Renaissance Texts*, ed. Patricia Parker and David Quint (Baltimore: Johns Hopkins University Press, 1986).

163. Anne McClintock, *Imperial Leather: Race, Gender and Sexuality in the Colonial Contest* (New York: Routledge, 1995), 5.

164. Ibid., 8.

165. Ibid.

166. Judith Butler, *Gender Trouble* (New York: Routledge, 1989), 8.

167. Ibid., 16.

168. Ibid., 18.

169. Ibid., 33.

170. Ibid., 25.

171. Ibid., 139.

DECONSTRUCTION OF THE SOCIAL RELATION I: HEIDEGGER AND SEX

172. Gilles Deleuze, *Foucault* (Minneapolis: University of Minnesota Press, 1996), 115.

173. Jacques Derrida, "Différence sexuelle, différence ontologique," in *Psyché* (Paris: Galilée, 1986), 396. (My translation.)

174. Martin Heidegger, *The Metaphysical Foudations of Logic* (Bloomington: Indiana University Press, 1984), 136–37.

175. Derrida, "Différence sexuelle, différence ontologique," 402.

DECONSTRUCTION AND THE SOCIAL RELATION II: DERRIDA'S ITINERARIES

176. Catherine Malabou and Jacques Derrida, *Jacques Derrida: La Contre-Allée*, ed. Louis Vuitton (Paris: La Quinzaine, 1999).

177. Jacques Derrida, *Of Grammatology* (Baltimore: Johns Hopkins University Press, 1976), 45.

178. Ibid., 217.

179. Ibid., 142.

180. Ibid., 143.

181. Jacques Derrida, "Violence and Metaphysics," in *Writing and Difference* (Chicago: University of Chicago Press, 1980), 83.

182. Jacques Derrida, *Glas* (Paris: Galilée, 1974), 108a.

183. Ibid., 8b.

184. Jacques Derrida, *Specters of Marx* (New York: Routledge, 1990), 75.

185. Ibid., 92.

186. Jean-Luc Nancy, *The Sense of the World*, trans. J. Lebritt (Minneapolis: Minnesota University Press, 1997), 103.

DERRIDA AND THE POLITICAL

187. Elizabeth Grosz, "Ontology and Equivocation," *Diacritics* 25 (1995): 122–123.

188. Peggy Kamuf, "Deconstruction and Feminism," in *Feminist Interpretations of Jacques Derrida*, ed. Nancy Holland (University Park: Pennsylvania University Press, 1997), 117.

189. Ibid., 121.

190. Ibid.

191. Drucilla Cornell, *The Philosophy of the Limit*, 40.

192. Ibid., 47.

193. Ibid., 49.

194. Sartre often speaks of appropriation as a "having" that is particular to the existential problematic of "being." This has to be distinguished from Heidegger's understanding of appropriation (dis-concealment) in terms of Being in the ontological sense. As yet, there is no synoptic study of the philosophical issue of appropriation, which is one of the reasons the history of this concept is elusive.

195. Of particular interest to me is Slavoj Zizek, *For They Know Not What They Do* (London: Verso, 1991). See his discussion of Derrida in which he faults Derrida for eliding negativity as a true opposition within dialectics. Here, again, there is much more indebtedness to Sartre than people may suspect, since Sartre at least raised the problematic of negativity as crucial to the question of dialectical thinking in terms of a "knowing what they do."

196. Jacques Derrida, "Eating Well," 100–01. The interview is significant in that it provides a conceptual itinerary for Derrida's more recent writings of the 1990s.

197. Wendy Brown, *States of Injury* (Princeton: Princeton University Press, 1996). "In a reading that links the new identity claims to a certain relegitimation of capitalism, identity politics concerned with race, sexuality, and gender will appear not as a supplement to class politics, not as an expansion of left categories of oppression and emancipation . . . but as tethered to a formulation of justice that reinscribes a bourgeois (masculinist) ideal as its measure." (60) I think Brown is right in locating bourgeois consciousness as the root of current academic identity politics. Also see Jürgen Habermas, *The Inclusion of the Other* (Cambridge: The MIT Press, 1998) for a similar critique.

RECONCEIVING THE THEORY MESS

198. Jacques Derrida, "Some Statements and Truisms About Neologisms, Newisms, Postisms, Parasitisms, and Other Small Seismisms," in *The States of "Theory": History, Art, and Critical Discourse*, ed. David Carroll (New York: Columbia University Press, 1990), 84. In fact, Derrida does quite a bit of "brain storming" in this essay about what theory might mean.

199. Derrida, "Some Statements and Truisms," 85, 88.

200. Jan Patocka, *Papiers phénoménologiques* (Grenoble: Jérôme Millon, 1995), 216.

201. For a brilliant and sustained account of "tradition" within an epistemic and semiotic hermeneutic that includes readings of Gadamer, Benjamin, Freud, Novalis, and Kant, see Angelika Rauch, *The Hieroglyph of Tradition* (New York: Farleigh Dickinson University Press, 2000).

202. Derrida, "Some Statements and Truisms," 93.

203. Jacques Derrida, "Biodegradables," *Critical Inquiry* 15, no. 4 (Summer 1989): 850.

POSTSCRIPT

204. R. Harris? "Fiddle, Fiddle, Fiddle," *Times Literary Supplement*, March 21, 1997.

205. Edward Said, "An Unresolved Paradox," *MLA Newsletter* (Summer, 1999): 3.

Abrams, Meyer. "The Deconstructive Angel." *Critical Inquiry* 3 (1977).

Adorno, Theodor. *Negative Dialectics.* Translated by E.B. Ashton. New York: Continuum, 1973 [1966].

Althusser, Louis. *Ecrits sur la psychanalyse: Freud et Lacan.* Paris: Stock/IMEC, 1993 [Originally written, 1966].

——. "Freud and Lacan." *Lenin and Philosophy.* New York: Monthly Review Press, 1971 [1964].

——. "Ideology and Ideological State Apparatuses (Notes Towards an Investigation)." In *Lenin and Philosophy.* New York: Monthly Review Press, 1971 [1970].

Bate, Walter Jackson. "The Crisis in English Studies." *Scholarly Publishing: Journal for Authors and Publishers* 14, no. 3(April, 1983).

Bennett, Tony. "Putting Policy Into Cultural Studies." In *Cultural Studies.* Edited by Lawrence Grossman, Cary Nelson, and Paula Treichler. New York: Routledge, 1992.

Bennington, Geoffrey and Jacques Derrida. *Jacques Derrida.* Paris: Seuil, 1991.

Bhabha, Homi. *The Location of Culture.* New York: Routledge, 1994.

Bloom, Allan. *The Closing of the American Mind: How Higher Education Has Failed Democracy and Impoverished the Souls of Today's Students.* Foreward by Saul Bellow. New York: Simon and Schuster, 1987.

Bloom, Harold. *Shakespeare: The Invention of the Human.* New York: Riverhead, 1999.

Braidotti, Rosi. *Patterns of Dissonance.* New York: Oxford, 1991.

Brown, Wendy. *States of Injury.* Princeton: Princeton University Press, 1996.

Butler, Judith. *Bodies That Matter.* New York: Routledge, 1993.

——. *Excitable Speech.* New York: Routledge, 1997.

——. *Gender Trouble.* New York: Routledge, 1989.

Caputo, John. *The Prayers and Tears of Jacques Derrida.* Bloomington: Indiana University Press, 1997.

Cixous, Hélène. *Rootprints*. New York: Routledge, 1997 [1994].

Cornell, Drucilla. *The Philosophy of the Limit*. New York: Routledge, 1992.

Coward, Rosalind and John Ellis. *Language and Materialism*. London: Routledge Kegan Paul, 1977.

Critchley, Simon. *Ethics, Politics, Subjectivity*. London: Verso, 1999.

Culler, Jonathan. *On Deconstruction*. Ithaca: Cornell University Press, 1982.

———. *Structuralist Poetics*. Ithaca: Cornell University Press, 1975.

D'Souza, Dinesh. *Illiberal Education*. New York: Random House, 1991.

de Certeau, Michel. *Art de faire*. Paris: Union Générals, 1980.

de Man, Paul. *Blindness and Insight*. New York: Oxford University Press, 1971.

de Saussure, Ferdinand. *Course in General Linguistics*. New York: McGraw Hill, 1966 [1915].

Deleuze, Gilles. *Foucault*. Translated and edited by Seán Hand. Minneapolis: University of Minnesota Press, 1996 [1986].

Deleuze, Gilles and Felix Guattari. *A Thousand Plateaus*. Translated by Brian Massumi. Minneapolis: University of Minnesota Press, 1987 [1980].

———. *What Is Philosophy?* Translated by Hugh Tomlinson and Graham Burchell. New York: Columbia University Press, 1994 [1991].

Derrida, Jacques. "Afterword: Toward an Ethic of Discussion." In *Limited Inc*. Translated by Samuel Weber. Evanston: Northwestern University Press, 1988.

———. *Archive Fever*. Translated by Eric Prenowitz. Chicago: University of Chicago Press, 1995.

———. "Biodegradables." *Critical Inquiry* 15, no.4 (Summer 1989).

———. "Deconstruction in America." *Journal of the Society for Critical Exchange* 17 (Winter 1985).

———. "Des tours de Babel." In *Psyché*. Paris: Galilée, 1986.

———. "Deux mots pour Joyce." In *Ulysse grammophone*. Paris: Galilée, 1987.

———. "Différance." *Margins of Philosophy*. Translated by Alan Bass. Chicago: Chicago University Press, 1982.

———. "Différence sexuelle, différence ontologique." In *Psyché*. Paris: Galilée, 1986.

———. *Dissemination*. Translated by Barbara Johnson. Chicago: Chicago University Press, 1981 [1972].

———. "D'un ton apocalyptique adopté naguère en philosophie." In *Les Fins de l'homme*. Paris: Galilée, 1981.

——. "Eating Well." In *Who Comes After the Subject?* Edited by Eduardo Cadava. New York: Routledge, 1991.

——. "Force of Law." In *Deconstruction and the Possibility of Justice.* Edited by Drucilla Cornell, Michel Rosenfeld, and David Gray Carlson. New York: Routledge, 1992.

——. "From Restricted to General Economy." In *Writing and Difference.* Translated by Alan Bass. Chicago: Chicago University Press, 1978.

——. *Given Time: I. Counterfeit Money.* Translated by Peggy Kamuf. Chicago: Chicago University Press, 1992.

——. *Glas.* Paris: Galilée, 1974.

——. *La Carte postale.* Paris: Flammarion, 1980.

——. "Like the Sound of the Sea Deep Within a Shell: Paul de Man's War." In *Responses to Paul de Man.* Edited by Werner Hamacher, Neil Hertz, and Thomas Keenan. Lincoln: University of Nebraska Press: 1988.

——. "Limited Inc." In *Limited Inc.* Translated by Samuel Weber. Evanston: Northwestern University Press, 1988.

——. "Marx & Sons." In *Ghostly Demarcations.* Edited by Michael Sprinker. London: Routledge, 1999.

——. *Memoires for Paul de Man.* Translated by Cecile Lindsay, Jonathan Culler, and Eduardo Cadava. New York: Columbia University Press, 1986.

——. *Of Grammatology.* Translated by Gayatri Spivak. Baltimore: Johns Hopkins University Press, 1976 [1967].

——. *Of Spirit.* Translated by Geoffrey Bennington and Rachel Bowlby. Chicago: Chicago University Press, 1989 [1987].

——. *Passions.* Paris: Galilée, 1994.

——. *Points of Suspension.* Translated by Peggy Kamuf et al. Stanford: Stanford University Press, 1995 [1992].

——. *Politics of Friendship.* Translated by George Collins. London: Verso, 1997 [1994].

——. *Positions.* Translated by Alan Bass. Chicago: Chicago University Press, 1981 [1972].

——. *Schibboleth.* Paris: Galilée, 1986.

——. "Some Statements and Truisms About Neologisms, Newisms, Postisms, Parasitisms, and Other Small Seismisms." In *The States of 'Theory': History, Art, and Critical Discourse.* Edited by David Carroll. New York: Columbia University Press, 1990.

——. *Specters of Marx.* Translated by Peggy Kamuf. New York: Routledge, 1994 [1993].

——. *Speech and Phenomena.* Evanston: Northwestern University Press, 1973 [1967].

——. "Structure, Sign, and Play." In *The Structuralist Controversy.* Edited by José Harari and Richard Macksey. Baltimore: Johns Hopkins University Press, 1966.

——. "Three Questions to Hans-Georg Gadamer." In *Dialogue and Deconstruction.* Edited by Diane P. Michelfelder and Richard Palmer. Albany: State University of New York Press, 1989.

——. *The Truth in Painting.* Translated by Geoffrey Bennington and Ian McLeod. Chicago: University of Chicago Press, 1987 [1978].

——. "Violence and Metaphysics." In *Writing and Difference.* Translated by Alan Bass. Chicago: University of Chicago Press, 1980 [1962].

Donoghue, Dennis. "A Criticism of One's Own." *The New Republic* (1986).

duCille, Ann. "The Occult of True Black Womanhood." *Female Subjects in Blackand White.* Edited by Elizabeth Abel, Barbara Christian, and Helene Moglen. Berkeley: University of California Press, 1997.

Eagleton, Terry. *Literary Theory: An Introduction.* Oxford: Oxford University Press, 1983.

Fish, Stanley. *Is There a Text in This Class?* Cambridge: Harvard University Press, 1980.

Fisk, John. "Cultural Studies and the Culture of Everyday Life." *Cultural Studies.* Edited by Lawrence Grossberg, Cary Nelson, and Paula Treichler. New York: Routledge, 1992.

Foucault, Michel. *The Archaeology of Knowledge.* London: Tavistock, 1972 [1969].

Frith, Simon. "The Cultural Study of Popular Music." *Cultural Studies.* Edited by Lawrence Grossberg, Cary Nelson, and Paula Treichler. New York: Routledge, 1992.

Fuss, Diana. *Essentially Speaking.* New York: Routledge, 1989.

Fynsk, Christopher. "Community and the Limits of Theory." *Community at Loose Ends.* Edited by Maimi Theory Collective. Minneapolis: University of Minnesota Press, 1991.

Gadamer, Hans-Georg. "Conversation and Shared Understanding." In *Plato's Dialectical Ethics.* New Haven: Yale University Press, 1991 [1932].

——. *Truth and Method.* New York: Continuum. 1975 [1960].

Gallop, Jane. *Feminist Accused of Sexual Harassment*. Durham: Duke University Press, 1998.

Gasché, Rodolphe. "Deconstruction as Criticism." *Glyph* 6 (1979).

——. *The Tain of the Mirror*. Cambridge: Harvard University Press, 1986.

Giroux, Henry A. "Resisting Difference: Cultural Studies and the Discourse of Critical Pedagogy." In *Cultural Studies*. Edited by Lawrence Grossman, Cary Nelson, and Paula Treichler. New York: Routledge, 1992.

Graff, Gerald. *Literature Against Itself*. Chicago: University of Chicago Press, 1979.

——. *Professing Literature*. Chicago: University of Chicago Press, 1987.

Greenblatt, Stephen. *Learning to Curse*. New York: Routledge, 1990.

Grosz, Elizabeth. "Ontology and Equivocation." *Diacritics* 25 (1995).

Grover, Jan Zita. "AIDS, Keywords, and Cultural Work." *Cultural Studies*. Edited by Lawrence Grossberg, Cary Nelson, and Paula Treichler. New York: Routledge, 1992.

Habermas, Jürgen. *The Philosophical Discourse of Modernity: Twelve Lectures*. Cambridge: MIT Press, 1987 [1985].

Hall, Catherine. "Missionary Stories." In *Cultural Studies*. Edited by Lawrence Grossberg, Cary Nelson, and Paula Treichler. New York: Routledge, 1992.

Hall, Stuart. "The Toad in the Garden." *Marxism and the Interpretation of Culture*. Edited by Lawrence Grossberg and Cary Nelson. Chicago: University of Illinois Press, 1988.

Hartman, Geoffrey. *Saving the Text*. Baltimore: Johns Hopkins University Press, 1981.

Heidegger, Martin. *The Metaphysical Foudations of Logic*. Bloomington: Indiana University Press, 1984 [1928].

Hillis Miller, J. "Deconstructing the Deconstructor." *Diacritics* 5 (Summer 1975).

Hirsch, E. D. *Validity in Interpretation*. New Haven: Yale University Press, 1967.

Hobson, Marian. *Jacques Derrida: Opening Lines*. New York: Routledge, 1999.

Husserl, Edmund. *Experience and Judgment*. Evanston: Northwestern University Press, 1973 [1948].

Jameson, Fredric. *Late Marxism: Adorno, or, the Persistence of the Dialectic*. London: Verso, 1990.

——. *Marxism and Form*. Princeton: Princeton University Press, 1971.

———. *The Prison-House of Language*. Princeton: Princeton University Press, 1972.

Johnson, Barbara. *A World of Difference*. Baltimore: Johns Hopkins University Press, 1987.

———.*The Critical Difference*. Baltimore: Johns Hopkins University Press, 1980.

Kamuf, Peggy. "Deconstruction and Feminism." In *Feminist Interpretations of Jacques Derrida*. Edited by Nancy Holland. University Park: Pennsylvania University Press, 1997.

Kaplan, Alice. *French Lessons*. Chicago: Chicago University Press, 1993.

Kolodny, Annette. "Dancing Through the Minefield." In *Feminisms*. Edited by Robyn R. Warhol and Diane P. Herndl. New Brunswick: Rutgers University Press, 1997.

Krieger, Murray. *Theory of Criticism*. Baltimore: Johns Hopkins University Press, 1976.

Lacan, Jacques. *Ecrits I*. Paris: Points, 1970.

———. *Le Séminaire XVII: L'envers de la psychanalyse*. Paris: Seuil, 1991.

Laclau, Ernesto. *Politics and Ideology in Marxist Theory*. London: Verso, 1977.

Laclau, Ernesto and Chantal Mouffe. *Hegemony and Socialist Strategy*. London: Verso, 1985.

Lehman, David. "Deconstructing de Man's Life." *Newsweek*, February 15, 1988.

Leitch, Vincent. *Deconstructive Criticism: An Advanced Introduction*. New York: Columbia University Press, 1983.

Lentricchia, Frank. *After the New Criticism*. Chicago: Chicago University Press, 1980.

Lyotard, Jean-Francois. *Le Différend*. Paris: Minuit, 1983.

Malabou, Catherine and Jacques Derrida, *Jacques Derrida: La Contre-Allée*. Paris: La Quinzaine, 1999.

Marin, Louis. *Portrait du Roi*. Paris: Minuit, 1981.

McClintock, Anne. *Imperial Leather: Race, Gender and Sexuality in the Colonial Contest*. New York: Routledge, 1995.

Mehlman, Jeffrey. "Perspectives: On de Man and Le Soir." *Responses: On Paul de Man's Wartime Journalism*. Edited by Werner Hamacher, Neil Hertz, and Tom Keenan. Lincoln: University of Nebraska Press, 1989.

Menke, Christoph. *Die Souveränität der Kunst: Äesthetische Erfahrung nach Adornound Derrida*. Frankfurt, Athenäum Verlag, 1988.

Morley, David and Kuan-Hsing Chen, eds. *Stuart Hall: Critical Dialogues in Cultural Studies*. London: Routledge: 1996.

Mouffe, Chantal. "Hegemony and New Social Subjects." *Marxism and the Interpretation of Culture*. Edited by Lawrence Grossberg and Cary Nelson. Chicago: University of Illinois Press, 1988.

Nancy, Jean-Luc. *The Inoperative Community*. Minneapolis: University of Minnesota Press, 1991 [1986].

——. *The Sense of the World*. Translated by Jeffrey Lebritt. Minneapolis: Minnesota University Press, 1997 [1993].

Nealon, Jeffrey. *Double Reading*. Ithaca: Cornell University Press, 1995.

Norris, Christopher. *Jacques Derrida*. Cambridge: Harvard University Press. 1987.

Ott, Hugo. *Martin Heidegger: A Political Life*. Translated by Allan Blunden. New York: Harper Collins, 1993.

Patocka, Jan. *Papiers phénoménologiques*. Grenoble: Jérôme Millon, 1995.

Poster, Mark. *Critical Theory and Poststructuralism*. Ithaca: Cornell University Press, 1989.

Pritchard, William H. "The Hermeneutical Mafia or After Strange Gods at Yale." *Hudson Review* 28 (Winter 1975–76).

Rauch, Angelika. *The Hieroglyph of Tradition*. New York: Farleigh Dickinson University Press, 2000.

Readings, Bill. *The University in Ruins*. Cambridge: Harvard University Press, 1996.

Roudinesco, Elizabeth. *Jacques Lacan and Company*. Chicago: Chicago University Press, 1990.

Ryan, Michael. *Marxism and Deconstruction: A Critical Articulation*. Baltimore: Johns Hopkins University Press, 1982.

Said, Edward. "An Unresolved Paradox." *MLA Newsletter* (Summer, 1999).

——. "Restoring Intellectual Coherence." *MLA Newsletter* (Spring 1999).

Sartre, Jean-Paul. *L'Etre et le néant*. Paris: Gallimard, 1943.

Searle, John. "Reiterating the Differences: A Reply to Derrida." *Glyph* 2 (1977).

Shattuck, Roger. "How to Rescue Literature." *The Innocent Eye*. New York: Washington Square Press, 1986.

Spivak, Gayatri Chakravorty. "Can the Subaltern Speak?" In *Marxism and the Interpretation of Culture*. Edited by Lawrence Grossberg and Cary Nelson. Chicago: University of Illinois Press, 1988.

———. "Feminism and Critical Theory." *In Other Worlds.* New York: Methuen, 1986.

———. "Finding Feminist Readings: Dante-Yeats." In *In Other Worlds: Essays in Cultural Politics.* New York: Methuen, 1987 [1980].

———. "Ghost Writing." *Diacritics* 25 (1995).

———. "Imperialism and Sexual Difference." *Oxford Literary Review* 8, no. 1 (1986).

———. *Outside in the Teaching Machine.* New York: Routledge, 1993.

———. *The Post-Colonial Critic.* New York: Routledge, 1990.

———. "Translator's Preface." *Of Grammatology* by Jacques Derrida. Baltimore: Johns Hopkins University Press, 1976.

Ulmer, Gregory. *Applied Grammatology.* Baltimore: Johns Hopkins University Press, 1985.

Vendler, Helen. *The Art of Shakespeare's Sonnets.* Cambridge: Harvard University Press, 1997.

Watts, Philip. *Allegories of the Purge.* Stanford: Stanford University Press, 1998.

Wellek, René. "Destroying Literary Studies." *The New Criterion*, 2, no. 4 (December, 1983).

Žižek, Slavoj. *For They Know Not What They Do.* London: Verso, 1991.

———. *The Sublime Object of Ideology.* London: Verso, 1989.

INDEX

DATE DUE

HIGHSMITH #45115